Lewis and Clark Meet Oregon's Forests

Lessons from Dynamic Nature

Gail Wells

Dawn Anzinger

OREGON FOREST
RESOURCES INSTITUTE

Rediscover Oregon's Forests

Copyright© 2001 Oregon Forest Resources Institute
808 SW Third Avenue, Suite 480
Portland, Oregon 97204

503/229-6718

*All rights reserved. No part of this publication may be reproduced
  in any form without permission from the publisher.*

Produced by Forestry Communications Group
  College of Forestry
  Oregon State University
  Corvallis, Oregon

  Caryn Davis, Editor
  Gretchen Bracher, Designer

Printed by Printing Today, Portland, Oregon
ISBN 0-87437-003-5

On the cover: Valley of the Willamette River.
            Painting by Henry J. Warre, 1845

Contents

Preface

We all treasure the magnificent trees and forests of the Pacific Northwest. We value these green landscapes for scenery, recreation, and wildlife, as well as for the products we use every day. The human inhabitants of the Pacific Northwest have valued and relied on forest resources for thousands of years. But human interaction with the forests surrounding us has changed over time, and today discussions about how to manage our forests can be contentious and divisive.

To help inform our choices about forest management in the future, authors Gail Wells and Dawn Anzinger suggest that we roll back the clock of ecological history to an earlier era for a look at our forests before European-American settlement. What is revealed is a landscape of constant change. From glaciers, volcanic eruptions, and earthquakes to fires and management by native peoples, our forests have been constantly influenced and shaped by immense forces of nature and the human need for food and shelter.

Bob Zybach was an early researcher who raised awareness of our forests' dynamic past. He helped uncover some of the first explorers' journal entries and references to presettlement Pacific Northwest forests. His tenacity in digging through numerous historic documents and maps helped pique interest in this issue, and we thank him for that.

Disturbance and change is the story line behind *Lewis and Clark Meet Oregon's Forests*. The lure of the Lewis and Clark experience, especially Clark's journal entries, offers a great backdrop for reflection on Northwest forests 200 years ago.

Wells and Anzinger write of "dynamic nature" and its importance to the past and future of our forests. No matter how far back we go in history, our forests were in a state of flux. Our present-day forests in the Willamette Valley or on the Pacific Coast are just one phase on a continuum of change. The authors ask us to examine our assumptions as we reflect on thousands of years in which nature and humans have shaped the forests Lewis and Clark saw, as well as the forests we see today.

This book concludes with questions for the reader, questions that each of us needs to answer as we examine choices for the future of our forests. What does it mean for us to understand nature as fundamentally dynamic rather than static? How can we define what is "normal" in nature? What is desirable as a forest management goal? What is attainable? As in other areas of human endeavor, only through an understanding of history can we avoid repeating the mistakes of the past.

Barte Starker, Chairman
Oregon Forest Resources Institute
Richard Zabel, Executive Director
Western Forestry and Conservation Association

Acknowledgements

First, the authors are grateful to the Oregon Forest Resources Institute for their support of this project. The book was in many ways a labor of love, but it would not have been accomplished without the financial backing of OFRI, and we thank them.

We are grateful to the many people who graciously listened to our ideas, offered their comments on our initial conception of this book, and helped us go looking for information. In particular, we thank Ric Balfour, Brett Butler, Ken Carloni, Ron Doel, Paul Farber, Steve Hackel, Cliff Hedlund, Ed Jensen, Katy Kavanagh, Ted Kaye, Mary Kentula, Tim LeCain, Kathleen Moore, Tara Nierenberg, Valerie Rapp, Bill Robbins, Ann Rogers, Cliff Snider, Mark Spence, Brooks Stanfield, and Dick Waring.

We are grateful for those who reviewed the manuscript in whole or in part and offered their thoughtful comments: James Agee, John Beuter, Robert Boyd, Ron Doel, Bob Gilman, Dave Hibbs, Norm Johnson, Scott Marlega, Russ McKinley, Steve Radosevich, Barte Starker, and Fred Swanson.

People who went to some lengths to dig out archive materials or unpublished information for us were Mike Bordelon and Casey Pileggi of the Oregon Department of Forestry, Lisa Heigh of the Youngs Bay Watershed Council, Mark Koski of the Bureau of Land Management's Salem District office, John Kwait of the Siuslaw National Forest, Scott Marlega of Willamette Industries, Inc., Ted Nelson, Steve Reinberger of the Mount Hood National Forest, Ruth Rhodes of the Fort Vancouver National Historic Site, and Diane Smith of the Forest Service PNW Research Station.

We received valuable assistance with photos and maps from Jonathan Brooks of the OSU College of Forestry, Mike Hanemann and Andrew Herstrom of the Oregon Department of Forestry, William E. Hill, David Leach of the Willamette National Forest, Lois Mack and Larry Rank of the Vancouver National Historic Reserve Trust, Jan Prior of the Mount Hood National Forest, Diane Rainsford of the Siuslaw National Forest, and Steve Wyatt of the Oregon Coast History Center. Doris Bills, Cindy Miner, Gayle Saunders, and Frank Vanni of the PNW Station pointed us to a drawerful of historic photos, which proved to be a gold mine. The help of all these good people was invaluable.

We are grateful to the capable staff at the Oregon History Center photograph and map library, and especially for the kind attention of Mikki Tint, whose thorough knowledge of the OHC archives helped us immensely.

Finally, we thank the capable editing and graphics staff at the Oregon State University Forestry Communications Group for their work on layout and production of the book. We are especially grateful for the sensitive and thoughtful editing of Caryn Davis, the inspired design of Gretchen Bracher, and the cartographic skills of Tristan Bähr.

Introduction

...the water passing with great velocity forming & boiling in a most horriable manner.

—William Clark, assessing the Cascades of the Columbia in October 1805

William Clark.

When Meriwether Lewis and William Clark steered their canoes down the tumultuous narrows and rapids of the lower Columbia River, they were entering a country where trees dominated the landscape. The shift was abrupt. The river carried them out of the virtually treeless desert east of the mountains, bumped them down the "Great Shute," as they called it, below present-day Cascade Locks, and spilled them out into tidewater and an utterly changed landscape.[1]

The Land

The topography of that landscape—now known as western Washington and Oregon—falls into three parallel sub-regions: the Coast Range, the interior valleys, and the Cascade Range. The Coast Range is a low mountain range composed of basalt, sandstone, and siltstone, extending from south of the Olympic Peninsula to the Klamath Mountains of southern Oregon. Coast Range summits are located toward the eastern edge of the range, with the highest point at 4,097-foot Marys Peak.

Meriwether Lewis.

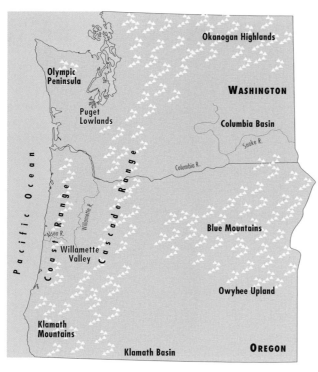
Physiographic features of Oregon and Washington.

The Willamette Valley and Puget Lowlands are interior valleys lying east of the Coast Range. The Willamette Valley extends from the Columbia River south to Eugene. The broad, flat river valley is 20 to 30 miles wide and 110 miles long. The river meanders north through the valley at a low gradient, descending over Willamette Falls and the Clackamas Rapids to join the Columbia River north of Oregon City.[2] The rich Willamette Valley soils are composed of silty deposits from ancient and modern floods.

The Puget Lowland region lies north of the Columbia River in southern Washington, beginning about 15 miles south of Olympia. It is a broad, flat valley of glacier-deposited rocks, gravel, sand, and silt, with numerous lakes and poorly drained depressions scattered throughout.[3]

The Cascade Range lies east of the Willamette Valley and Puget Lowlands. These mountains have moderately steep slopes and ridges averaging 4,500 feet.[4] Numerous volcanic peaks—Mount Rainier is the highest at 14,410 feet—tower above the lower slopes. The Columbia River cuts from east to west through both mountain ranges, flowing through a steep gorge carved by ancient floodwaters. Past the Cascades, the Columbia slows and meanders its way to the ocean.

The Forests

To get an idea of how the forests of the Pacific Northwest looked to Lewis and Clark and their Corps of Discovery, we have to peel away, in our imagination, the layers of change wrought by

European-American settlement—the cities built along the banks, the highways and railroad tracks following the channel on both sides, the effects of upriver dams in slowing the river's flow and simplifying its course. If we can envision the river as it might have existed 200 years ago— swift-flowing down from the Cascades, its banks thick with willows and alders and dotted with Indian villages—the words of William Clark, a

Big trees near Seaside, Oregon. The Douglas-fir in the foreground was standing when Lewis and Clark arrived. When this photo was taken in 1941, the tree was one of the last veterans of the coastal old-growth forest.

diligent journal keeper during his time here, can help us clothe its landscape in our imagination.

Here was a thickness and diversity of forest such as they had not seen since they left the oak, chestnut, walnut, and hickory woods of their native state of Virginia—much of which had been cleared by then to make room for settlers and their farms.[5] The Columbia's banks were covered with ash, alder, cottonwood, fir, and spruce, and the heights above the river clothed with conifers. "The mountains and bottoms thickly timbered with Pine Spruce Cotton and a kind of maple… the mountains are low on each Side & thickly timbered with pine," wrote Clark in his journal entry of November 2, 1805. The party was near Beacon Rock, on the Washington side of the river. Two days later he described the north bank as "an open Prarie for 1 mile back of which the wood land commence riseing back, the timber on the edge of the Prarie is white oke, back is Spruce pine & other Species of Pine mixed."[6]

Clark used "pine" in a generic sense (as many people do today) to refer to any of several conifers. Here, "spruce pine" may mean

A forest on the western flank of the Oregon Cascades. These forests are dominated by Douglas-fir in the lower elevations; true firs and hemlocks appear at higher elevations.

A forest in the Willamette Valley foothills. Douglas-fir is more abundant along the valley margins today than it was 200 years ago, when periodic fire, both natural and Indian-caused, discouraged it from encroaching.

Douglas-fir.[7] Of the landscape across the river from Beacon Rock, near Crown Point, Clark wrote, "here the mountains leave the river on each Side, which from the great Shute to this place is high and rugid; thickly Covered with timber principalley of the Pine Species. The Bottoms below appear extensive and thickly Covered with wood."[8]

Along the western flanks of the Cascades, the trees grew huge, tall and thick and dense. The forests were dominated by Douglas-fir along the lower slopes, with intermingled western hemlock and western redcedar. In the luxuriant understory were salal, rhododendron, Oregongrape, vine maple, and oceanspray. In the higher-elevation forests, Douglas-fir was mingled with silver fir, subalpine fir, and mountain hemlock. Douglas-fir also dominated the forests along the eastern and the upper western slopes of the Coast Range. A narrow belt of forest near the coast was dominated by western hemlock, Sitka spruce, and western redcedar, with considerable Douglas-fir also in the mix. Understories included swordfern, salal, mosses, and red and black (or evergreen) huckleberry.[9]

In contrast to its mountainous flanks, the Willamette Valley was sparsely forested. The riverbanks were covered by wide, thick "gallery forests" of deciduous hardwoods such as ash, alder, willow, maple, and cottonwood, with conifers such as Douglas-fir and western hemlock interspersed. The valley was a prairie, dominated by native bunchgrasses and fescues.[10] Groves of oak mixed with Douglas-fir grew on the tops and sides of the hills, and maple, cedar, and hemlock dominated the foothill forests encircling the valley.

Dynamic Landscapes

This land was far from being an unbroken blanket of forest from river to river and from ridge to ridge. On the contrary, the forest along the mountain ridges and on the Willamette Valley foothills lay in swaths and patches of differing sizes and compositions across the landscape. The diversity of these forests as they existed 200 years ago reflected the effects of natural and human-caused disturbances over many millennia. Floods, windstorms, volcano-induced mud flows, landslides, and fire—both natural wildfire and fires set deliberately by the Indians as part of their cultural practices—all had been working over many, many years to shape the forests Lewis and Clark saw.

These forests represented a snapshot in time of a landscape that had been continuously shaped by incremental, dramatic, and catastrophic events for a long time, long before Lewis and Clark arrived on the scene. In subsequent chapters of this book, we will explore the natural and human-caused influences that shaped and continue to shape the forests of the Pacific Northwest. We will look at prehistoric landscape dynamics, which included some extremely large-scale and catastrophic events. We will look at the incremental, but over time significant, changes brought by the first humans to live in this region. And we will examine the pervasive processes of change brought by European-American settlement, taking a look at how these processes shaped the landscape in three different northwestern Oregon locations—the area around Astoria and Tillamook Head, the lower Willamette Valley and the west slopes of the Cascades, and the Alsea River country of the central Coast Range.

Finally, we will discuss what the dynamic character of the Pacific Northwest's landscapes can teach us about how to think about, come to terms with, manage, and cherish our forests and our other natural surroundings. We will consider what the land's history has to show us about how we can live in our landscape, shaping it and being shaped by it, in a manner that sustains both its vital processes and our own.

Notes to Introduction

1. The men portaged the canoes and baggage around the most threatening rapids, but managed to run the rest—sometimes by passing the gear through with elkskin ropes. Stephen E. Ambrose, *Undaunted Courage: Meriwether Lewis, Thomas Jefferson, and the Opening of the American West* (New York: Simon & Schuster, 1996), p. 302.

2. J. F. Franklin and C. T. Dyrness, *Natural Vegetation of Oregon and Washington*, USDA Forest Service General Technical Report PNW-8 (Portland, OR: USDA Forest Service Pacific Northwest Forest and Range Experiment Station, 1973).

3. Ibid.

4. Ibid.

5. Michael Williams, *Americans and Their Forests: A Historical Geography* (Cambridge: Cambridge University Press, 1989), pp. 60–65.

6. Ambrose, *Undaunted Courage*, p. 303.

7. Gary E. Moulton, ed., *The Journals of the Lewis & Clark Expedition*, vol. 6 (Lincoln: University of Nebraska Press, 1990), p. 19n; and Elbert L. Little, Jr., *Conifers and Important Hardwoods*, vol. 1 of *Atlas of United States Trees* (Washington, DC: USDA Forest Service, 1971), cited in Moulton, *Journals*, p. 19.

8. Moulton, *Journals*, pp. 7–9.

9. Franklin and Dyrness, *Natural Vegetation of Oregon and Washington*.

10. Jerry C. Towle, "Changing Geography of Willamette Valley Woodlands," *Oregon Historical Quarterly* LXXXIII, no. I (spring 1982), p. 67–87; and Franklin and Dyrness, *Natural Vegetation of Oregon and Washington*.

Chapter 1

Pacific Northwest Forests Through Time

As a result of major climatic changes over the last 20,000 years and more, the Northwest Coast has undergone major environmental changes. Some of these, such as sea level fluctuations, have a direct effect on the archaeological record. All of them presented the coast's ancient and not so ancient peoples with problems to solve. Some changes may have been so rapid as to be seen in an individual's lifetime, while others spanned millennia, and would have been invisible to any given generation. Some changes may have had profound regional effects, while others, such as the abrupt drowning of a marsh as the result of an earthquake, may have been only of local effect, though still as profound to the people so affected. The Northwest Coast was not a uniform environment, either in time or space.

—Kenneth Ames and Herbert Maschner, *Peoples of the Northwest Coast*

Measured on a geological time scale, the forests and woodlands described by Lewis and Clark were young. Trees and other forest plants have been associated in specific locations on the landscape for only a few thousand years. Pacific Northwest forests have changed continuously for thousands of years. Most of this change has been gradual, in response to long-term climatic fluctuations, but periods of extreme disturbance and rapid environ-

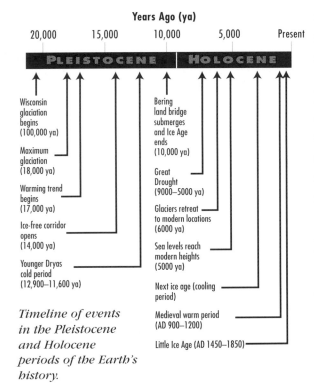

Years Ago (ya)

| 20,000 | 15,000 | 10,000 | 5,000 | Present |

PLEISTOCENE | HOLOCENE

Wisconsin glaciation begins (100,000 ya)

Maximum glaciation (18,000 ya)

Warming trend begins (17,000 ya)

Ice-free corridor opens (14,000 ya)

Younger Dryas cold period (12,900–11,600 ya)

Bering land bridge submerges and Ice Age ends (10,000 ya)

Great Drought (9000–5000 ya)

Glaciers retreat to modern locations (6000 ya)

Sea levels reach modern heights (5000 ya)

Next ice age (cooling period)

Medieval warm period (AD 900–1200)

Little Ice Age (AD 1450–1850)

Timeline of events in the Pleistocene and Holocene periods of the Earth's history.

mental change also have shaped the composition and development of these forests.

Pacific Northwest forests appear to have been in an almost continuous state of flux since the Earth began to warm after the last Ice Age, about 13,000 years ago. Plant communities have formed and re-formed, shifting their composition in response to changing environmental conditions, prompted in turn by changes in climate. During cold, glacial periods, bands of vegetation slide south and toward lower elevations, and during warmer, drier periods, they move north and toward higher elevations. Many of the trees that occupied the lower elevations during the last Ice Age now grow near timberline in the Cascade Mountains.

Climate Change

The Earth's climate exhibits a cyclical pattern of warming and cooling. During the cool periods, huge ice sheets develop and expand in the polar regions. When the Earth warms, the glaciers melt, and an interglacial warming period ensues. We are now experiencing just such a warming period, called the Holocene, which began at the close of the last ice age, 10,000 years ago.

The Last Ice Age

Repeated ice ages have occurred over the last several million years. The most recent was the Fraser Glaciation, which began about 28,000 years ago and ended roughly 10,000 years ago, with glacial maximum occurring between 20,000 and 16,800 years ago. During this period the Cordilleran Ice Sheet, which covered southwestern

Canada and much of the northwestern United States, advanced south into the Puget Lowlands and west across the northern Olympic Peninsula into the ocean. The ice sheet in the northern portion of the Puget Lowlands was 5,200 or more feet thick.[1]

Because so much water was locked up in glacial ice, sea levels dropped by 20 to 30 feet during the Fraser Glaciation, exposing 30 miles of continental shelf along the Pacific Coast. Lowered sea levels also uncovered a land mass 1,000 miles wide along the floor of the Bering Strait between about 25,000 and 10,000 years ago. This land mass shared many environmental characteristics with the contiguous lands, and so the whole sweep of land across northeastern Asia and northwestern North America, including the Bering land bridge, has been called by modern scholars *Beringia*. It is thought that the first humans to arrive in America crossed this land bridge 11,000 years ago.[2]

The climate of the Pacific Northwest during the Fraser Glaciation was much colder and drier than today's— more like the current climate of Alaska's northern interior. Average temperatures during glacial expansion were 9 to 14 degrees Fahrenheit colder than today's, and air temperatures near the glacier may have been 18 degrees lower still. Air movement along the ice sheet probably created squalls and

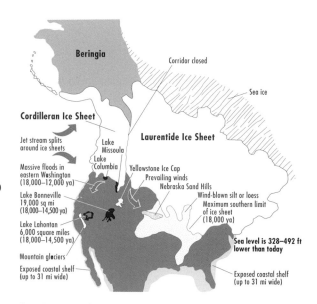

Ice Age North America about 18,000 years ago.

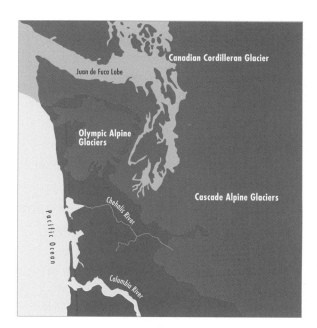

Glaciers covering western Washington between about 20,000 and 16,800 years ago, during the coldest part of the most recent Ice Age, the Fraser Glaciation.

Milankovitch cycles

Long-term, roughly cyclical fluctuations in the Earth's orbit around the Sun and its rotation about its axis are responsible for the pattern of warming and cooling over roughly 100,000 years that cause ice ages to come and go. These fluctuations are called Milankovitch cycles, after the Yugoslavian astrophysicist who discovered the connection among them.

First, the shape of the Earth's orbit around the Sun changes from a wider to a flatter ellipse over a 90,000- to 100,000-year period, the result of tugging from other planets. Because the ellipse is longer at one end than at the other, the Earth is carried farther from the Sun during the winter, and winters are colder and longer than summers.

As the Earth orbits about the Sun, it also spins on an axis that tilts lower and then higher during a 41,000-year cycle. The tilt ranges between 22 and 25 degrees. At times of greatest tilt, there is more contrast between winter and summer near the North and South Poles.

Finally, the Earth wobbles as it spins about its axis, much the way a spinning top wobbles and then returns to a stable position. The wobble, which takes place in a 22,000-year cycle, also produces greater contrast between winter and summer temperatures.

When these three cycles coincide—when the orbital ellipse is flattest, the axial tilt is strongest, and the wobble is most pronounced—the Earth enters an ice age. The whole cycle of cooling and warming takes roughly 100,000 years. Glaciers dominate the land for 60,000 to 90,000 years, and the warm phase lasts for 10,000 to 40,000 years.

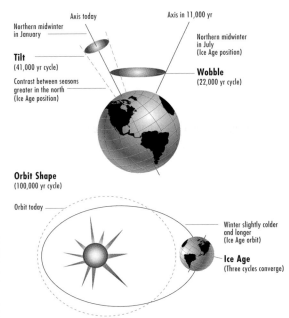

Milankovitch cycles. Ice ages are influenced by coinciding points in the cyclical patterns of the tilt and wobble of the Earth's axis and of its orbit around the Sun.

cold, dry winds. Timberline in the Cascade and Coast Ranges was 2,000 feet lower than it is now.

The chilly air over the ice sheets covering the northern half of North America may have caused a split in the jet stream, an important influence on North American weather patterns. The jet stream is a huge river of fast-moving air that flows west to east through the upper atmosphere above North America. Today, the jet stream is responsible for bringing cyclonic storms towards the Pacific Northwest, and it carries the region's famed winter rains. During the Fraser Glaciation, the southern branch of the jet stream may have moved south of its

Missoula floods

Lake Missoula was a huge interior lake formed by glacial meltwater trapped behind ice dams. Lake Missoula was formed and reformed when a lobe of the Cordilleran Ice Sheet repeatedly blocked the Clark Fork Valley, in present-day Idaho.[1] At its maximum size, roughly 17,000 years ago, the lake covered 3,000 square miles and was 2,000 feet deep, as large as present-day Lake Ontario and Lake Erie combined. When the ice dam crumbled, as it did repeatedly, a torrential flood of icy water would pour through the gap, flowing so fast that the entire lake would be drained in two days. Lake Missoula was filled and emptied numerous times during the last ice age.

The largest of the Missoula floods occurred 17,000 to 18,000 years ago, the last one about 13,000 years ago. During the biggest flood, a 100-mile-wide wall of water raced across Idaho and eastern Washington at speeds of up to 60 miles an hour.[2] The rushing water, hundreds of feet deep, filled all the river and stream drainages and cut new channels across divides. The distinctive scablands of eastern Washington were created when topsoil and bedrock were eroded by the violence of the floodwaters.

The topography channeled the floodwaters toward the Columbia Gorge. Water shot through the gorge at about 90 miles an hour, scouring the walls to 1,000 feet, eroding tributary stream channels to bedrock, and creating the spectacular waterfalls seen along the Columbia Gorge today.[3] At the end of the Gorge, a 400-foot wall of water spilled into area now occupied by east Portland. The floodwaters slowed and spread, depositing boulders, rocks, and gravel in a large alluvial fan. Alameda Ridge in east Portland is a 300-foot gravel bar deposited by Lake Missoula floodwaters.

Floodwaters flowed up the Willamette, Tualatin, and Clackamas river valleys. Water poured into the Willamette Valley, creating another temporary lake 400 feet deep. Suspended soil materials were deposited on the valley floor, making a layer several meters to tens of meters deep. Icebergs carried by swiftly moving floodwaters dropped large boulders along the valley margins.[4]

Much of the soil, gravel, and boulders picked up by the floodwaters has been found in western Oregon, but most of the material removed from eastern Washington is unaccounted for. It may be located offshore, beyond the mouth of the Columbia. The Columbia River's many islands and offshore river bars may be composed of Missoula flood deposits.[5]

[1] Thomas M. Bonnicksen, *America's Ancient Forests: From the Ice Age to the Age of Discovery* (New York, NY: John Wiley & Sons, Inc., 2000).

[2] J. Newman, producer, "The Missoula Flood", a television program (Oregon Field Guide #1001. Portland, OR: Oregon Public Broadcasting, Oct. 4, 1998).

[3] L. Bogart, "Geological and Exploration Associates," on the Web at http://ewu63562.ewu.edu/map.htm, 3/24/2000.

[4] Cliff Hedlund, personal communication, January 2000; and Newman, "The Missoula Flood."

[5] L. Bogart, "Geological and Exploration Associates," on the Web at http://ewu63562.ewu.edu/map.htm, 3/24/2000.

Ice Age forests

How do we know what Ice Age forests were like? Scientists can infer the forest composition of the past and, by extension, the likely climate by analyzing layers of lakebed sediments. Over time, pollen grains, plant material, volcanic ash, and charcoal are deposited on lake surfaces and settle in layers on the bottom.

Paleoecologists—scientists who study prehistoric plant communities—extract sediment cores from 40,000- to 50,000-year-old lakes and analyze and date the layers. They look for pollen grains and plant fossils, such as cones and leaves, and from these make educated guesses about past forest environments. Sediment cores have so far been analyzed from lakes in the Puget Lowlands, the Olympic Peninsula, and the Oregon Coast Range. Conclusions from these studies are necessarily tentative; paleoecological evidence is limited in time and space, and subsequent events like floods erase some of the record. Scientists must often reconstruct conditions on landscapes by extrapolating findings from neighboring areas.

- Ice sheets and alpine glaciers
- Mixed conifer forest
- Mixed conifer-oak forest
- Coastal redwood forest
- Pinion-juniper forest
- Juniper-sage woodland
- Subalpine & mixed conifer forest
- Brushland & grassland
- Ponderosa pine forest
- Pygmy conifer-oak woodland
- Grass tundra & cold steppes
- Tundra and cold steppes
- Sagebrush-grassland
- Grassland
- Sedge tundra and cold steppes
- White spruce forest
- Jack pine forest
- Southern pine-oak forest
- Sand dune-scrub

Cordilleran Ice Sheet

Sea ice

Laurentide Ice Sheet

Forests extend over exposed coastal shelf

America's Ice Age forests. Land cover shifted constantly in response to climate change during the Pleistocene, 20,000 to 10,000 years ago.

present position, causing storms to be deflected away from the Pacific Northwest and reducing precipitation levels by as much as half. As the climate warmed, the two branches of the jet stream reunited. The last glacial advance of the Fraser Glaciation, about 14,500 years ago, may have happened because of the increase in winter precipitation after the return of the jet stream to the Pacific Northwest.[3]

Western Washington

Forest conditions during glacial maximum (28,000 to 10,000 years ago) varied across the landscape. Near the edge of the ice sheet, in modern-day southern Washington, temperatures were very cold, and the ground was permanently frozen. A huge ice lobe extending into the ocean to the west prevented the moderating influence of the ocean from reaching the Puget region until about 13,000 years ago. As the climate warmed, glacial meltwater fed numerous rivers, ponds, and marshes in the southern Puget Lowlands. Tundra vegetation—grasses, sedges, willow, sagebrush, and dwarf birch—was abundant.[4]

Not many trees grew in the Puget Lowlands between 20,000 and 15,000 years ago, although birch and cottonwood may have grown along the edges of rivers and marshes, and patches of Engelmann spruce and lodgepole pine may have grown in some locations.[5] Then, during a warming trend about 15,000 years ago, an open woodland of Engelmann spruce and lodgepole pine, with lesser amounts of mountain hemlock and cottonwood, developed in the Puget Lowlands.[6]

The last advance of the Puget lobe of the Cordilleran Ice Sheet, roughly 14,500 years ago, prompted a shift from trees to tundra vegetation. After 500 years, open woodlands of Engelmann spruce returned, but lodgepole pine did not come back until much later, and mountain hemlock retreated to the Cascades.[7]

Western Oregon

The land that is now called Oregon lay to the south, away from the immediate climatic influence of the glacier. During the height of the Fraser Glaciation, the Oregon Coast Range was covered with open woodlands of Engelmann spruce, lodgepole pine, and mountain hemlock, as well as tundra vegetation such as grasses, sedges, and sagebrush.[8] The Willamette Valley may also have had scattered Engelmann spruce and lodgepole pine and an understory of tundra vegetation during this time.

Years Ago	Oregon Coast Range	Southern Puget Trough	Olympic Peninsula
Present	Douglas-fir, western hemlock, and western redcedar forest	Douglas-fir and western redcedar forest	W. hemlock, w. redcedar, and spruce forest
5,000	Douglas-fir, western hemlock, cedar, and alder forest		
		Douglas-fir and oak savannah	
10,000	Douglas-fir, alder, and western redcedar forest		Open Douglas-fir and alder forest
	Pine, fir, and hemlock forest	Forest of temperate and subalpine taxa	Lodgepole pine, spruce, and mountain hemlock forest
	Forest of Douglas-fir, alder, fir, and hemlock		
15,000	Forest of spruce, fir, and hemlock		
			Parkland/tundra with mountain hemlock and lodgepole pine
20,000	Parkland forest of Engelmann spruce, lodgepole pine, and mountain hemlock	Parkland of mountain hemlock, fir and pine	
25,000			Open forest with mountain hemlock and lodgepole pine
30,000		Hemlock, fir and pine forest	Hemlock and spruce forest
		Pine, spruce, and fir forest	
35,000	Western white pine, fir and western hemlock forest		
40,000			Tundra
45,000			Western hemlock, spruce, and pine forest

Shifts in forest composition over time in western Oregon and Washington.

Glacial refugia

During the Ice Age, where were the species that were later to dominate Pacific Northwest forests? Many of these species had moved far to the south. Others were located in small, protected "islands" where mild climatic conditions persisted. These areas are called *refugia* because they provided a place of refuge for warm-weather species during the bitter cold years of the Ice Age. Wide bands of vegetation adapted to progressively warmer climates arrayed themselves south of the glaciers. Refugia for the warm-weather tree species now found in the Pacific Northwest were located to the south and to the west, on the exposed continental shelf. The Klamath Mountains of southern Oregon and northern California, with their diversity of conifer and hardwood species, may have been an important refugium during the last Ice Age.

About 15,000 years ago a late-glacial warming trend began, allowing closed forests of western hemlock, silver fir, and noble fir to spread into the Coast Range from locations farther to the south. These forests had lesser amounts of Engelmann spruce, lodgepole pine, and mountain hemlock. Near the streams and rivers were Sitka spruce, red alder, and willow.[9] These forests were very similar to the high-elevation silver fir forests growing in the Cascades today.

A few hundred years later, there came a period of frequent fire in parts of the central Oregon Coast Range, and Douglas-fir and red alder forests became established in the disturbed areas and were dominant for 350 years. Understory plants in these Douglas-fir forests included swordfern, elderberry, and brackenfern.[10]

Between 14,400 and 14,250 years ago, the forests again shifted from warmer-weather to cooler-weather species. The swiftness with which this happened suggests that these species—Engelmann spruce, lodgepole pine, and mountain hemlock—were living close by, possibly on the few high-elevation slopes of the Coast Range, during the previous warm period. Or they may have been abundant in the Coast Range throughout the entire glacial period.[11]

Undisturbed forests of the Coast Range between 14,000 and 13,000 years ago were composed of mountain hemlock, western hemlock, noble fir, grand fir, and possibly Pacific silver fir.[12] During glacial times, a narrow band of Sitka spruce and western hemlock forest may have grown on the edge of the continental shelf, which was exposed by lowered sea levels.

Post-glacial Forests

The last Ice Age began to die about 17,000 years ago, but it took 4,500 years for the Cordilleran Ice Sheet to melt back into Canada and another 1,500 years for the ice to shrink up into the high mountains. Enormous quantities of meltwater were trapped in the interior west, where they formed over 100 inland seas. The landscape the receding glacier left behind was covered with piles and ridges of rocks, gravel, and sands, as well as sheets of sand and silt.[13] Huge rocks called glacial erratics were scattered across the landscape where they were dropped by the melting ice sheet.

A fringe of tundra vegetation sprang up in the wake of the retreating glacier. Gradually, shrubs colonized the exposed landscape. It is thought that lodgepole pine was the first tree species to become established in the coarse glacial soils, followed by spruce—the cold, dry conditions suggest Engelmann spruce.[14] Red alder and brackenfern soon became part of the community.

Between 12,000 and 10,000 years ago, the Pacific Northwest's climate warmed significantly, although annual temperatures may still have been 7 to 9 degrees Fahrenheit colder than today's. The warming climate caused a major expansion of temperate-forest species in many locations in the Pacific Northwest. At the beginning of this period, a forest of lodgepole pine, Sitka spruce, Engelmann spruce, western hemlock, mountain hemlock, and subalpine fir grew in the Puget Lowlands. Willow thickets and red alder were common in riparian areas, and western white pine was also abundant in some locations.[15] First Engelmann spruce, then subalpine fir retreated to the Cascades as the climate warmed. Sitka spruce became increasingly restricted to its present location along the coast. Lodgepole pine and western white pine also gradually decreased in abundance.[16]

In the Oregon Coast Range, lodgepole pine and western white pine first increased, then declined. Douglas-fir and red alder also temporarily declined, possibly because of colder temperatures.[17] Between 11,000 and 10,000 years ago, Douglas-fir and red alder again increased, while spruce, mountain hemlock, and true fir declined. Noble fir retreated to the highest reaches of the Coast

Succession

Ecological succession means the sequence of plant (and animal and microbial) communities that successively occupy an area over a period of time. It also means the process of change by which these communities replace each other and by which the environment itself is changed.[1] The product of succession is called a *sere*, and the various communities that make up a sere are called *seral stages*.

Plants in forest communities both cause and respond to changes in the physical environment. When a disturbance, such as fire, removes the canopy of a forest, species adapted to the newly changed environment colonize the site or become more abundant. Over time, the presence of the early-seral species changes the physical environment by (among other things) shading the site and reducing the amount of sunlight that can reach the ground. Early-seral species, which are often shade-intolerant and fast-growing, give way to other, usually longer-lived species more suited to shady environments.

Examples of early-seral species in Northwest forests are Douglas-fir, salmonberry, lodgepole pine, and red alder. Species adapted to environments highly modified by vegetation are called *late-successional species*. Late-successional species include western hemlock, western redcedar, and Pacific yew.

Not all species fit neatly into any one seral category. For example, Douglas-fir seedlings require a disturbed, high-light environment to become established and grow, but mature Douglas-fir trees are extremely long-lived and become an important component of old-growth (late-successional) forests.

Succession is the basis for predicting what will happen in a forest after disturbance. Seral stages are intimately related one to another; forest conditions before a disturbance have a strong influence on how early-seral communities will develop, and the characteristics of early-seral communities in turn affect later stages of succession.[2] Understanding succession is critical for understanding the history of a forest, or of any other plant community.

[1] J.P. Kimmins, *Forest Ecology: A Foundation for Sustainable Management,* 2nd ed. (Upper Saddle River, NJ: Prentice Hall, 1997).

[2] J.F. Franklin and C.T. Dyrness, *Natural Vegetation of Oregon and Washington, USDA Forest Service General Technical Report PNW-8* (Portland, OR: USDA Forest Service Pacific Northwest Forest and Range Experiment Station,1973).

Range, such as Marys Peak, where it grows today. Swordfern and brackenfern also became increasingly common, and tundra species declined.[18]

By 10,500 years ago, a forest of Sitka spruce and western hemlock very much like today's coastal forests grew along the Washington and Oregon coastlines. These forests have remained relatively stable for thousands of years, although the component species have shifted in abundance as the climate has fluctuated.

Between 10,500 and 7,000 years ago, a warm spell accompanied by a severe drought gripped the Pacific Northwest. The conditions encouraged frequent, low-severity fires that maintained open and early-seral forest communities throughout the Pacific Northwest. Brackenfern, a shade-intolerant plant, was abundant during this time, suggesting that there were many forest openings. Oregon white oak, a drought-tolerant species, spread rapidly across the Puget Lowlands, the Willamette Valley, and the Oregon Coast Range.[19]

The ranges of Douglas-fir, western hemlock, and red alder also quickly expanded early in this period. These species completely

A 100-year-old spruce-hemlock stand on Cascade Head on the Oregon Coast. Hemlock seedlings have germinated in the shady understory.

Douglas-fir seedlings germinating thickly on a site that was logged and slash-burned. This photo was taken in 1919 on the Columbia National Forest, now the Gifford Pinchot National Forest, in southern Washington.

Extent of old-growth forests before settlement

How much old-growth forest was there in the Pacific Northwest before European-Americans settled here? Several studies have tackled this question. Some researchers have analyzed historic stand maps drawn before large-scale timber harvesting; others have derived an estimate from mathematical models based on the known fire-return interval. Utilizing these separate approaches, researchers have estimated that old-growth forests probably accounted for 40 to 70 percent of the total forested land base prior to settlement. The location and the amount of old forest varied at any given moment in history, because the disturbances that set the stage for it are unpredictable in both time and space.[1]

[1]D.E. Booth, "Estimating prelogging old-growth in the Pacific Northwest," *Journal of Forestry* 89 (1991), pp. 25–29; William J. Ripple, "Historic Spatial Patterns of Old Forests in Western Oregon," *Journal of Forestry* 92, no. 11 (1994), pp. 45–49; T. Spies, D. Hibbs, J. Ohmann, G. Reeves, R. Pabst, F. Swanson, C. Whitlock, J. Jones, B.C. Wemple, L. Parendes, B. Schrader, "The Ecological Basis of Forest Management in the Oregon Coast Range," in *Forest and Stream Management in the Oregon Coast Range* (in press); P.D.A. Teensma, "Fire History and Fire Regimes of the Central Western Cascades of Oregon" (Ph.D. dissertation, University of Oregon, Eugene, OR, 1987); and Michael C. Wimberly, Thomas A. Spies, Colin J. Long, and Cathy Whitlock, "Simulating Historical Variability in the Amount of Old Forests in the Oregon Coast Range," *Conservation Biology* 14, vol. 1 (2000), pp. 1–15.

displaced Engelmann spruce, mountain hemlock, and lodgepole pine from the Puget Lowlands, the Washington Coast Range, and the western slope of the Cascades. Douglas-fir and red alder also continued to increase in the Oregon Coast Range. These forests had an understory composed of California hazel and vine maple. Oregon ash became prevalent in riparian areas.[20]

Between 7,000 and 5,000 years ago, the climate became cooler and moister. Fire frequency declined, and Pacific Northwest forests became more closed. By 6,000 to 5,000 years ago, the forests of the Pacific Northwest assumed the composition we are familiar with today, although the mix of species has changed by as much as 50 percent over the last several thousand years. The abundance of Douglas-fir and bracken fern decreased, while red alder, western hemlock, Sitka spruce, and swordfern gradually increased. Western redcedar very slowly expanded from scattered locations along moist stream bottoms and gulches to become an increasingly important component of the spruce-hemlock forests of the Puget Lowlands and the Oregon and Washington Coast Range.[21]

Pollen records for the Oregon Coast Range suggest that 5,000 years ago, Douglas-fir grew on dry and fire-prone slopes, while red alder, western hemlock, western redcedar, Pacific yew, Oregon ash, and bigleaf maple grew in moist and riparian areas. Small amounts of grand fir were also present. Oregon white oak and California hazel reached their maximum extent in the Willamette Valley and in prairies of the Puget Lowlands.[22]

Between 5,000 and 4,000 years ago, the climate cooled and became wetter. Engelmann spruce and subalpine fir moved back down to the mid-elevations from the upper reaches of the Cascade Range, and moisture-loving, late-successional conifers such as western redcedar and western hemlock expanded throughout low-elevation forests. Fire frequency declined everywhere except in the Puget Lowlands and the Willamette Valley. Fires that did occur were severe and of the stand-replacing type.[23]

The high frequency of fire in the Willamette Valley and Puget Lowlands during the last 2,000 years may be attributable to Native American burning practices. Certain Indian tribes, chiefly those who depended for their subsistence on valley environments, regularly burned the prairies of the Willamette Valley and other Northwest river valleys as part of their food-gathering practices.[24] Some of these fires probably spread to the eastern slopes of the Coast Range and the western slopes of the Cascades.

Late-successional species such as western hemlock and Sitka spruce may have increased in abundance between 3,000 and 2,000 years ago, perhaps owing to a cooling period that dampened the frequency of fires.[25] Between 3,000 and 1,500 years ago, grand fir, Sitka spruce, and Douglas-fir increased and red alder decreased in abundance. The climate has undergone minor changes over the last 1,000 years with little effect on forest composition.

There is, however, good evidence that the climate is warming once again. Glaciers in the Cascades have been melting for 200 years,[26] and they are now melting at an unparalleled rate. Global climate models are detecting a warming trend that is taking place faster than any natural

A retreating glacier in the North Cascades Range of Washington.

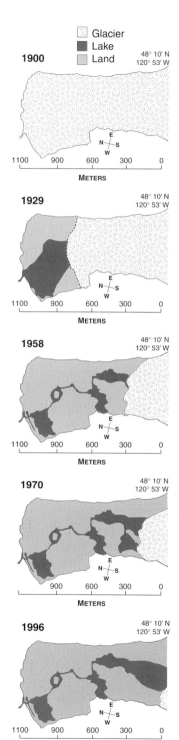

warming trend of the past, so far as we know.[27] Global climate change may significantly alter the species composition of forests within the next 20 to 30 years, perhaps changing environments faster than species can adapt or migrate.[28]

Geological Change

One major disturbance affected the coastal forests of Oregon and Washington just 300 years ago. There is evidence that a huge earthquake hit the coast of Oregon and Washington in the year 1700. The earthquake may have triggered the massive sinking of numerous coastal marshes and forested lowlands into the Pacific Ocean, in locations ranging from Vancouver Island to Humboldt Bay.[29]

Many submerged lowlands off the coast of southern Washington bear snags and stumps of trees that died suddenly about 300 years ago. Remnants of western redcedar and Sitka spruce 300 years old have been recovered from estuaries in Willapa Bay and from the mouth of the Columbia. Buried salt marshes with leaves and stems of tufted grass have been found. These marshes are covered with a layer of coarse sand, which may have been deposited at the time of the coastal submergence by a 30-foot tsunami. Further evidence for the massive wave comes from as far away as Japan, where a 6- to 9-foot tsunami was recorded by coastal villagers in January of 1700.[30] Computer models indicate that an earthquake of magnitude 9 on the Richter Scale along the Pacific Northwest Coast would be strong enough to cause a tsunami of that magnitude in Japan.[31]

The seaward edge of the Cascadia subduction zone. A massive earthquake 300 years ago probably triggered a sinking of forested lands along the Northwest Coast.

The Pacific Northwest has experienced many disturbances during the last several millennia. Large-scale natural catastrophes, such as glaciations, floods, volcanic eruptions, prolonged droughts, subductions of the coastal margin, and tsunamis all have affected the forest landscape. The forests of the region have been in an almost continual state of flux since the end of the last Ice Age. Thus very little may be said about what constitutes a "normal" forest community or disturbance regime. Tree species have moved into neighboring areas when conditions were favorable. They have moved about on the landscape. They have reshuffled their communities continuously in response to changing climatic conditions. Many of the old forests such as Lewis and Clark saw 200 years ago had their origin in fires occurring only a few hundred years before the Corps of Discovery arrived. The paleoecological evidence suggests that this kind of forest is only one of many kinds that have occupied this region since forests began to colonize land watered by melting glaciers.

Notes to Chapter 1

1. C.J. Heusser, "Quaternary Palynology of the Pacific Slope of Washington," *Quaternary Research* 8 (1977), pp. 282–306.

2. Kenneth M. Ames and Herbert D.G. Maschner, *Peoples of the Northwest Coast: Their Archaeology and Prehistory* (London: Thames and Hudson, 1999).

3. M.A. Worona and C. Whitlock, "Late Quaternary Vegetation and Climate History near Little Lake, Central Coast Range, Oregon," *Geological Society of America Bulletin* 107 (1995), pp. 867–876.

4. Thomas M. Bonnicksen, *America's Ancient Forests: From the Ice Age to the Age of Discovery* (New York: John Wiley & Sons, Inc., 2000); and M. Tsukada, S. Sugita, and D.M. Hibbert, "Paleoecology in the Pacific Northwest. I. Late Quaternary Vegetation and Climate," *Proceedings— International Association of Theoretical and Applied Limnology, 1980*, vol. 21, pt. 2 (1981), pp. 730–737.

5. Tsukada et al.,"Paleoecology in the Pacific Northwest"; and L.D. Grigg and C. Whitlock, "Late-glacial Vegetation and Climate Change in Western Oregon," *Quaternary Research* 49, no. 3 (1997), 287–298.

6. Tsukada et al., "Paleoecology in the Pacific Northwest"; and Worona and Whitlock, "Late Quaternary Vegetation and Climate History."

7. Tsukada et al., "Paleoecology in the Pacific Northwest."

8. Grigg and Whitlock, "Late-glacial Vegetation and Climate Change in Western Oregon"; and Worona and Whitlock, "Late Quaternary Vegetation and Climate History."

9. Grigg and Whitlock, "Late-glacial Vegetation and Climate Change in Western Oregon."

10. Ibid.

11. Ibid. See also Worona and Whitlock, "Late Quaternary Vegetation and Climate History."

12. Worona and Whitlock, "Late Quaternary Vegetation and Climate History."

13. Bonnickson, *America's Ancient Forests.*

14. James K. Agee, personal communication, June 2000.

15. Tsukada et al., "Paleoecology in the Pacific Northwest"; and Grigg and Whitlock, "Late-glacial Vegetation and Climate Change in Western Oregon."

16. Bonnickson, *America's Ancient Forests*; Grigg and Whitlock, "Late-glacial Vegetation and Climate Change in Western Oregon"; and Tsukada et al., "Paleoecology in the Pacific Northwest."

17. Grigg and Whitlock, "Late-glacial Vegetation and Climate Change in Western Oregon."

18. Worona and Whitlock, "Late Quaternary Vegetation and Climate History."

19. Colin J. Long, Cathy Whitlock, Patrick J. Bartlein, and Sarah H. Millspaugh, "A 9000-year Fire History from the Oregon Coast Range, Based on a High-resolution Charcoal Study," *Canadian Journal of*

Forest Research 28 (1998), pp. 774–787; Tsukada et al., "Paleoecology in the Pacific Northwest"; and Cathy Whitlock and Lyn Berkley, "Fire and Vegetation History in the Cascade Range, Oregon," unpublished paper. Copy in possession of the authors. See also Worona and Whitlock, "Late Quaternary Vegetation and Climate History"; and Bonnickson, *America's Ancient Forests.*

20. Bonnickson, *America's Ancient Forests*; and Tsukada et al., "Paleoecology in the Pacific Northwest." See also Grigg and Whitlock, "Late-glacial Vegetation and Climate Change in Western Oregon"; and Worona and Whitlock, "Late Quaternary Vegetation and Climate History."

21. Long et al., "A 9000-year Fire History from the Oregon Coast Range"; T. Spies, D. Hibbs, J. Ohmann, G. Reeves, R. Pabst, F. Swanson, C. Whitlock, J. Jones, B.C. Wemple, L. Parendes, B. Schrader, "The Ecological Basis of Forest Management in the Oregon Coast Range," in *Forest and Stream Management in the Oregon Coast Range* (in press); Tsukada et al., "Paleoecology in the Pacific Northwest"; and Bonnicksen, *America's Ancient Forests.*

22. Tsukada et al., "Paleoecology in the Pacific Northwest."

23. Bonnicksen, *America's Ancient Forests*; Cathy W. Barnosky, "Late Quaternary Vegetation in the Southwestern Columbia Basin, Washington," *Quaternary Research* 23 (1985), pp. 109–122; and Spies et al., "The Ecological Basis of Forest Management."

24. Robert Boyd, ed., *Indians, Fire, and the Land in the Pacific Northwest* (Corvallis, OR: Oregon State University Press, 1999).

25. Worona and Whitlock, "Late Quaternary Vegetation and Climate History."

26. Ari Jumpponen, Kim Mattson, James M. Trappe, and Rauni Ohtonen, "Effects of Established Willows on Primary Succession on Lyman Glacier Forefront, North Cascades Range, Washington, U.S.A.: Evidence for Simultaneous Canopy Inhibition and Soil Facilitation," *Arctic, Antarctic, and Alpine Research* 30, no. 1 (February 1998), pp. 31–39. In their study of plant succession on the forefront of Lyman Glacier, Jumpponen et al. used historical photos and other sources to track the recession of the glacier over the past century.

27. Cliff Hedlund, personal communication, January 2000; and Richard Waring, personal communication, August 2000.

28. Daniel Botkin, *Discordant Harmonies: A New Ecology for the Twenty-first Century* (New York and Oxford: Oxford University Press, 1990), p. 194.

29. B.F. Atwater and D.K. Yamaguchi, "Sudden, Probably Coseismic Submergence of Holocene Trees and Grass in Coastal Washington State," *Geology* 19 (1991), pp. 706–709; G.C. Jacoby, "Tree-ring dating of coseismic coastal subsidence in the Pacific Northwest Region," Tree-ring Laboratory, Lamont-Doherty Earth Observatory, on the Web at http://erp.er.usgs.gov/reports/VOL37/PN/g2451.htm, 5/17/2000; and R.A. Kerr, "Faraway Tsunami Hints at a Really Big Northwest Quake," *Science* 267 (1995), p. 962.

30. Atwater and Yamaguchi, "Sudden, Probably Coseismic Submergence of Holocene Trees and Grass"; and James K. Agee, "Historic forest disturbance on Oregon's North Coast" (paper presented at the symposium, "Oregon's Forests as Encountered by Lewis and Clark," Seaside, OR, August 24, 2000, sponsored by Oregon Forest Resources Institute, Portland, OR).

31. Kerr, "Faraway Tsunami Hints at a Really Big Northwest Quake."

Chapter 2

Ecology of Pacific Northwest Forests

*The differences between trees of the same kind have
already been considered. Now all grow fairer and are
more vigorous in their proper positions; for wild, no less
than cultivated trees, each have their own positions:
some love wet and marshy ground, as black poplar,
abele, willow and in general those that grow by rivers;
some love exposed and sunny positions; some prefer a
shady place. The fir is fairest and tallest in a sunny
position, and does not grow at all in a shady one; the
silver-fir on the contrary is fairest in a shady place, and
not so vigorous in a sunny one.*

—Theophrastus, 300 B.C.

The forests encountered by Lewis and Clark at the far western
edge of North America were unfamiliar to their eyes. The
temperate forests of the Pacific Northwest are composed of
evergreen conifers—the warm, dry summers and cool, wet winters
of the region favor them—while the temperate forests they left
behind in the East were and are predominantly deciduous hardwoods.

Pacific Northwest conifers are big—taller and bigger in girth
than most other trees in the world. Many conifers continue to grow
throughout their long lifespans and achieve huge sizes. Trees in old
forests may be 3 to 6 feet in diameter at chest height and 180 to 240

feet tall. Douglas-fir, which can live for 700 to 1,000 years (although 300 to 500 is more typical), can grow to be 10 feet in diameter and 325 feet tall. Western redcedar, with a life span of up to 1,000 years, can grow to be 16 feet in diameter and 250 feet tall. Huge trees are not isolated in these forests; entire stands may be composed primarily of giant conifers.[1]

Besides the striking differences in the kinds and sizes of trees they encountered, Lewis and Clark no doubt marveled at the sheer quantity of *stuff* in these western evergreen forests. Conifer forests in this region may have as much as 1,000 times more biomass than hardwood forests. This biomass is contained not only in the huge tree boles but in dead branches, standing dead trees, logs on the forest floor, and understory plants. Because they are evergreens, conifers can photosynthesize and grow during the winter months when moisture is plentiful, and their waxy needles can tolerate drier weather in the summer.[2]

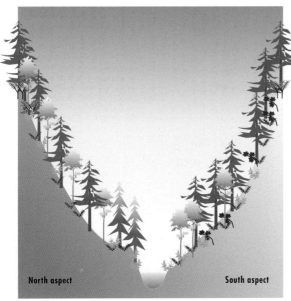

North aspect   South aspect

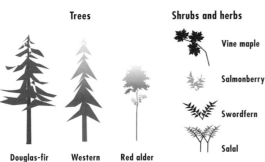

Trees			Shrubs and herbs	
				Vine maple
				Salmonberry
				Swordfern
				Salal
Douglas-fir	Western redcedar	Red alder		

Typical pattern of forest community development on north and south slopes in the western hemlock zone.

Forest Types

Several different forest *types*, or broad groupings of forest communities, are found in western Oregon and Washington. The most widespread is the western hemlock zone—so called because western hemlock becomes the most abundant tree species there after a very long time without disturbance. Despite the name, however, most western hemlock zone forests are composed primarily of Douglas-fir, and western hemlock is not present at all in some places.[3] The western hemlock zone is also called the Douglas-fir region. Western hemlock zone forests are found on the western slopes of the Cascades, the Puget Lowlands, and the Coast Range of Oregon and Washington.

The second forest type, the Sitka spruce zone, is found in a narrow band along the coastline of Oregon and Washington, and sometimes farther inland along river channels. The third type, composed of the Oregon white oak woodlands and grassland prairies, is found in the interior valleys of western Washington and Oregon.[4]

Many different plant communities are located within each forest type. In particular, riparian forests may be quite different from upland forest communities. Riparian forests grow alongside streams and rivers and in poorly drained soils. Riparian forests are typically composed of deciduous hardwood trees rather than conifers.

North aspect　　　　　　　South aspect

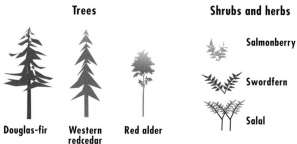

Trees: Douglas-fir, Western redcedar, Red alder

Shrubs and herbs: Salmonberry, Swordfern, Salal

Typical pattern of forest community development on north and south slopes in the Sitka spruce zone.

Disturbance

Disturbance is an essential component of forested ecosystems. Disturbance regimes are patterns of a particular type of disturbance (frequency, intensity, extent) in a particular location. Disturbance regimes are diverse across the landscape and through time, and they play a major role in shaping forest composition and structure.

Until the advent of large-scale logging, fire was the most influential disturbance factor in the development of Pacific Northwest

Disturbances in riparian forests

Riparian forests are subject to the same disturbance processes that affect upland forests, and they also experience disturbances related to their situation next to rivers. Fires may burn through riparian forests, or they may burn upland areas, contributing to landslides, which add sediment and woody debris to stream channels.[1]

Landslides may uproot trees and expose soils for colonization by early-seral species such as red alder. As a result, the streams of forested areas in western Washington and Oregon naturally contain large amounts of woody debris such as treetops, branches, rootwads, and entire trees. Where streams come together, riparian forest floors can be covered with downed logs, sediments, and woody debris.[2]

Localized disturbances, such as small landslides, stream channel migrations, minor floods, and ponding behind beaver dams, occur frequently in riparian forests. Many riparian plant species require disturbed environments to become established. Riparian forests usually contain a mixture of trees and shrubs with a wide range of ages.[3]

[1]Tara R. Nierenberg, "A Characterization of Unmanaged Riparian Overstories in the Central Oregon Coast Range" (master's thesis, Oregon State University, Corvallis, OR, 1996).

[1,2]Ibid. See also F.J. Swanson, G.W. Lienkaemper, and J.R. Sedell. *History, Physical Effects and Management Implications of Large Organic Debris in Western Oregon Streams.* USDA Forest Service General Technical Report PNW-56 (Portland, OR: USDA Forest Service Pacific Northwest Forest and Range Experiment Station, 1976); and T. Spies, D. Hibbs, J. Ohmann, G. Reeves, R. Pabst, F. Swanson, C. Whitlock, J. Jones, B.C. Wemple, L. Parendes, B. Schrader, "The Ecological Basis of Forest Management in the Oregon Coast Range," in *Forest and Stream Management in the Oregon Coast Range* (in press).

[3]Nierenberg, "A Characterization of Unmanaged Riparian Overstories"; and R.J. Pabst and T.A. Spies, "Distribution of Herbs and Shrubs in Relation to Landform and Canopy Cover in Riparian Forests of Coastal Oregon," *Canadian Journal of Forestry* 76 (1998), pp. 298–315.

forests. Fire affects the composition of forests by selectively favoring fire-resistant and early-successional species such as Douglas-fir over fire-sensitive and late-successional species like western hemlock. Fire consumes organic material on the forest floor, freeing nutrients that are then taken up by other plants or moved off the site by water. Fire kills mature trees and clears the land so that early-seral plant species can become established. Fire also kills individual tree seedlings and saplings, influencing the future composition and structure of the forest.[5]

Douglas-fir is an early-seral species that seeds naturally on soil exposed after a stand-replacing forest fire (that is, one that burns the forest to the ground). The presence of large areas of Douglas-fir forest in the Coast Range and western Cascades, noted by explorers and surveyors who arrived a few years after Lewis and Clark, indicates that fire was a natural part of the ecology of these forests. Contemporary research in forest ecology confirms this. Fires burn in Oregon's Douglas-fir-dominated forests about once every 150 years on average,

Fire regimes

A fire "regime" is the pattern of frequency and severity with which fire visits a given landscape. Fire regimes in the forests of the Northwest are categorized according to their severity.[1]

Forests growing in wet, cool environments are characterized by high-severity fire regimes. Forests of the Sitka spruce zone and the western redcedar forests of southern Washington are examples. Fires in these forests are severe but infrequent; the length of time between fire events (called the fire-return interval) is between 400 and 1,000 years. The forests are usually composed of thin-barked, fire-sensitive species. Fires in the high-severity regime usually occur when warm easterly winds blow at the ends of very dry summers. These fires may burn extremely hot for days to weeks, killing 70 percent or more of the trees.[2]

Moderate-severity fire regimes are typical of forests composed of both fire-resistant (thick-barked) and fire-sensitive (thin-barked) trees. Fire-return intervals typically range between 50 and 150 years. These forests live in areas of summer drought. The Douglas-fir forests of the eastern Coast Range, the Willamette Valley foothills, and the western Cascades are characterized by a moderate-severity fire regime. After the fire, the forest looks like a patchwork of more or less severely burned areas. Islands of trees usually survive the fire.

Low-severity fire regimes are characterized by short fire-return intervals—less than 25 years—in forests and woodlands composed of fire-resistant species. Oregon white oak woodlands had a low-severity fire regime before large-scale European-American settlement of the interior valleys. Fires of the low-severity regime kill understory plants and saplings, but over 80 percent of the mature trees typically survive.[3]

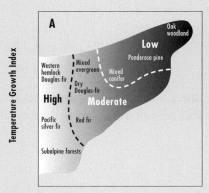

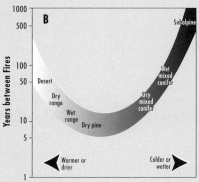

A. Various forest types classified according to fire regime. Forests of different fire regimes experience fires of differing severity.

B. Varying fire-return intervals associated with different environmental conditions.

[1] James K. Agee, *Wildfire in the Pacific West: A Brief History and Implications for the Future,* USDA Forest Service General Technical Report PSW-109 (Berkeley, CA: Pacific Southwest Research Station, 1989).

[2] Ibid. See also J.K. Agee, *Fire Ecology of Pacific Northwest Forests* (Covelo, CA: Island Press, 1993); and P.D.A. Teensma, "Fire History and Fire Regimes of the Central Western Cascades of Oregon" (Ph.D. dissertation, University of Oregon, Eugene, OR, 1987); and William G. Morris, "Forest Fires in Western Oregon and Western Washington," *Oregon Historical Quarterly* 35, no. 4 (1934), pp. 313–339.

[3] Agee, *Wildfire in the Pacific West;* and Agee, *Fire Ecology of Pacific Northwest Forests.*

although actual frequency varies widely from the average, and not every fire is a stand-replacing fire.[6]

Fires occur in an unpredictable pattern, but certain factors make them more likely to strike in certain locations. Ridges, south-facing slopes, and sites exposed to easterly winds are apt to have more fires and a shorter fire-return interval, while valley bottoms, north-facing slopes, and sites protected from easterly winds will generally have fewer fires and a longer fire-return interval.[7]

Fire regimes are also constantly changing, owing to natural climatic factors and, since European settlement, human activity. The Coast Range experienced extensive and severe fires during the nineteenth century as white settlers began to move into the area.[8] Fires have declined in both frequency and severity since the early 1900s, when timber owners and government agencies began to organize to suppress and prevent forest fires. (There are spectacular exceptions, such as the Tillamook Burns of 1933, 1939, 1945, and 1951.)

Recently, scientists have begun to reconstruct the presettlement fire history of western Oregon forests by investigating pollen and charcoal samples from ancient lakebeds and other sites, maps and other data from prelogging days, and growth rings of trees, as well as by using computers to model probable fire-return intervals of the past. These studies show that fire has visited western Oregon forests at varying frequencies throughout the past several centuries.[9]

Along the coast, especially in the spruce-hemlock forests to the north, wind is the primary disturbance factor. Coastal forests and forests located on mountain ridges, along forest edges, and near the Columbia Gorge have been greatly influenced by wind disturbance.[10] Violent

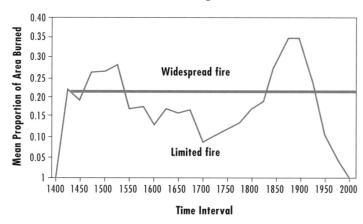

Varying frequency of fires in western Oregon and Washington from 1400 to present, as inferred from tree-ring studies.

windstorms disrupt the forest fabric by toppling trees in small groups or one at a time.

Effects of wind on forests varies with wind velocity and direction, the topography of the land, and the structure and species composition of the forest. High-velocity easterly winds are typical of winters in the Columbia Gorge, and winter storms with strong southwesterly winds typically hit the northern coast. The effects of wind on forests are most pronounced in these exposed places— along the coastline and the Gorge—and diminish as one moves inland and away from the river. Trees exposed on ridges and at the edges of forest stands, and trees of shallow-rooted species such as spruce and hemlock, are the most vulnerable to toppling by wind.

William Clark and his companions had firsthand experience with coastal winds at Fort Clatsop, in the present-day city of Astoria, where they made their winter camp. "The wind Shifted around to the N.W. and blew with Such violence that I expected every moment to See trees taken up by the roots, maney were blown down," Clark wrote in his journal on November 28, 1805.[11]

Wind disturbance over time creates small breaks in the forest cover, making a fine-scale patchiness that contrasts with the relatively homogeneous landscape created by a large forest fire. Thus, old coastal forests tend to have trees of a greater diversity of ages and sizes than old forests farther inland, which are hit more often by large-scale fires. The accumulation of wind-toppled trees over centuries gives the forest floor a rolling, uneven character, familiar to anyone who has walked through a patch of north-coastal old growth. When a big tree topples, it leaves a hole where the roots were. Over time, as the roots and trunk decompose, a pile of humus accumulates next to the hole, resulting in a recognizable "pit-and-mound" topography.[12]

Fire and Wind at Fort Clatsop

Fort Clatsop was somewhat sheltered from the prevailing southwesterly winter winds by a ridge to the west.[13] Lewis realized this; he noted on Feb. 15, 1806, that "the S.W. winds are frequently very violent on the coast when we are but little Sensible of them at Fort Clatsop. In Consequence of the lofty and thickly timbered fir country which Surrounds us from that quarter, from the South to the N. East."[14]

Without a long-term record it is impossible to say how often an area of Northwest coastal forest might have been flattened by wind—how long the average "canopy turnover time" was, in Agee's words.[15] One researcher hypothesizes that small-scale blowdowns probably have a greater impact over time than large-scale ones, and estimates that the forest canopy might be completely replaced at almost 400-year intervals from all windstorms.[16]

Fire and wind together shaped the forests that Lewis and Clark saw around Fort Clatsop. From charcoal samples taken from the Fort Clatsop site in 1988, Agee and his colleagues hypothesize that an ancient fire or series of fires occurred on that site several hundred to many hundreds of years ago. Analyzing the charcoal to determine what species of trees were burned, they found that hemlock, spruce, and cedar, all shade-tolerant species, predominated in the samples, while Douglas-fir, a shade-intolerant species, was completely absent. This suggests that the forest that was burned in the fire grew from hemlock, spruce, and cedar seedlings that germinated in the patchy openings left by small-scale wind disturbances. It also suggests that the forest was a late-successional or old-growth forest that was obliterated by a stand-replacing fire.[17]

The forest that grew in its place—the one Lewis and Clark saw—probably was dominated by Sitka spruce, western hemlock, and western redcedar. Douglas-fir was probably present but did not dominate. These trees may have been a century to several centuries old. Occasional windstorms probably created openings that allowed young hemlocks in the understory to grow into the forest's canopy. "The forest at the time of Lewis and Clark's visit probably had characteristics of old growth forest: large live trees, some large dead standing trees, large downed log material, and a multilayered under-story, much of which was small trees."[18]

Fire and wind disturbance has been the key dynamic influencing forest composition and structural age. Although wind was a

critical shaper of coastal forests, fire has been the single most important disturbance in the Pacific Northwest region, and multiple fire
regimes over diverse topography have produced a highly variable
structure and composition in the region's forests.

Notes to Chapter 2

1. R.H. Waring and J.F. Franklin, "Evergreen Coniferous Forests of the
    Pacific Northwest," *Science* 204 (1979), pp. 1380–386; W.M. Harlow and
    E.S. Harrar, Textbook of Dendrology (New York: McGraw-Hill Book
    Company, Inc., 1941); and J.F. Franklin and C.T. Dyrness, *Natural
    Vegetation of Oregon and Washington*, USDA Forest Service General
    Technical Report PNW-8 (Portland, OR: USDA Forest Service Pacific
    Northwest Forest and Range Experiment Station, 1973).

2. Franklin and Dyrness, *Natural Vegetation of Oregon and Washington*;
    and Waring and Franklin, "Evergreen Coniferous Forests of the Pacific
    Northwest."

3. Franklin and Dyrness, *Natural Vegetation of Oregon and Washington*;
    and J.K. Agee, *Fire Ecology of Pacific Northwest Forests* (Covelo, CA:
    Island Press, 1993).

4. Franklin and Dyrness, *Natural Vegetation of Oregon and Washington*.

5. Agee, *Fire Ecology of Pacific Northwest Forests*.

6. Ibid.

7. P.D.A. Teensma, "Fire History and Fire Regimes of the Central Western
    Cascades of Oregon" (Ph.D. dissertation, University of Oregon, Eugene,
    OR, 1987).

8. William G. Morris, "Forest Fires in Western Oregon and Western Wash-
    ington," *Oregon Historical Quarterly* 35, no. 4 (1934), pp. 313–339.

9. Colin J. Long, Cathy Whitlock, Patrick J. Bartlein, and Sarah H.
    Millspaugh, "A 9000-year Fire History from the Oregon Coast Range,
    Based on a High-resolution Charcoal Study," *Canadian Journal of*

Forest Research 28 (1998), pp. 774–787; Cathy Whitlock and Lyn Berkley, "Fire and Vegetation History in the Cascade Range, Oregon," unpublished paper. Copy in possession of the authors; Peter D.A. Teensma, John T. Reinstra, and Mark A. Yeiter, *Preliminary Reconstruction and Analysis of Change in Forest Stand Age Classes of the Oregon Coast Range from 1850 to 1940,* BLM Technical Note T/N OR-9 (Portland, OR: USDI Bureau of Land Management, 1991); Peter J. Weisberg and Frederick J. Swanson, "Regional Synchronicity in Changing Fire Regime Patterns of the Western Cascades, U.S.A." Paper in review. Copy in possession of the authors; and Michael C. Wimberly, Thomas A. Spies, Colin J. Long, and Cathy Whitlock, "Simulating Historical Variability in the Amount of Old Forests in the Oregon Coast Range," *Conservation Biology* 14, vol. 1 (2000), pp. 1–15.

10. James K. Agee, *A Conceptual Plan for the Forest Landscape of Fort Clatsop National Memorial,* Report CPSU/UW 89-1 (Seattle, WA: U.S. Department of Interior, National Park Service and University of Washington, College of Forest Resources, 1989), p. 7; Agee, *Fire Ecology of Pacific Northwest Forests*; E.W. Hewson, J.E. Wade, and R.W. Baker, *Vegetation as an Indicator of High Wind Velocity.* Phase I Final Report (Oregon State University, Department of Atmospheric Sciences, prepared for the U.S. Department of Energy, DOE Contract EY-76-226, 1977); and F.J Swanson, J.A. Jones, and J.K. Agee. *Analysis of Disturbance History by Fire, Windthrow, and Related Land Management Activities in the Bull Run Watershed, Mt. Hood National Forest, Oregon* (submitted to the City of Portland Water Bureau and Mt. Hood National Forest in partial fulfillment of cooperative agreement PNW 92-0220, 1998).

11. Gary E. Moulton, ed., *The Journals of the Lewis & Clark Expedition,* vol. 6 (Lincoln: University of Nebraska Press, 1990), p. 92.

12. Agee, *A Conceptual Plan for the Forest Landscape,* p. 7.

13. Ibid., p. 9.

14. Moulton, *Journals,* p. 314.

15. Agee, *A Conceptual Plan for the Forest Landscape.*

16. P.A. Harcombe, "Stand Development in a 130-year-old Spruce-hemlock Forest Based on Age Structure and 50 Years of Mortality Data," *Forest*

Ecology and Management 14 (1986), pp. 41–58, cited in Agee, *A Conceptual Plan for the Forest Landscape*, p. 9.

17. Agee, *A Conceptual Plan for the Forest Landscape*, pp. 7, 13.

18. Ibid., p. 15.

Chapter 3

Early European Eyewitnesses

Entering the lower reaches of the Columbia, Lewis and Clark had come once again into a landscape observed and mapped by Europeans. From ships' logs and explorers' journals, we can glean a fragmentary but revealing picture of the Northwest forest landscape and the influences that shaped it before the changes that came with European-American settlement.

Treasure Hunters

More than 250 years before Lewis and Clark departed from St. Louis, European sea captains had begun poking their way up the west coast of North America. The Spanish explorers Juan Rodriguez Cabrillo and Bartoleme Ferrelo sailed north from Baja California in 1542. Ferrelo may have come within sight of the southern Oregon coastline, but he never came ashore. In 1579, the Englishman Sir Francis Drake sailed north perhaps as far as Cape Arago, Oregon, looking for a safe anchorage to repair his ship, the *Golden Hind*. Some say he came as far north as Whale Cove, near present-day Depoe Bay. He made no landings until he got back to Point Reyes, just north of San Francisco.[1]

European interest in the west coast of America waned during the seventeenth and early eighteenth centuries. The Pacific Northwest was a long way from home, the weather was chancy, and there was yet no profitable fur trade to lure wealth-seekers west. But in the eighteenth century, the Spanish, British, and Russians, inspired by a new expansionist mood, goaded by imperial rivalry, and aided by improved navigational technology, turned their attention again to the Northwest Coast.[2] The Russians pushed into Siberia and across the Pacific in search of furs. Spain, anxious to protect her claims to the lands of the Northwest, sent several expeditions northward from New Spain, her territories in present-day Mexico and California.

The *Santiago,* commanded by Juan Perez, reached the coast of British Columbia in 1774. Father Juan Crespi was aboard. As the ship returned along the Washington Coast, Crespi observed that "the land was well forested with trees all the way from the snow covered peak [Mount Olympus]. ... All through the mountains we can see the smokes of many fires, showing that the country is populated." Along the Oregon shore, Crespi noted "low land, but parts rise somewhat, all covered with trees." Farther south: "we saw some level country on the shore, without trees but with plenty of grass."[3]

The three voyages of Captain James Cook, a renowned navigator and explorer, did much to expand European knowledge of the Pacific Coast's natural features and commercial possibilities. The British government, bent on Britain's being first to find the fabled Northwest Passage, offered a prize of 20,000 pounds for its discovery.[4] Cook was trying to find the Northwest Passage in 1778 when he landed at Nootka Sound on what is now Vancouver Island. There he dispatched his men ashore to fell trees for masts. Cook's crew members became the first European loggers in the Northwest.[5]

Cook's crew also acquired sea otter furs from the Indians, paying for them with bits of metal.[6] The next winter the men sold the furs in Canton, China, for $100 or more each.[7] Thus began the Pacific Northwest fur trade, which set the course for the economic expansion and exploitation of the Northwest Coast in the early nineteenth century.

Sailing past a rocky headland on the northern Oregon coast on March 7, 1778, Cook named it Cape Perpetua, after the saint commemorated on that day in the liturgical calendar. Cook described the land near it and Cape Foulweather, which he also named, as "diversified with a great many rising grounds and small hills; many of which are covered with tall straight trees; and others which are lower, and grew like coppices; but the interspaces and sides of many of the rising grounds were clear."[8]

Cook was followed by British traders, including Captain John Meares, who visited the Northwest Coast in 1788. He was the one who named the promontory north of the Columbia's mouth Cape Disappointment, because, like Vancouver, he had missed the river he was looking for. Sailing along the Olympic Peninsula in July, Meares wrote, "The appearance of the land was wild in the extreme . . . immense forests covered the whole of it within our sight down to the very beach . . . the force of Southerly storms was evident to every eye; large and extensive woods being laid flat by their power, the branches forming one long line to the North West, intermingled with roots of enumerable trees, which had been torn from the beds. . . ."[9] Meares provides a vivid description of the effects of wind, the primary natural disturbance that has shaped the Northwest's coastal forests.

Early in 1792, also in search of the Northwest Passage, the British sea captain George Vancouver entered Puget Sound through the Strait of Juan de Fuca. He described the landscape along the strait as "well covered with a variety of stately forest trees." Like Cook, Vancouver logged some of the timber, which furnished stout spars to replace some of his ship's defective yardarms. "[I]t was a very fortunate circumstance, that these defects were discovered in a country abounding with materials to which we could resort; having only to make our choice from amongst thousands of the finest spars the world produces," he wrote.[10]

Thick as the forest was in places, it "did not conceal the whole face of country in one uninterrupted wilderness, but pleasantly clothed its eminences, and chequered the valleys; presenting in many directions, extensive spaces that wore the appearance of having been cleared by art." Vancouver may not have been aware that the open landscape he so admired was indeed brought about by "art," namely the burning of the prairies by the Indians. He did speculate that the Indians felled some trees: "It is possible that most of the clear spaces [around the Indians' villages] may have been indebted, for the removal of their timber and underwood to manual labor."[11]

Further glimpses of the Northwest landscape through European eyes comes to us from Lieutenant William Broughton, attached to Captain Vancouver's expedition.[12] Broughton and Vancouver barely missed being the first European explorers to enter the Columbia. Vancouver's flagship, *Discovery,* passed the river's mouth on the morning of April 27, 1792. Vancouver was on orders not to "pursue any inlet or river further than it shall appear to be navigable by vessels of such burthen as might safely navigate the Pacific Ocean."[13]

Captain Robert Gray's ship, Columbia Rediviva, *the first to enter the Columbia's mouth.*

Captain Gray

As he sailed past the Columbia's mouth, he could see from the change in the water that a river emptied into the ocean there. However, "not considering this opening worthy of more attention," he sailed north without investigating further.[14] Two weeks later, on May 11, 1792, the American fur trader Robert Gray, commanding the *Columbia Rediviva,* noted the same flume of muddy water coming from the shore and decided to follow it. At eight o'clock in the morning, Gray's ship crossed the bar, and Gray became the first European-American to see the banks of the Great River of the West.[15] He named the river after his ship.

It was not Captain Gray's first visit to the Northwest. A few years earlier, he had sailed along the southern Oregon Coast in the Boston trading ship *Lady Washington.* His first mate, Robert Haswell, kept a journal of the trip. Haswell wrote that the shore near Cape Blanco was "beautifully diversified with forists and green verdant

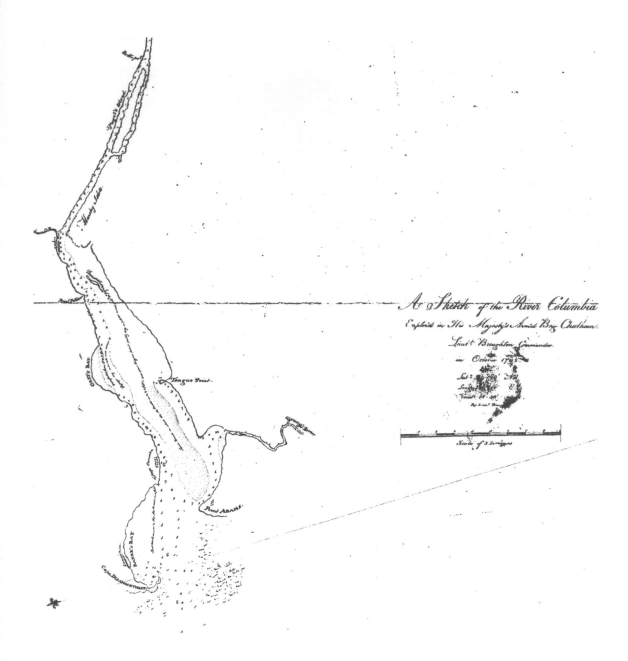

Map of the mouth of the Columbia River drawn by Lieutenant William Broughton, who came with Captain George Vancouver's expedition of 1792. Broughton sailed the armed brig Chatham *up the Columbia as far as the mouth of the Sandy River.*

lawns." He also noted that "the countrey must be thickly inhabited by the fires we saw in the night and the culloms of smoke we could see in the day time."[16] Haswell was correct to assume that the country was inhabited, but the smoke he saw may also have come from wildfires sparked by lightning.

In October of 1792, Vancouver sent Broughton up the Columbia in the *Chatham* with orders to explore the river and take possession of the land through which it flowed. The *Chatham,* like many ships after her, had a rough time crossing the Columbia's bar.[17] "I never felt more alarmed & frightened in my life," wrote one of Broughton's clerks in his journal. "The Channel was narrow, the water very Shoal, and the Tide running against the Wind . . . raised a Surf that broke entirely around us, and I am confident that in going in, we were not twice the Ship's length from Breakers, that had we struck on, we must inevitably have gone to pieces."[18] From this and many subsequent disasters and near-misses, the dangers attending the crossing of the Columbia's bar became well known among sea captains.

Broughton sailed the *Chatham* up to about the mouth of the Sandy River, opposite a projection on the north bank which he named Point Vancouver.[19] He found the country much to his liking. Describing the wooded islands and the groves of alder, maple, birch, willow, poplar, oak, and fir along the shore, he said it was, "the most beautiful landscape that can be imagined."[20]

Fur trader Alexander Mackenzie was the first European to travel overland through the Columbia Basin to the Pacific. In 1793 he paddled and walked the 1,200 miles from Fort Chipewyan in Alberta, over the Canadian Rockies, down the Fraser River—which he called by its Indian name, Tacouche Tesse—and thence overland by Indian trail to the ocean.[21] He accomplished the round trip in 107 days.[22] Mackenzie thought, erroneously, that the Tacouche Tesse was the upper part of the Columbia. Yet he proved, finally, that there was no Northwest Passage. An account of his explorations, *Voyages,* was published in 1801. Thomas Jefferson was familiar with the book, as were Lewis and Clark, who carried a copy of it on their expedition to the Pacific Northwest.[23]

Notes to Chapter 3

1. Herbert K. Beals, *The Last Temperate Coast: Maritime Exploration of Northwest America, 1542-1794,* annotated poster (Portland, OR: Oregon Historical Society, 1990).

2. James H. Hitchman, *Maritime History of the Pacific Coast, 1540-1980* (Lanham, MD: University Press of America, 1990), pp. 4-5.

3. Juan Crespi, *Missionary Explorer on the Pacific Coast: 1769-1774* (Berkeley, CA: University of California Press, 1927).

4. Dorothy O. Johansen, *Empire of the Columbia*, 2d ed. (New York: Harper & Row, 1967), p. 31.

5. Robert Reed Bunting, "Landscaping the Pacific Northwest: A Cultural and Ecological Mapping of the Douglas-fir Region, 1778-1900" (Ph.D. dissertation, University of California, Davis, 1993), p. 80.

6. Hubert Howe Bancroft, *History of the Northwest Coast, Vol. 1: 1543-1800* (San Francisco: A.L. Bancroft & Company, 1884).

7. Hitchman, *Maritime History of the Pacific Coast.*

8. Bancroft, *History of the Northwest Coast.*

9. Robert E. Ficken, *This Forested Land: Lumbering in Washington* (Seattle, WA: University of Washington Press, 1987).

10. Edmund S. Meany, *Vancouver's Discovery of Puget Sound* (New York: The Macmillan Company, 1915).

11. Ibid.

12. Terence O'Donnell, *That Balance So Rare: The Story of Oregon* (Portland, OR: Oregon Historical Society Press, 1988), p. 16.

13. Johansen, *Empire of the Columbia*, p. 44.

14. Ibid.

15. O'Donnell, *That Balance So Rare*, p. 16.

16. Robert Haswell, *Voyages of the Columbia to the Northwest Coast, 1787-1790 and 1790-1793*, Frederic W. Howay, ed. (Portland, OR: Oregon Historical Society and Massachusetts Historical Society, 1990).

17. Johansen, *Empire of the Columbia*, p. 46.

18. J. Nielson Barry, ed., "Columbia River Exploration, 1792," Oregon Historical Quarterly, March 1932. Cited in Johansen, *Empire of the Columbia*, p. 46.

19. Johansen, *Empire of the Columbia*, p. 46.

20. O'Donnell, *That Balance So Rare*, p. 16.

21. Johansen, *Empire of the Columbia*, p. 46.

22. Thomas M. Bonnicksen, *America's Ancient Forests: From the Ice Age to the Age of Discovery* (New York: John Wiley & Sons, Inc., 2000), p. 347.

23. Johansen, *Empire of the Columbia*, p. 67.

Chapter 4

What Lewis and Clark Saw

For the next week and more, they were pinned down by the tide, the waves, the wind, at Point Ellice. They were unable to go forward, to retreat, to climb out of their campsite because of the overhanging rocks and hills, to do anything except endure pure misery. It rained for eleven days. At high tide, gigantic waterborne trees of cedar, fir, and spruce, some of them almost two hundred feet long and up to seven feet in diameter, crashed into the camp. Fires were hard to start, difficult to maintain. The captains and men of the expedition looked more like survivors from a shipwreck praying for rescue than the triumphant members of the Corps of Discovery.

—Stephen Ambrose, *Undaunted Courage*

On November 3, 1805, the party set out late from their camping spot under the towering basalt column now known as Crown Point. "The fog So thick this morning we did not think it prudent to Set out untill (it Cleared away at) 10 oClock ..." wrote Clark.[1]

That day's journey took them past the mouth of the Sandy River, which Clark called the "quick Sand" river because of the "emece quanty of (quick) Sand" it had discharged into a sandbar long and high enough to steer the river's current toward the north bank. The sand may have been mixed with volcanic ash from an eruption of Mount Hood in the 1790s, which would have sent enormous mudflows down the glacial rivers.[2]

They landed on the north side of Lady Island, downstream from the Sandy's mouth. Accompanied by some Indian acquaintances from upriver, Clark walked along the island's south bank. "The under groth rushes, vines &c. in the bottoms too thick to pass through," he wrote. To the southeast he saw a mountain "which we Suppose to be Mt. Hood."[3]

The next day the party camped on Government Island. "The Country is low rich and thickly timbered on each Side of the river, the Islands open & Some ponds." There were waterfowl everywhere: "Swan, geese, Brants, Cranes, Stalks [storks], white guls, comerants & plevers &c." A couple of days later, Clark complained, "I could not Sleep for the noise kept by the Swans, Geese … they were emensely numerous and their noise horrid."[4]

A few miles downriver on the north bank, he saw open country, "a small Prarie in which there is a pond … here I landed and walked on Shore, about 3 miles a fine open Prarie for about 1 mile, back of which the countrye rises gradually and wood land comencies. . . ."

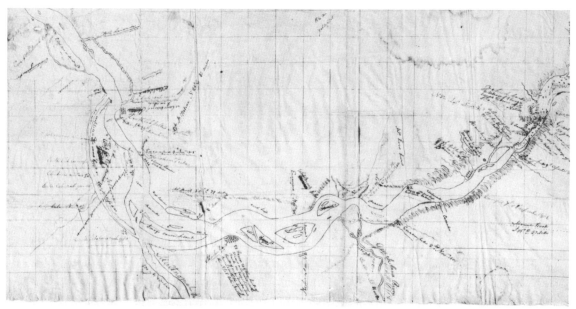

William Clark's map of the Columbia River from The Dalles to the mouth of the Cowlitz River.

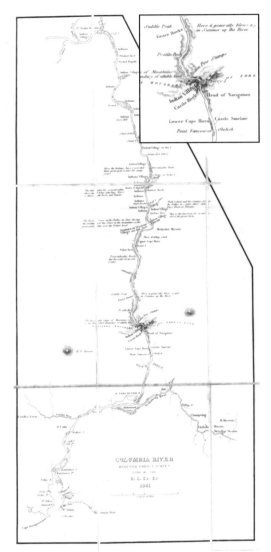

Charles Wilkes's 1841 map of the Columbia River from Fort Walla Walla to The Dalles, showing Indian villages all along the shoreline.

Human-caused fire

According to the anthropologist Robert Boyd, "The traditional stereotype of non-agricultural foraging people was that they simply took from the land and did not have the tools or knowledge to modify it to suit their needs." On the contrary, Native Americans "did indeed have a tool—fire—and they knew how to use it in ways that not only answered immediate purposes but also modified their environment."[1]

A large body of archaeological, ecological, and historical evidence indicates that the Indians living in and around the Willamette Valley and Puget Lowland prairies regularly burned the prairies as part of their food-gathering practices. Indian-set fires probably escaped into the surrounding foothill forests at times, although there is no way to know the extent, frequency, or precise location of these events.[2]

Fires became rarer in the valleys with the plummet in Native American populations in the early 1800s owing mainly to disease, and with fire suppression by settlers, begun in the mid-1840s.[3]

[1] Robert Boyd, ed., *Indians, Fire, and the Land in the Pacific Northwest* (Corvallis, OR: Oregon State University Press, 1999), p. 2.

[2] Boyd, *Indians, Fire, and the Land*, p. 10; and Thomas M. Bonnicksen, *America's Ancient Forests: From the Ice Age to the Age of Discovery* (New York: John Wiley & Sons, Inc., 2000), p. 153.

[3] Boyd, *Indians, Fire, and the Land*, pp. 99–100.

Clark mentioned white oak, different species of conifers, cotton-wood, ash, and "Several Species of undergroth of which I am not acquainted… ." He also noted wild crabapple, *Malus diversifolia*, and his "maple" was probably bigleaf maple, *Acer macrophyllum*. Both species were until then unknown to science.[5]

Clark was seeing the site of the future city of Vancouver, Washington. The pond he mentions is Vancouver Lake. It is likely that the Indians who lived there kept the prairie clear of trees and brush by periodic, intentional burning. This practice of burning may have begun as long as 5,000 years ago.[6]

Interior of a longhouse.

The rivers tributary to the Columbia from the north were the home of the Klikitats and their close linguistic relatives, the Cowlitz. Unlike their Chinookan neighbors upstream, who took most of their sustenance from the river, the Klikitats and Cowlitz looked to the prairies to furnish them with the camas roots, hazelnuts, acorns, huckleberries, and venison they lived on. Camas is a low-elevation meadow plant, huckleberry a high-elevation one, but both are enhanced by periodic fire, and deer congregate in areas of brush or forest interspersed with open areas of succulent young plants. Oaks produce more acorns when subjected to fires that burn the undergrowth and scorch the tree's bark.[7] The Indians of the Northwest used fire in a deliberate and strategic way to alter their prairie environments to their own advantage.

On the south shore, the Corps of Discovery encountered a Chinookan village of 25 wooden houses. They bought four bushels of wapato roots (*Sagittaria latifolia*). Wapato was a staple of the Chinookan diet. "It has an agreeable taste and answers verry well in place of bread," wrote Clark.[8] Most of the houses in the Indian village were dug partway into the earth, as was common among Northwest Indians and others. These houses were sided with bark and thatched with straw. One large house was 50 feet long, built above the ground, "and covered with broad Split boards." The remains of this village probably lie on the site now occupied by the Portland Airport.[9]

The Indians built their plank houses of a post-and-beam framework made of squared logs, sheathing the framing timbers with planks. They split the planks from fallen cedar logs, and sometimes standing trees, using wedges made from stone and antlers. Lacking nails, they lashed the lumber together with cords of cedar bark.[10] The historian Stephen Dow Beckham describes the arduous process of splitting off the planks:

> [T]hey took several elk horn or bone wedges and drove them along the edge of a log. Gradually as they forced open a crack in the wood, they placed larger wedges made of yew wood. Eventually the soft cedar or redwood split and a long plank popped free from the log. Then the men took a stone-tipped adze. Slowly, with much labor, they thinned and smoothed the board.[11]

Wood, particularly redcedar, was very important in the lives of the Chinook and other Northwest coastal tribes. According to the anthropologist Robert Boyd, redcedar "was so important to Northwest Coast Indian cultures that its use is considered one of the hallmarks of the culture area. If you were to superimpose a map of the Northwest Coast culture area over a map of western redcedar distribution, they would coincide almost exactly."[12]

From cedar logs the Indians crafted dugout canoes, using only stone and bone tools and fire. Robert Stuart, one of John Jacob Astor's fur-company employees, marveled at the skill it took to produce these boats, and to pilot them in the Columbia's churning waters:

> Their Canoes for the most part are made of Cedar, and altho' possessed of no other instrument than a small chisel, it would be in vain for any White (with every tool he could wish) to set up a competition with them in this art; if perfect symmetry, smoothness and proportion constitute beauty, they surpass anything I ever beheld: I

have seen some of them as transparent as oiled paper, thro' which you could trace every formation of the inside; and the natives of this river & its vicinity are the most expert paddle men any of us had ever seen.... [13]

From cedar bark the Indians made fabric for clothing, nets, and line for fishing. From the ash and willow trees that lined the rivers, they made paddles for their canoes, scoops for bailing, pole frames for drying fish and meat, bowls and kitchen utensils, and watertight wooden boxes for storing household goods. They made cedar boxes for stewing meat or fish, using hot stones to bring the water to a boil. They made bows of cedar and arrows of pine and hardwood. [14]

On to Fort Clatsop

Racing downstream, the Corps of Discovery was making 30 miles a day. [15] Setting out at sunrise from their camp on the Washington shore below Vancouver, on November 5, the expedition passed the mouth of the Kalama River, noting steep, rocky banks on both sides. "Here the river is about one and a half miles wide, and deep," wrote Clark. "The high Hills which run in a N.W. & S.E. derection form both banks of the river the Shore boald and rockey, the hills rise gradually & are Covered with a thick groth of Pine &c." He estimated the Columbia's drainage basin to be 60 miles wide, "rich thickly Covered with tall timber, with a fiew Small Praries bordering on the river and on the Island… ." [16]

Clark found the prospect much to his liking. "This is certainly a fertill and a handsom valley, at this time Crouded with Indians." However, in what would become a weary refrain over the next four months, he observed, "Cloudy with rain … we are all wet cold and disagreeable." [17]

Clark's drawing of a trout, from his journal. Lewis and Clark brought back many detailed and accurate drawings and descriptions of the Northwest's flora and fauna.

On November 6, Clark's journal records an exultant shout: "Ocian in view! O! the joy." His jubilation was premature—he was seeing the Columbia's broad estuary. For the next week the party would be stranded on a narrow crescent of beach at Point Ellice, on the river's north bank, backed up against "a Clift of Purpendicular rocks or steep assents to the hight of 4 or 500 feet" lashed by rain, battered by high winds, assaulted by the immense drift logs that slammed into the riverbank at high tide.[18] On November 10, Clark wrote peevishly, "The logs on which we lie is all on flote ever high tide—The rain Continud all day—we are all wet, also our beding and many other articles. we are all employed untill late drying our bedding. nothing to eate but Pounded fish."[19]

Three of the expedition's men rounded the point on November 13, looking for a better campsite. They found one at present-day Fort Canby State Park, and on the 17th the party gathered there. Separately, Lewis and then Clark climbed Cape Disappointment, the headland that marks the north boundary to the Columbia's estuary, and carved their names into a tree. Clark added to his, with a flourish: "By Land from the U. States in 1804 & 1805."[20]

The land along the river was hilly—more so on the north bank—and thickly timbered with big, old trees. Behind the hills to the north and south lay lower, sometimes marshy ground, covered with brushy forest so thick the men couldn't walk through it. To the southwest lay the marshy, shrubby Clatsop Plains, extending south along the coast from the river's mouth.

On the 19th, Clark explored the hills north of Cape Disappointment. "I proceeded on through ruged Country of high hills and Steep hollers ... to the Commencement of a Sandy Coast." He found "... different Species of pine of 3 or 4 feet through growing on the bodies of large trees which had fallen down, and covered with moss and yet part Sound."[21]

Beyond these hills was long, sandy beach, present-day Long Beach, Washington, leading into "a low pondey countrey, maney places open with small ponds in which there is a great number of fowl."[22]

On the 22nd, the party took a vote on where to spend the winter. The choices were to stay where they were, go back upriver to the Cascades of the Columbia, or cross to the south shore in search of a good wintering site before deciding. The vote was almost unanimous in favor of the third alternative. The opinion of York, Clark's slave, was counted, and so was that of Sacagawea, the Shoshone woman who had been with the Corps of Discovery almost since the beginning. Using her nickname, Clark wrote, "Janey in favour of a place where there is plenty of Potas [evidently roots]."[23] "This was the first vote ever held in the Pacific Northwest," says the historian Stephen Ambrose. "It was the first time in American history that a black slave had voted, the first time a woman had voted."[24]

On the 26th, the party crossed to the south shore. A few days later Lewis explored Youngs Bay, into which flowed a river which he called "Ne-tul," thinking that was the Indians' name for it.[25] His journal reads, at intervals along the way, "land not very high and open woods a little back from the bay ... marshey ground ... to a marshey point passing the arm of the bey ... the country to the S.E. appears to be low for a great distance and is marshey and untimbered for three miles back ...."[26]

The windy, miserable weather continued: "about 12 o'Clock [on the 28th] the wind Shifted around to the N.W. and blew with Such violence that I expected every moment to See trees taken up by the roots, maney were blown down" wrote Clark. "This wind and rain Continued with Short intervales all the latter part of the night. O! how disagreeable is our Situation dureing this dreadfull weather."[27]

The party also found the forest understory heavy going. On the 26th, they were only a few miles from the ocean—they could hear the waves breaking. Lewis sent three men to explore the country to the south and west. They returned after two hours and informed him that "the wood was so thick and obstructed by marrasses & lakes that they were unable to proceed to the ocean."[28]

Finally, early in December, Lewis chose a spot on the river now called Lewis and Clark. The site was "a thick groth of pine about 200 yards from the river, ... thickly Covered with lofty pine," wrote

William Clark. "this is certainly the most eligible Situation for our purposes of any in its neighbourhood."[29]

Building the Fort

On December 8, Clark took five men and set out for the ocean to find a good place to make salt. This was done, Ambrose explains, by boiling seawater in iron kettles until it evaporated, and then scraping the salt crystals from the sides.[30] Clark was looking for a place close to the sea that had abundant firewood. They set out to the southwest, "on a dividing ridge through lofty piney land much falling timber." After wading two streams and rafting a third, the party spotted a herd of elk and chased it "through verry bad Slashes [swamps] and Small ponds. . . ."[31]

Clark marveled at the depth of the swamp and the nimbleness of the elk. "It is almost incredeable to assurt the bogs which those animals Can pass through, I prosue'd this gang of Elk through bogs which the wate of a man would Shake for 1/2 an Acre, and maney places I Sunk into the mud and water up to my hips. . . ." The bogs were covered with cranberries, and the higher ground with "pine Common to the Countery & Lorel."[32] Typically, Clark used "pine" to refer to any of several evergreen trees; "Lorel" is probably coast rhododendron (*Rhododendron macrophyllum*). Says Moulton: "The men were probably familiar with the Eastern species mountain laurel, *Kalmia latifolia* L., which is similar to the rhododendron in appearance, hence the use of the term laurel."[33]

On his return, Clark found Lewis and the rest of the men cutting down trees to build their winter fort. "We Continue to put up the Streight butifull balsom pine on our houses—and we are much pleased to find that the timber Splits most butifully and to the width of 2 feet or more."[34] According to Moulton's notes, the wood they were using could have been Douglas-fir, grand fir, or Sitka spruce; others think it was more likely western redcedar, the best splitter of all the trees that grow along the north coast and a species much used by the Indians.[35]

The Corps received a visit from a party of Clatsop Indians on the 12th of December. "We gave a Medal to the principal Chief named Con-ny-au or Com mo-wol," wrote Clark. The leader's name has come down to us as Coboway, and it was to him the captains made a gift of Fort Clatsop when they departed the following spring. According to his descendents, Coboway used the fort during the next several hunting seasons.[36]

The building of the fort continued through December. "All the men at work about the houses, Some Chinking, Dobbing, Cutting out dores &c. &c." On December 23, the captains moved into their quarters, as yet unfinished; the next day the men moved into theirs, as yet unroofed. On the 30th the fort was completed.[37]

In Search of Whale

Early in January, the Clatsops informed the captains that a whale had come ashore on the beach near Tillamook Head. Clark set out with a party of eleven—including Sacagawea, who had begged to come along "and was therefore indulged"—in the hope of obtaining whale meat or oil. Their journey took them on a trek down the beach at Seaside, followed by an arduous climb over Tillamook Head. "We proceeded on the round Slipery Stones under a high hill which projected into the ocian about 4 miles further than the direction of the Coast." Their Indian guide halted after 2½ miles, pointed to the top of the mountain, and indicated that the party had to leave the beach and climb. "I hesitated a moment & view this emence mountain the top of which … was obscured in the clouds, and the assent appeard. to be almost perpindecular." At one point "we were obliged to Support and draw our Selves up by the bushes & roots for near 100 feet, and after about 2 hours labour and fatigue we reached the top of this high mountain, from the top of which I looked down with estonishment to behold the hight which we had assended … ."[38]

Climbing to a promontory open to the sea, Clark beheld the ocean from Tillamook Head's 500-foot height, "the grandest and most pleasing prospects which my eyes ever surveyed, in my frount a boundless Ocean; to the N. and N.E. the coast as far as my sight

Could be extended ...." The ruggedness of the shoreline "gives this Coast a most romantic appearance."[39] The high ground of Tillamook Head was covered with a heavy growth of conifers, some of which Clark estimated to be 210 feet tall and 8 to 12 feet in diameter.

Clark returned to the fort with 300 pounds of blubber and a few gallons of whale oil. These he had to buy from the Indians, who had stripped the whale's carcass before he arrived. Lewis found the whale meat agreeable, "very palitable and tender," resembling "the beaver or dog in flavor."[40] For everyone it was likely a welcome change from elk, the expedition's dietary staple throughout the long winter.

Lewis and Clark left Fort Clatsop in March of 1806. They had endured a cold, wet, tedious winter: in 20 weeks they had seen only 12 days without rain, only 6 without clouds. Their supplies were low, their trade goods nearly depleted. "Two handkerchiefs would not contain all the small articles of merchandize which we possess," wrote Lewis on March 16.[41] In an act that leaves a stain on the Corps' otherwise honorable reputation, they stole a canoe from a Clatsop Indian because they couldn't afford to buy it. When the four men who did the deed got back to the fort, they found the Clatsop leader Coboway visiting. Awkwardly hiding their deception, the captains tendered to Coboway the fort's building and furniture, along with "a cirtificate of [Coboway's] good conduct." He had been, wrote Lewis, "much more kind an hospitable to us than any other indian in this neighbourhood."[42]

Before they left, Lewis posted on the wall in his quarters a list of the names of the men of the Corps of Discovery. He left a copy of the list with Coboway. The object of the list, he wrote, was to prove to any "civilized person who may see the same" that the party sent out by the U.S. government in May of 1804 to explore the continent "did penetrate the same...[to] the Pacific Ocean."[43]

Notes to Chapter 4

1. Gary E. Moulton, ed., *The Journals of the Lewis & Clark Expedition*, vol. 6 (Lincoln: University of Nebraska Press, 1990), p. 9.

2. Ibid., p. 11; and Bob Zybach, "Historical Overview of Columbia Gorge Forestlands: Dynamics and Fragmentation, 1792–1996." Unpublished report. Copy in possession of the authors, p. 1.

3. Moulton, *Journals*, p.12.

4. Ibid., pp. 13–14. Clark was seeing sandhill cranes, wood storks, double-crested cormorants, and trumpeter and whistling swans; the other references are too obscure to identify.

5. Ibid., pp. 17, 19.

6. Ibid., p. 20; and Kenneth M. Ames and Herbert D.G. Maschner, *Peoples of the Northwest Coast: Their Archaeology and Prehistory* (London: Thames and Hudson, 1999), p. 142.

7. Helen H. Norton, Robert Boyd, and Eugene Hunn, "The Klikitat Trail of South-central Washington: A Reconstruction of Seasonally Used Resource Sites," in *Indians, Fire, and the Land,* ed. Robert Boyd (Corvallis, OR: Oregon State University Press, 1999), p. 66; and Ames and Maschner, *Peoples of the Northwest Coast*, p. 142.

8. Moulton, *Journals*, p. 17.

9. Ames and Maschner, *Peoples of the Northwest Coast*, p. 151; and Moulton, *Journals*, p. 20.

10. Ames and Maschner, *Peoples of the Northwest Coast*, p. 151; and Olin D. Wheeler, *The Trail of Lewis and Clark 1804–1904*, vol. II. (New York: G.P. Putnam's Sons, 1904), p. 220.

11. Stephen Dow Beckham, *The Indians of Western Oregon: This Land was Theirs* (Coos Bay, OR: Arago Books, 1977), p. 59.

12. Robert Boyd, personal communication, June 2000.

13. Philip Rollins, ed., "Robert Stuart's Narratives," in *The Discovery of the Oregon Trail* (New York, NY: Charles Scribner's Sons, 1935).

14. Moulton, *Journals*, pp. 32, 211; Gabriel Franchere, *Adventure at Astoria, 1810–1814,* Hoyt C. Franchere, tr. and ed. (Norman, OK: University of Oklahoma Press, 1967), p. 113; Oregon Council for the Humanities, *The First Oregonians: An Illustrated Collection of Essays on Traditional Lifeways, Federal-Indian Relations, and the State's Native People Today* (Portland: Oregon Council for the Humanities, 1991), p. 5; Ames and Maschner, *Peoples of the Northwest Coast,* p. 151; and Wheeler, *The Trail of Lewis and Clark*, p. 223.

15. Stephen E. Ambrose, *Undaunted Courage: Meriwether Lewis, Thomas Jefferson, and the Opening of the American West* (New York: Simon & Schuster, 1996), p. 305.

16. Moulton, *Journals*, pp. 23–24.

17. Ibid., p. 24.

18. Ambrose, *Undaunted Courage*, p. 308; and Moulton, *Journals*, p. 39.

19. Moulton, *Journals*, p. 39.

20. Ibid., p. 66; and Ambrose, *Undaunted Courage*, p. 309.

21. Moulton, *Journals*, pp. 69–70.

22. Ibid., *Journals*, p. 70.

23. Ambrose, *Undaunted Courage*, p. 311; and Moulton, *Journals*, p. 84.

24. Ambrose, *Undaunted Courage,* p. 311.

25. Wheeler, *The Trail of Lewis and Clark,* p. 224. According to the grandson of Coboway, the Clatsop leader who befriended Lewis and Clark during their winter stay, Indians were not in the habit of giving names to rivers. "Netul" most likely referred to a place along the river, and not to the river itself.

26. Moulton, *Journals*, p. 95.

27. Ibid., p. 92.

28. Ibid., p. 95.

29. Ibid., p. 114.

30. Ambrose, *Undaunted Courage,* p. 313.

31. Moulton, *Journals,* p. 116.

32. Ibid., p. 117.

33. Ibid., p. 28.

34. Ibid., p. 124.

35. Ibid., p. 124; and James Agee, personal communication, July 2000.

36. Moulton, *Journals,* p. 123; and 37. Kelly Cannon, *Administrative History: Fort Clatsop National Memorial* (U.S. Department of Interior, National Park Service, Seattle, WA, 1995), p. 15.

37. Moulton, *Journals,* p. 127; and Ambrose, *Undaunted Courage,* p. 314.

38. Moulton, *Journals,* pp. 171, 177–178.

39. Ibid., p. 182.

40. Ambrose, *Undaunted Courage,* p. 323.

41. Ibid., p. 330.

42. Ibid., pp. 330–331.

43. Ibid., p. 331.

Chapter 5

The Lower Columbia, Astoria, and Tillamook Head

A bluff of yellow Clay and Soft Stone from the river to the Comencement of this nitch below the Country rises to high hills of about 80 or 90 feet above the water.... Here I found Capt Lewis name on a tree. I also engraved my name & by land the day of the month and year, as also Several of the men."

—Journal of William Clark, Monday, November 18, 1805

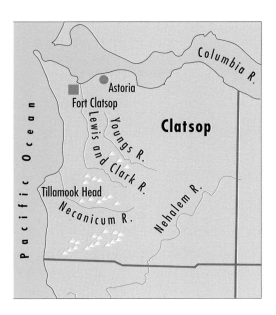

I f Meriwether Lewis and William Clark climbed the basalt bluff of Cape Disappointment today, they would not find the tree (or maybe more than one) into which they carved their names. They would still recognize some of the prominent features of the lower Columbia River, the ones we now call Crown Point, Beacon Rock, Coffin Rock, the mouth of the Sandy. They would recognize the islands in the estuary near Astoria. Other landmarks, like Celilo Falls, are gone, drowned under a dam-created lake. Much would be unfamiliar.

Clatsop County, northwestern Oregon.

The face of the landscape has changed greatly in the 200 years since Lewis and Clark's canoes plied the Columbia's swift waters. The noise of the waterfowl that kept Clark awake all night at the mouth of the Willamette now is drowned in the noise of airplanes taking off and landing at Portland Airport. Damming, diking, dredging, building of levees, and filling of wetlands have transformed the river's channel and streambank, simplifying the river, curbing its tendency to braid and meander, and taking away much of the marshy, brushy bottomland that Lewis and Clark had such trouble walking through.[1] The "emence" trees near Fort Clatsop are gone, replaced with younger, naturally seeded and planted Douglas-firs, cedars, hemlocks, and spruces. Settlement and development—the realization of President Thomas Jefferson's dream for the Northwest—have wrought dramatic changes to the lower Columbia.

Fur Trade and Early Settlement

One of Jefferson's motives for sending Lewis and Clark to the Pacific was to strengthen U.S. claims on the Pacific Northwest. British fur traders had been in the area since the North West Company's Alexander Mackenzie traveled from Fort Chipewyan down the Fraser and across to the Pacific Ocean by Indian trail in 1793.[2] The Montreal-based North West Company and its rival, the British-chartered Hudson's Bay Company, plied a web of river-based trapping routes through eastern and central Canada. These were held together by a network of trading posts, or "factories," along the major rivers.

Lewis and Clark's successful return to the United States not only reinforced their country's claim on the territory but made it known that the Northwest was a place suitable for settlement. In 1810, the Winship family of Boston gave it a try. They made a deal with the Russians in Alaska to hire Aleut hunters to hunt sea otters off the California Coast for the Chinese market. They needed a post midway between Alaska and California, and the Columbia suited them well. In May of that year, the *Albatross,* captained by Nathan Winship, set out to establish a settlement at Oak Point, 40 miles upriver from Fort Clatsop. They began building a fort, but a late-spring flood washed out their garden and forced them to move a quarter-mile downstream.[3] Indians' threats against them finally prompted the Winships to abandon the venture.

The next attempt at settlement was made by employees of John Jacob Astor's Pacific Fur Company. Astor, a German immigrant who had begun his empire as a seller of flutes, sent two parties to the Northwest, one overland, the other in the *Tonquin,* commanded by the intemperate—some say psychopathic—Jonathan Thorn. "Through his madness eight men were lost at sea before he reached his destination," says the historian Terence O'Donnell.[4]

The *Tonquin* made a very rough crossing of the Columbia bar in March of 1811. "On approaching the bar, the terrific chain of breakers, which keep rolling one after another in awful succession, completely overpowered us with dread," wrote Alexander Ross, one of the company's clerks. The ship hit hard on a reef and stayed there for hours "until the tide providentially beginning to flow, just at a time when it appeared as if no earthly power could save us from a watery grave, brought about our deliverance by carrying the ship along with it into Baker's Bay, snug within the Cape, where we lay in safety."[5]

For their fort, the Astorians chose a heavily wooded site on the south shore, on Smith Point, where the city of Astoria now stands. Accustomed to the spare landscape of his native Scotland, Ross took in the dark cloak of forest with wonder: to him it was both awesome and forbidding, and his practical mind wrestled with the difficulties of clearing and building on

Fort Astoria in 1841, from the Wilkes Expedition report.

it. "Toward the south, the impervious and magnificent forest darkened the landscape as far as the eye could reach," he wrote. "The place thus selected for the emporium of the of the West might challenge the whole continent to produce a spot of equal extent presenting more difficulties to the settler: studded with gigantic trees of almost incredible size, many of them measuring fifty feet in girth, and so close together, and intermingled with huge rocks, as to make it a work of no ordinary labor to level and clear the ground."[6]

His words were prophetic. Two months later, barely an acre had been cleared. Three men had been killed by the Indians, two had been wounded by falling trees, one had blown his hand off with gunpowder. It sometimes required two days to fell one tree, and then, more often than not, it would hang up on the other trees on its way down. "Sometimes a number of them would hang together, keeping us in awful suspense," Ross wrote, recounting the arduous task. "Many of the party had never handled an axe before . . . [T]here is an art in felling a tree as well as in planting one, but unfortunately none of us had learned that art . . . it would have made a cynic smile."[7]

It should be noted that Gabriel Franchère, a young French-Canadian member of the company, mentioned none of these gloomy events in his journal, and indeed described the landscape in rosier tones than Ross did: "The weather was superb and all nature smiled. We imagined ourselves to be in an earthly paradise—the forests looked like pleasant groves, the leaves like brilliant flowers." The party set to work "with enthusiasm," he wrote, "and in a few days cleared a point of land covered by underbrush and half-burned tree trunks."[8]

The Astorians' venture too was star-crossed. The *Tonquin's* Captain Thorn was killed by Indians on Vancouver Island and his ship blown up after he struck an Indian leader in the face with a roll of fur. The overland party, plagued with illness and scarce game, split up in the Snake River canyon. The main group arrived at Fort Astoria in February of 1811; the others, Ramsay Crooks and John Day, staggered in three months later. They were naked and nearly starved, and John Day had gone insane.[9]

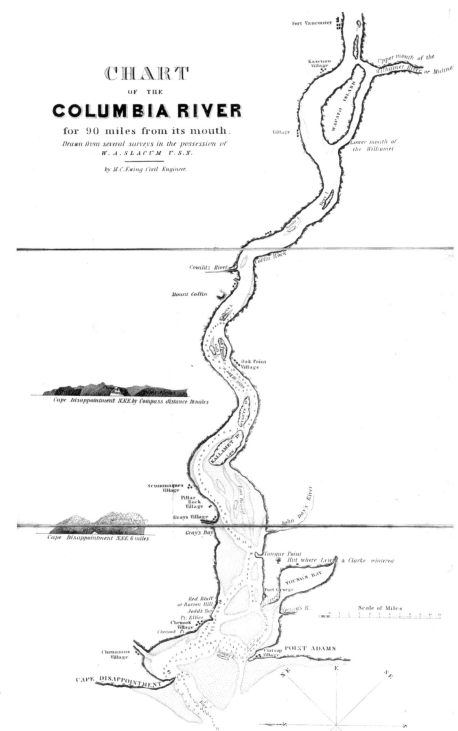

CHART
OF THE
COLUMBIA RIVER
for 90 miles from its mouth.
Drawn from several surveys in the possession of
W. A. SLACUM U.S.N.

by M.C.Ewing Civil Engineer.

Fort Vancouver

Kasenow Village

Upper mouth of the Willamet River or Multno

WAPATO ISLAND

Village

Lower mouth of the Willamet

Coffin Rock

Cowlitz River

Mount Coffin

Oak Point Village

Cape Disappointment N.N.E. by Compass distance 10 miles

KALLAMET R.

Scummaques Village

Pillar Rock Village

Grays Village

Cape Disappointment N.N.E. 6 miles

John Days River

Gray's Bay

Tongue Point

Hut where Lewis & Clarke wintered

YOUNG'S BAY

Fort George

Youngs R.

Red Bluff or Barren Hill

Jodd's Bay

Pt. Ellice

Chenook Village

Chenook Pt.

Chenamus Village

Chatsop Village

POINT ADAMS

Scale of Miles

CAPE DISAPPOINTMENT

N.W.   E.   S.E.

S.

William Slacum's 1837 chart of the Columbia's mouth, showing "Hut where Lewis & Clarke wintered."

The final blow to Astor's scheme came when the United States declared war on Britain in 1812. Fearful the British would show up and take the fort, the Astorians decided to sell it to the British-owned North West Company instead. In December of 1813, Fort Astoria became Fort George, flying the Union Jack, and for the next three decades Britons, not Americans, dominated the region. Although the fort itself was returned to the Americans in connection with the treaty ending the war, the North West Company continued to be based there. When the Hudson's Bay Company merged with the North West Company in 1821, Fort George was part of the package.[10]

The Hudson's Bay Company was after beaver furs to supply the demand for fashionable beaver hats among the gentlemen of London and New York. In 1823 the company moved its headquarters from Fort Astoria (as it was renamed) to Fort Vancouver, 100 miles upriver. Astoria, being at least nominally American, seemed a less favorable place to stay, and besides, the prairie land along the Columbia's up-stream banks was better for establishing the self-sufficient farm that the fort's charming, iron-willed chief factor, John McLoughlin, desired.[11]

A pair of naturalists, botanist Thomas Nuttall and ornithologist John Kirk Townsend, were visitors to Fort Vancouver in 1834. They came west with another American fur venture headed by a Massachusetts ice merchant, Nathaniel J. Wyeth. Townsend's first glimpse of the Columbia, from the high desert west of Walla Walla, filled him with delight. "I gazed upon the magnificent river, flowing silently and majestically on, and reflected that I had actually crossed the vast American conti-

John McLoughlin, the Hudson's Bay Company's chief factor at Fort Vancouver.

nent, and now stood upon a stream that poured its waters directly into the Pacific. This, then, was the great Oregon, the first appearance of which gave Lewis and Clark so many emotions of joy and pleasure...."[12]

In December of 1834, Townsend visited the site of Astoria, by that time under the care of a single superintendent: "Fort George, as it is called, although perhaps it scarcely deserves the name of a fort, being composed of but one principal house of hewn boards, and a number of small Indian huts surrounding it.... This is the spot where once stood the fort established by the direction of our honored countryman, John Jacob Astor." One chimney of the old fort was still standing, "a melancholy monument of American enterprise and domestic misrule." The stockade that once surrounded the fort "is now overgrown with weeds and bushes, and can scarce be distinguished from the primeval forest which surrounds it on every side."[13]

Homesteaders and Farmers

The treaty ending the War of 1812 had done nothing to settle the growing rivalry between Britain and the United States over possession of the Pacific Northwest. Both the United States and Britain sent out emissaries to gather information on the territory—in the case of the Americans, on its potential for white settlement; in the case of the British, on the defensibility of the lower Columbia, "in case of any hostile aggression upon Her Majesty's dominions on the western coast of America."[14]

In 1836, President Andrew Jackson sent William A. Slacum, a purser in the U.S. Navy, to spy out Oregon and bring back "[a] full and accurate report ... in regard to the country and its inhabitants," including "all such information, political, physical, statistical, and geographical as [might] prove useful and interesting to this government."[15]

When Slacum saw it, the landscape around the mouth of the Columbia had not changed much from the time Lewis and Clark were there. "The pines, firs, and the most beautiful variety of flowers, grow to an extraordinary size, whilst the finest grasses are seen at this season fringing the sides of the hills to the water's edge." At Oak Point, site of the short-lived Winship settlement, "the oak is first seen: from thence the oak, ash, laurel, cotton wood, beach [sic], alder, pines, firs, yew, and cedar. . . ."[16]

A lone homesteader's cabin in the deep woods of northwestern Oregon.

Navy lieutenant Neil M. Howison was dispatched by the Secretary of the Navy under President Polk early in 1846 to examine the situation in Oregon. Howison visited "all settled spots on the Columbia below the Cascades, the Wilhammette valley for sixty miles above Oregon City, and the Twality [Tualatin] and Clatsop plains." Like others before him, Howison took particular note of the danger of the Columbia bar crossing; he provided detailed navigation notes in his report. Like William Clark, he mentioned the windy, rainy weather and the primeval character of the forest and its animal inhabitants. "Elk are still numerous, but very wild, living in the depths of the forests, or near those openings which the white man has not yet approached. An Indian hunter often brought elk meat to us at Astoria, which he had killed in the unexplored forests between Clatsop Plains and Young's river."[17]

Like other early European-American visitors who marveled at the huge trees and impenetrable thickets, Howison had a hard time imagining that this forest would ever amount to anything of value. "Although most descriptions of timber grow in this country, and grow to a great size, its quality and usefulness are in nowise comparable to that produced in the United States." Howison was partial to the hardwoods he was familiar with back home. "Neither hickory, walnut, nor locust has yet been found here; they would doubtless, if introduced and proper soil selected for them, thrive prosperously. . . . Perhaps a critical exploration would find timber of durable fibre in the less genial atmosphere of the mountain ridges; the cause of its bad quality in the low lands is the rapidity of its growth, which in all countries produces the same disqualifying effects."[18]

Astoria Settled

The superintendent whom Townsend encountered at Fort Astoria in 1834 may have been the only white man in the neighborhood, for the first European-American settlers and missionaries did not come until the 1840s. An agent of the Hudson's Bay Company was still in residence at Fort Astoria in 1846, according to Lieutenant Howison, but the company was preparing to transfer him to a warehouse being built at Cape Disappointment. By then, missionaries had established a settlement 18 miles southwest of Fort Astoria. By February of 1841 they had built a one-story log building and started two farms. That summer the missionaries opened a trail to the Willamette Valley and brought back livestock.[19]

By this time, emigrants from the United States were beginning to come into the Oregon country in some numbers. The first large influx was the "Great Migration" of 1843. About 875 people, mostly women and children, came in that train, along with some 200 wagons, plus cattle, horses, and household goods. They arrived late in the year, exhausted and broke, and, like many who followed, were indebted to the generous hand of John McLoughlin of the Hudson's Bay Company, who fed them, lent them boats to travel up the river, and gave them credit to tide them over until the next growing season.

Between 1840 and 1860, 53,000 Americans came west over the Oregon Trail.[20] Most of them settled in the Willamette Valley, but Astoria received a few immigrants. Homesteaders began to settle

Sitka spruce zone

The Sitka spruce zone is a band of vegetation only a few miles wide, lying along the coast of Oregon and Washington and extending a bit up Coast Range river valleys. The climate in this zone is fairly stable owing to the moderating influence of the Pacific Ocean. Precipitation averages 80 to 150 inches annually, most of which falls during the winter months. Fog and low clouds are typical during the summer months, helping to keep trees from becoming moisture-stressed.[1]

Forests of the Sitka spruce zone are dense and tall, and trees grow rapidly. Sitka spruce, western hemlock, and western redcedar are most abundant tree species. Seedlings of all three species are able to grow in the partial shade of the small gaps typical of mature coastal forests, and as a result, old Sitka spruce forests are composed of trees of many ages and sizes. Douglas-fir and grand fir are also fairly common in Sitka spruce forests. Lodgepole pine (shore pine) grows on sand dunes and boggy sites within the Sitka spruce zone.[2]

The understory in a Sitka spruce forest is lush and dense, with shrubs (huckleberry, salal, vine maple, salmonberry, devil's club) and ferns (swordfern, lady fern, deer fern) growing in abundance. Herbs, such as violet and woodsorrel, also are abundant. Live trees and downed logs are covered with conifer seedlings, mosses, club mosses, and liverworts.[3]

In the Sitka spruce zone and the Coast Range in general, riparian forests, those found near streams, are most often composed of single-aged stands of red alder. Red alder stands are typically associated with a dense salmonberry understory that keeps conifer seedlings from becoming established. Red alder seedlings are unable to grow under the shade of mature forests; therefore, red alder stands occupy a given site for only about 80 to 100 years, the life span of a typical red alder. Sites occupied by aging red alder stands are eventually replaced by salmonberry or conifers. Lesser amounts of Sitka spruce, western redcedar, Douglas-fir, and bigleaf maple may also be present in coastal riparian forests. Steeper streams and narrower stream channels tend to support riparian forests with more conifers.[4]

[1] J.F. Franklin and C.T. Dyrness, *Natural Vegetation of Oregon and Washington,* USDA Forest Service General Technical Report PNW-8 (Portland, OR: USDA Forest Service Pacific Northwest Forest and Range Experiment Station, 1973).

[2] Ibid. See also J.K. Agee, *Fire Ecology of Pacific Northwest Forests* (Covelo, CA: Island Press, 1993).

[3] Franklin and Dyrness, *Natural Vegetation of Oregon and Washington.*

[4] D.E. Hibbs and P.A. Giordano, "Vegetation Characteristics of Alder-dominated Riparian Buffer Strips in the Oregon Coast Range," *Northwest Science* 70 (1996), pp. 213–222; Franklin and Dyrness, *Natural Vegetation of Oregon and Washington;* D. Minore and H.G. Weatherly, "Riparian Trees, Shrubs, and Forest Regeneration in the Coastal Mountains of Oregon," *New Forests* 8, no. 3 (1994), p. 249; and Tara R. Nierenberg, "A Characterization of Unmanaged Riparian Overstories in the Central Oregon Coast Range" (master's thesis, Oregon State University, Corvallis, OR, 1996).

around the Columbia's mouth in the 1840s, claiming land under one of several homestead laws. By 1844 there were at least three permanent white families in Astoria proper. Howison reported 20 or 30 families in Astoria and the Clatsop Plains to the southwest, and perhaps as many on the north side of the river. The site of the fort and surrounding lands, Howison wrote, had been claimed by two Americans, Welch and Maclure.[21]

Astoria was still not much more than a clearing in the deep woods, consisting of "ten houses, including a warehouse, Indian lodges, a cooper's and a blacksmith's shop; it has no open ground except gardens within less than a mile of it." About 30 white people lived there along with two lodges of Chinook Indians. Howison considered the town to be "in a state of transition, exhibiting the wretched remains of a bygone settlement, and the uncouth germ of a new one."[22]

Clearing the land proved as monumental a task for the homesteaders as it had for the Astorians. Many of the hemlocks, spruces, and cedars were 12 feet thick at the base. The homesteaders could not cut them down, so they burned them down. According to one pioneer's memoirs, the men would bore two tunnels into the tree, one atop the other, the first at 45 degrees and the second horizontal, so that they would meet at an angle in the tree's heart. Then they would drop hot coals into the tunnels and blow on them with a hand bellows until the coals ignited the surrounding wood. The fire would burn inside the tree for many days, constantly enlarging the cavity "until there was within that tree a good-sized room, around the walls of which the fires would continue to blaze until, with a terrific roar, the huge forest giant fell with earth-shaking reverberations."[23]

Astoria saw its first dairy farm in 1845, started with cows brought to the area by ship. The moist climate was perfect for growing grass, which provided good grazing on the tidal margins. There were still wolves in the area to threaten livestock. What Howison wrote about the Willamette Valley may also have been true on the coastal river plains: "Wolves are numerous, and prey upon other animals, so that the plains are entirely in their possession."

Another threat to livestock was water. Farmers who grazed their animals on the tidal marshes had to watch that they did not get swept away by tides, storm surges, or floods.[24]

To increase their usable acreage, farmers built extensive dikes and filled in sloughs along the tidal lowlands and the river mouths. About 5,000 acres of wetlands had been diked by 1888, for meadow, pasture, and grain and vegetable crops. These land reclamation efforts, along with grazing and the introduction of exotic grass and weed species, greatly changed the character of the lowland plant communities around Astoria. Because the wetland vegetation was not surveyed in detail before the land was developed, it is hard to know exactly how extensive the impact has been.[25]

Homesteaders at Fort Clatsop

While European-Americans had been settling the area around Astoria, the timbers of Lewis and Clark's Fort Clatsop had been returning to the earth. A visitor who hiked up from Fort Astoria in 1813 to see the site described the fort as "in total ruins, the wood having been cut down and destroyed by the Indians; but the remains are still visible. In the fort are already grown up shoots of willows 25 feet high."[26]

The site along the Lewis and Clark River that contained the ruins of the fort was homesteaded in 1849 by S.M. Henell of Astoria, under a land claim law passed by the Oregon provisional government. The next year Thomas Scott jumped Henell's claim under the federal Donation Land Claim Act of 1850. Scott soon traded the property to Carlos Shane. Shane built a house nearby, and then set out to burn the fort's timbers because he was trying to clear the land to farm it—which was, after all, what homesteaders were supposed to do.[27] He told the story in 1900:

A few feet from where I built my house there were at that time the remains of two of the Lewis and Clark cabins. They lay east and west, parallel with each other, and ten or fifteen feet apart. Each cabin was sixteen by

*thirty feet; three rounds of the south cabin and two
rounds of the north cabin were then standing. In the
south cabin stood the remains of a large stump. The
location of the old stockade was indicated by second
growth timber, while all around it was the original
growth, or the stumps of trees which had been cut. In
clearing away for my house I set fire to the remains of
the old cabins and endeavored to burn them.*[28]

The presence of a large stump in the south cabin was explained by Chief Coboway's grandson, Silas B. Smith. In a statement made around 1900, he remembers his mother, Celiast, the chief's second daughter, telling him about her memories of Lewis and Clark's arrival. "Mother said that in one of the houses they used was the large stump of a tree, which had been cut smooth, and which was used as a table. The tree had been cut down and then the house built, enclosing the stump."[29]

A couple of years after he claimed the 320-acre homestead, Carlos Shane gave it to his brother, Franklin, and moved up the river. In 1852, Richard Moore made an agreement with Franklin Shane to build a sawmill at Lewis and Clark's former canoe landing site. Shane agreed to move the boundary slightly to the north so Moore could claim the landing. Moore built the mill. From 1852 to 1854, the forest around the mill was logged and the lumber sent by ship to San Francisco. The mill closed in 1853 when the lumber market took a downturn.[30]

By the mid-1860s, Lewis and Clark's canoe landing site had become part of the land route used by travelers from Portland to Seaside. The Oregon Steam and Navigation Company ran a carriage service from Portland to Fort Clatsop, and in 1875 the company bought 5 acres along the river from the current owner, William Smith, Franklin Shane's son-in-law.[31]

Through the nineteenth century, the location of the site of Fort Clatsop was generally known to local people. By 1899 the Lewis and Clark centennial was approaching, and public interest in everything having to do with Lewis and Clark was growing. Franklin Shane's daughter, Mary Shane Smith, who spent a good deal of her childhood at the homestead, had identified a decaying, half-buried log near their house and had told her son that it was the last remaining timber of the fort's ruins.[32]

In 1899 a writer for the Northern Pacific Railway set out to find the site. He took with him four long-time Astorians, including Silas Smith, Coboway's grandson.

Identifying the site of Fort Clatsop, 1899.

Smith showed them where he remembered the fort to be. The next year another group that included Smith and Carlos Shane came out again and placed stakes at the southwest corner, which they remembered seeing on the previous visit. Then they put stakes at where they speculated the other three corners would have been.[33] In 1912, the county historical society put a bronze marker at the site.

Logging and Sawmilling

Eventually Astoria's big trees began to be seen as an asset rather than a liability. Logging in the Youngs Bay watershed began about 1850 to supply the market that had suddenly boomed with the discovery of gold in California, where lumber was selling for $600 a thousand board feet. Some logs were also milled and sold locally, more after the California market declined in the early 1860s.[34] Early logging used simple technology: two-man crosscut saws ("Swede fiddles"), a greased skid road to slide the logs down to the water, and the river to carry them to a mill or a ship on the bay.

Toward the end of the century, a visitor could see how logging and homesteading were altering the landscape. In 1872, the writer

Frances Fuller Victor described Smith Point, the site of the old Fort Astoria and subsequently the town of Astoria, which by then had between 400 and 500 inhabitants. "The whole point was originally covered with heavy timber, which came quite down to high-water mark; and whatever there is unlovely in the present aspect of Astoria, arises from the roughness always attendant upon the clearing up of timbered lands." However, if the viewer were to look out toward the river, "with your back to half-cleared lots, made unsightly by the blackened stumps of trees, the view is one of unsurpassed beauty."[35]

Victor visited the ruins of Fort Astoria, noting the smoothing veneer of civilization in a tone of approval tinged with wistfulness: "Nothing now remains . . . except some slight indentations in the ground where were once the cellars of the now vanished fort, and a few graves. Perhaps the only enduring memorial is the smooth turf and fine grass of civilization, which Time does not eradicate, and which grows here in strong contrast to the rank, wild grasses of the uncultivated country."[36]

By 1861, there were 150 settlers of European descent in Clatsop County, many of them Swedish and Finnish immigrants. In 1898 the Columbia River Railroad Company built a passenger rail line between Portland and Seaside. By 1900 there were 27 dairies supplying milk to Astoria. By 1930, the population of Clatsop County had risen to 21,124. Astoria had a population of 10,349. There were 1,565 people in Seaside, and the rest of Clatsop County's population lived in small villages, on farms, or in logging camps.[37]

In the 1880s railroads began to penetrate the hills, making logging above tidewater much more feasible and efficient. The Eastern and Western Railroad ran from south of Fort Clatsop up the west bank of the Lewis and Clark River to its source near Saddle Mountain. Another significant logging rail line ran up the west bank of the Youngs River, just to the east of the Lewis and Clark River. Numerous spurs ran from both lines up into headwater creeks. In 1889, steam donkeys replaced ox teams for yarding logs. That technological improvement along with rail transportation made it possible to do extensive logging away from the Columbia and up into the interior. John Chitwood, who logged the Saddle Mountain

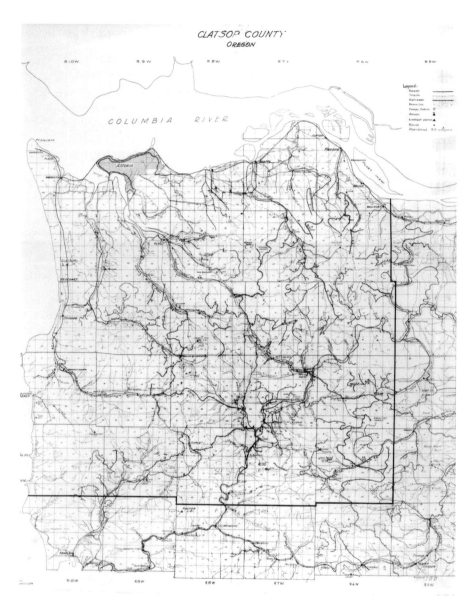

A network of logging railroads crisscrossing Clatsop County forests.

area from 1884 to the 1890s, is credited with being the first logger in Clatsop County to use a steam donkey. By the 1890s Clatsop County was webbed with many miles of track.[38]

Some of the forest around Astoria had been burned during the last decades of the century. On a steamer trip up from Astoria to Portland,

Frances Fuller Victor noted the "desolated appearance" of the hills "in consequence of fires, which every year spread through and destroy large tracts of timber ... the naked trunks alone of the towering firs being left standing to decay." After a few years, "a new growth covers the ground, but the old trees remain unsightly objects still."[39]

Even so, by the turn of the century, logging and fires had not made many holes in Clatsop County's heavy forest fabric. "Thousands of square miles of hemlock, spruce and fir forests are found near the vicinity of Astoria, and the quality of the timber here is the same high quality found on the best parts of Puget Sound Country," said an 1894 publication. Clatsop County was one of the state's most heavily forested. An 1898 *Portland Oregonian* article put the county's timber land acreage at 530,000.[40] Of the county's total land area of 873 square miles, 838 were forested.

According to a 1902 report, Clatsop County had 16.7 million board feet of standing timber, with an average of 37,400 board feet to the acre. Only Lane County, with more than five times the land area, had more total standing timber, and only Tillamook County, lying south of Clatsop along the rain-soaked north coast, had more board footage to the acre (39,500). "The forests are extremely dense and heavy, and, compared with the area of the county, but little cutting has been done, and the burned areas, although numerous, are small and collectively amount to less than 5 per cent of the area of the county."[41]

The Dry '30s

By 1938 the forests of Clatsop County were no longer dense and unbroken, and officials and citizens were beginning to worry about deforestation. A Forest Service inventory in that year shows a decline in forest land area and standing timber and an increase in the amount of deforested land. Clatsop County then had a total forest land area of 478,375 acres, or 747 square miles—down from the 530,000 reported by the *Portland Oregonian* in 1898. Immature forest occupied 171,500 acres. About 79 percent of this represented logged forest; the rest, burns. Trees of less than 6 inches average diameter covered 45 percent of the immature-forest acreage. The forest was mostly privately owned—87 percent of the land and 94 percent of the timber volume was in private hands.[42]

The total volume of conifer trees big enough to log in 1938 was 7.9 billion board feet, Scribner rule.[43] The *Portland Oregonian* in 1898 had reported a volume of

Log dump at Young's Bay, 1937.

18.5 billion board feet. Forty years later there were 79,000 acres of deforested, nonrestocked land, not counting acres clearcut and naturally reforested since the beginning of 1930.[44]

Of that 79,000 acres, 50,000 had been logged and were not growing trees. The rest of the land was designated "deforested burns." Most of the latter acreage had been burned in the 60,000-acre Wolf Creek fire of 1933. At the time of the survey, five years after the fire, the burned land was regenerating only sparsely. The average site had between

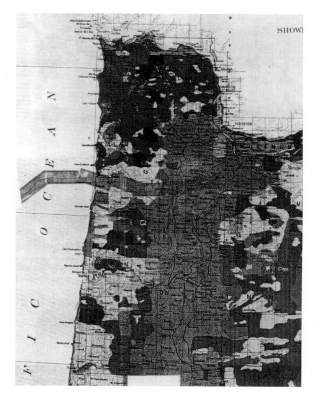

Forest Service map of northwestern Oregon forest cover in 1901. The yellow swath in the middle is the Willamette Valley. Green patches denote merchantable timber; darker-green patches indicate older forest. Red horizontal stripes denote "cut timber, not restocking."

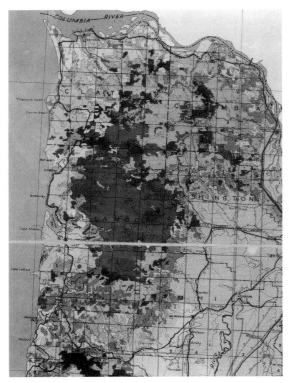

Forest Service map of northwestern Oregon forest cover in 1936. The large Africa-shaped patch in the center is the Tillamook Burn of 1933.

U.S. Geological Survey map showing logged-off lands (the green-shaded areas) in Clatsop County, 1939.

30 and 40 percent of the seedlings it needed to be considered satisfactorily stocked.[45] In those days most cut-over or burned-over forest land was left alone in the hope that it would regenerate naturally from seeds blown in from nearby forest stands.

Conditions in the county's forests were cause for alarm. "The gravity of the situation developing from the removal of so great a percentage of the county's merchantable timber is recognized by public officials and many individuals," said the author of the 1938 Forest Service report.[46] The biggest problem was how to grow trees again on the logged-over or burned-over private land. In those days slash burning after logging was mandatory—the intent was to eliminate the dry fuels that could feed a major forest fire. But many of the slash fires escaped and repeatedly burned cut-over land, making it very resistant to natural regeneration and regrowth of the forest. Much of this land ended up in county ownership, forfeited by the owners for nonpayment of taxes.

Eventually a solution was found. About 550,000 acres of cut-over and burned timber lands were transferred to the state of Oregon under a land acquisitions law passed in 1939.[47] The state forestry department turned these lands

New public-domain land in Columbia County, 1934. During the Depression, many thousands of acres of cut-over and burned lands were forfeited to northwestern Oregon counties for nonpayment of taxes.

into state forests. They reforested the lands with the promise that the eventual revenues from the maturing timber would mostly go to the counties in which the forests lie.

The planted seedlings on these state forests are now fast-growing young trees beginning to reach a merchantable size. The Clatsop and Tillamook state forests are now being managed for multiple use, including timber harvesting, under a plan that promises to keep the land in a forested condition and to maintain a relatively constant distribution of forest ages and sizes across the landscape.[48]

Along the Whale Walk

The forest of the outer bank of Tillamook Head, through which William Clark and his party walked in search of whale meat, has not changed much in 200 years. Within the 1,300-acre Ecola State Park, which now occupies the westernmost point, the forest has never seen large-scale commercial logging, but trees have been cut to make way for roads, and the area has been salvage-logged after windstorms, especially the big 1962 Columbus Day Storm. A small area was cleared during World War II to build a military observation bunker. That site, now the location of the park's hike-bike campground, is covered with trees of about 50 years old.[49] The rest of the forest along the headland is dominated by hemlocks and spruces of between 100 and 150 years old. Most older trees have been blown down over the years. A large number might have been toppled by a massive earthquake that shook the Pacific Coast in 1700, or they may have been burned in a subsequent wildfire. Along the Olympic Peninsula, a massive fire or fires occurred around the same time as

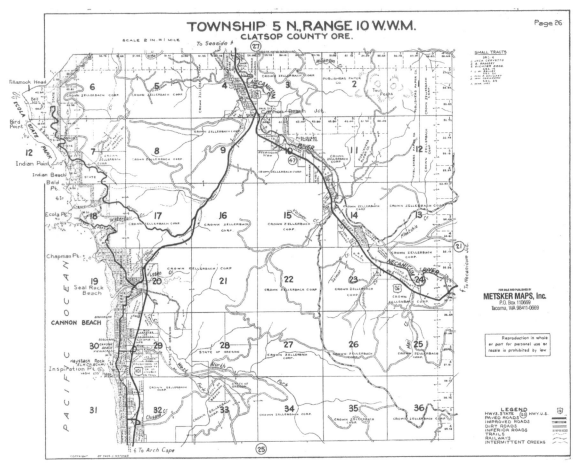

Much of northwestern Oregon's timber land is owned by large companies. The Crown Zellerbach holdings shown on this 1956 map are now owned by Willamette Industries.

the earthquake—probably fueled by the large quantities of dead "earthquake-thrown" trees. Tillamook Head might also have been hit by wildfire, because the oldest trees appear to be about 300 years old.[50] A few trees 250 to 300 years old are still standing. These might have been—when they were younger and smaller—among those that Clark and his party saw.

In the early twentieth century, to the north of Tillamook Head, there was some selective logging of coastal spruces in the small watersheds near Seaside. The big trees were cut and hauled out of the woods by soldier-loggers of the U.S. Army Spruce Division during the last year of World War I. The Army needed spruce to build strong, lightweight airplanes for the war. Wing beams, in particular, had to be made from straight-grained, clear wood that was tough but supple, and the lumber had to be in lengths of at least 40 feet. The Sitka spruce in the Coast Range of Oregon and Washington answered the need. At the time, private mill owners could not meet the Army's specifications, and the industry was involved in a disastrous strike besides. So the Army set up its own military division to get the job done. They built 13 short-line railroads to haul the giant cants—the huge logs were split into quarters in the woods—to the Spruce Division's mill at Fort Vancouver.[51] Several Spruce Division logging camps operated up the Necanicum River from Seaside and along other streams in the western part of the county.

East of Ecola State Park, the forest land on Tillamook Head has been in private ownership for a long time. The lands a mile or more east of the park were railroad-logged in the late 1920s, and those nearer the park were logged in the '50s and '60s, after trucks replaced railroads as the main means of log hauling. These lands were subsequently seeded or planted with Douglas-fir, western hemlock, and Sitka spruce. Most of the land had belonged to the timber giant Crown Zellerbach and the company's predecessors since the 1920s. The company owned 118,800 acres in Clatsop County by the end of 1946. The Clatsop Tree Farm, as it was called, was one of 10 operated by the company. At the time Crown Zellerbach owned a total of 675,000 acres of timber land in Oregon and Washington along both sides of the Columbia and on Puget Sound.[52]

1949

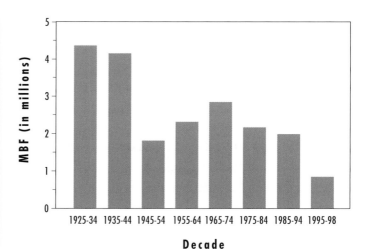

Sawlog production and timber harvest by decade in Clatsop County from 1925 to 1998. Figures for Columbia County were combined with Clatsop County's for the years 1932, 1933, 1938, 1940, and 1943.

1966

In 1978, 605 acres of Crown Zellerbach land was purchased and added to the northeast boundary of Ecola Park. Portland artist and jewelry heiress Louise Feldenheimer gave money to the state parks department to buy the tract, which was named the Elmer Feldenheimer Forest Preserve, in honor of Feldenheimer's late brother. In 1990, Louise Feldenheimer was instrumental in adding another 871 acres of former forest industry land east and south of the first addition. This complicated deal involved the Nature Conservancy, the state parks department, and Cavenham Forest Industries, which by then owned the land.[53]

The land added to Ecola State Park, along with the land to the east of it, had been logged in tracts

1998

Aerial photos of forests on Tillamook Head in 1949, 1966, and 1998. The darker, more textured-looking cover, indicating older coniferous forest, increases in the later photos. The web of logging roads, sharply defined in the 1966 photo, has been almost obliterated by forest regrowth 32 years later.

between 1943 and 1962 and subsequently reseeded or replanted. The area now is covered with stands of mostly Douglas-fir, western hemlock, and red alder, ranging from 20 to 50 years in age. According to Feldenheimer's wishes, the forest will be left to grow toward old-growth conditions. The parks department may even push it toward that goal by having foresters thin the young trees to accelerate the forest toward developing old-growth structural conditions.[54]

Reconstructing Fort Clatsop

In contrast to the outer reach of Tillamook Head, the landscape around Fort Clatsop has been dramatically altered. By the time the mid-twentieth century arrived, nothing about the site was the same as it had been when Lewis and Clark were there. Settlers had pulled down the old fort, built houses on the land, logged it, farmed it, burned charcoal, and mined clay. The Lewis and Clark River had been used as a log dump and boom highway. Farmers had built dams and levees along the river. According to a 1995 history of the site, "The manipulation of the natural resources of the area greatly altered the landscape from the coastal forest environment that had existed at the time of the Expedition's winter encampment."[55]

Not much had been done to commemorate the Fort Clatsop site since the Clatsop County historical society installed the bronze marker in 1912. In the early 1950s, spearheaded by the Astoria Jaycees and helped by the local historical society, citizens began to plan a reconstruction of the site.[56] They built a replica of the fort, locating it according to experts' best guesses as to where the original fort had stood. They installed a split-rail fence and planted native vegetation.

The site was donated to the National Park Service in 1958. Park officials commissioned a study of native plants and animals, and they began planting trees—more than 15,000 Sitka spruce, western hemlock, and Douglas-fir—in an effort to reforest fields that had been cleared by homesteaders. The tree-planting program worked so well "that vistas between the fort and the river needed to be thinned

Lewis and Clark Trail Commission in 1966 at the reconstructed Fort Clatsop, now a national memorial site.

to keep river views open."[57]

In 1989, James Agee, a forest ecologist at the University of Washington, developed a plan to recreate, as nearly as possible, the forest that existed in 1805–1806. Agee identified historic native species of northern Oregon coastal forests and considered the agents of disturbance that have shaped those forests through time—principally wind, fire, and human manipulation.[58]

It is clear from Agee's report, which heavily emphasizes disturbance factors, that the vision of a "reconstructed" forest is at best a moving target. Forest ecosystems, "are dynamic and ever-changing," he wrote. "There is no single point in time from which forest composition and structure can be recreated and 'frozen.'" The 1805 forests of Fort Clatsop, he concluded, are not a mere snapshot, but a "moving picture" of natural forest species composition and structure.[59]

Notes to Chapter 5

1. Gary E. Moulton, ed., *The Journals of the Lewis & Clark Expedition*, vol. 6 (Lincoln: University of Nebraska Press, 1990), p. 12.

2. Terence O'Donnell, *That Balance So Rare: The Story of Oregon* (Portland, OR: Oregon Historical Society Press, 1988), p. 27; and Dorothy O. Johansen, *Empire of the Columbia*, 2d ed. (New York: Harper & Row, 1967), p. 66.

3. O'Donnell, *That Balance So Rare*, p. 18; and Johansen, *Empire of the Columbia*, pp. 61-62.

4. O'Donnell, *That Balance So Rare*, p. 19.

5. Alexander Ross, *Adventures of the first settlers of the Oregon or Columbia River: being a narrative of the expedition fitted out by John Jacob Astor, to establish the "Pacific Fur Company;" with an account of some Indian tribes on the coast of the Pacific* (1849; reprint, New York: The Citadel Press, 1969) pp. 63, 67-68.

6. Ibid., p. 77.

7. Ibid., pp. 78-80, 109-110. Alexander Ross was ambivalent about the settlement prospects of the Northwest, even after seeing the Willamette Valley, which he pronounced "one of the finest valleys west of the Rocky Mountains." He wrote, "But however inviting may be the soil, the remote distance and savage aspect of the boundless wilderness along the Pacific seem to defer the colonization of such a region to a period far beyond the present generation; and yet, if we consider the rapid progress of civilization in other new and equally remote countries, we might still indulge the hope of seeing this, at no distant time, one of the most flourishing countries on the globe."

8. Gabriel Franchère, *Adventure at Astoria*, 1810-1814, Hoyt C. Franchère, tr. and ed. (Norman, OK: University of Oklahoma Press, 1967), p. 46.

9. O'Donnell, *That Balance So Rare*; and Johansen, *Empire of the Columbia*, p. 97.

10. O'Donnell, *That Balance So Rare*, p. 22; and Johansen, *Empire of the Columbia*, 110-111.

11. O'Donnell, *That Balance So Rare,* pp. 22-23; *Patricia C. Erigero, Cultural Landscape Report: Fort Vancouver National Historic Site*, vol. 2 (Seattle, WA: U.S. Department of Interior, National Park Service, 1992), pp. 14, 19. The site had three large open meadows, called Fort Plain, Lower Plain, and Mill Plain, flanked by the river to the south and dense forest to the north. Fourth Plain Boulevard and Mill Plain Boulevard are now major arterials in the city of Vancouver, Washington.

12. John Kirk Townsend, *Narrative of a journey across the Rocky Mountains, to the Columbia River, and a visit to the Sandwich Islands, Chili &c., with a scientific appendix* (1839; reprint, Corvallis: Oregon State University Press, 1999), p. 110.

13. Ibid., p. 132.

14. Henry Warre and Mervyn Vavasour, "Documents relative to Warre and Vavasour's military reconnoissance in Oregon, 1845-6," reprinted in *Oregon Historical Quarterly* X, no. 1 (1909), p. 22.

15. William A. Slacum, "Slacum's Report on Oregon 1836-7," reprinted in *Oregon Historical Quarterly* XIII, no. 2 (1912), p. 175.

16. Slacum, "Slacum's Report on Oregon," p. 200.

17. Neil Howison, "Report of Lieut. Neil M. Howison, United States Navy, to the commander of the Pacific Squadron; being the result of an examination in the year 1846 of the coast, harbors, rivers, soil, productions, climate, and population of the Territory of Oregon" (30th Cong., 1st Sess., United States House of Representatives, 1848; reprint, Portland, OR: *Oregon Historical Quarterly* XIV, no. 1, 1913), pp. 3, 16-17. Howison noted that the winter of 1846–47 was unusually severe: "The river is often frozen over in the neighborhood of Fort Vancouver. Even in Baker's bay, the schooner we were on board of was in January belted around with ice at the water's edge, fully eighteen inches thick; this was, however, considered by the old residents an unusual and extraordinary spell of cold weather."

18. Howison, "Report of Lieut. Neil M. Howison," pp. 49-50.

19. Lisa Heigh, "Unpublished draft report on Young's Bay history." Copy in possession of the authors; and William Adrian Bowen, "Migration and Settlement on a Far Western Frontier: Oregon to 1850," (Ph.D. dissertation, University of California, Berkeley, 1972), pp. 21–22.

20. William E. Hill, *The Oregon Trail: Yesterday and Today* (Caldwell, ID: The Caxton Printers, Ltd., 1992), p. 17; Warre and Vavasour, "Documents," pp. 48–49) ; and O'Donnell, *That Balance So Rare*, p. 35.

21. Jan M. Prior, "Kinship, Environment, and the Forest Service: Homesteading in Oregon's Coast Range" (master's thesis, Oregon State University, Corvallis, OR, 1998), pp. 27–44; and Heigh, "Unpublished draft report on Young's Bay history." One early settler, William Hobson, homesick for familiar plants, sent back to Europe for seeds of Scots broom. No one knows whether he was the first one, or the only one, to introduce this highly invasive species, but it is hard to miss the masses of mustard-yellow blossoms that emerge all over western Oregon in May. Those with pollen allergies are acutely aware of the ubiquitous shrub. See also Howison, "Report of Lieut. Neil M. Howison," p. 25.

22. Howison, "Report of Lieut. Neil M. Howison," p. 41.

23. Heigh, "Unpublished draft report on Young's Bay history."

24. Heigh, "Unpublished draft report on Young's Bay history"; and Howison, "Report of Lieut. Neil M. Howison," p. 49.

25. Heigh, "Unpublished draft report on Young's Bay history."

26. Olin D. Wheeler, *The Trail of Lewis and Clark 1804-1904,* vol. II (New York: G.P. Putnam's Sons, 1904), pp. 197–98.

27. Kelly Cannon, *Administrative History: Fort Clatsop National Memorial* (U.S. Department of Interior, National Park Service, Seattle, WA, 1995).

28. Wheeler, *The Trail of Lewis and Clark*, p. 198.

29. Ibid., p. 197.

30. Cannon, *Administrative History*, pp. 15-1; and Heigh, "Unpublished draft report on Young's Bay history."

31. Cannon, *Administrative History*, p. 17.

32. Ibid., pp. 16–17, 19.

33. Ibid., p. 19.

34. Heigh, "Unpublished draft report on Young's Bay history"; and Frances Fuller Victor, *All over Oregon and Washington: Observations on the Country, its Scenery, Soil, Climate, Resources, and Improvements* (San Francisco, CA: John G. Carmany & Co., 1872), p. 46.

35. Victor, *All over Oregon and Washington*, pp. 45, 48.

36. Ibid., p. 48.

37. Heigh, "Unpublished draft report on Young's Bay history"; and USDA Forest Service, *Forest Statistics for Clatsop County, Oregon* (Portland, OR: Pacific Northwest Forest and Range Experiment Station, 1938), p. 2.

38. Heigh, "Unpublished draft report on Young's Bay history."

39. Victor, *All over Oregon and Washington*, p. 57.

40. Heigh, "Unpublished draft report on Young's Bay history"; and John Minto, "From Youth to Age as an American," *Oregon Historical Quarterly* IX, no. 1 (March 1908), p. 14.

41. Henry Gannett, *The Forests of Oregon* (Washington, DC: U.S. Department of Interior, U.S. Geological Survey, 1902), p. 15, 18; and James K. Agee, personal communication, July 2000. Forest ecologist Agee notes that board-foot measures of the day were different from those currently in use because the efficiency with which the raw material was utilized at the time—much lower than it is today—was incorporated into the board-foot scaling rule. Hence, "the figures are a large underestimate by today's Scribner rule."

42. USDA Forest Service, *Forest Statistics for Clatsop County, Oregon*, pp. 2, 4, 11. The ownership balance has since changed. Of the county's 425,043 acres of timberland, about one-third is privately owned, and the next largest component, 133,000 acres, is state-owned and -managed. During the Depression, a lot of once-private forest land throughout the Coast Range was abandoned by the owners for non-payment of taxes. The Oregon Department of Forestry took over

ownership of many thousands of acres of these lands and now manages them as state forests. The 154,000-acre Clatsop State Forest, lying in Clatsop and Columbia counties, is one of these. About 364,000 acres, most of them burned in the infamous series of fires known as the Tillamook Burn, now make up the Tillamook State Forest, in Tillamook and Washington counties. See USDA Forest Service, *County Portraits of Oregon and Northern California,* General Technical Report PNW-GTR-377 (Portland, OR: USDA Forest Service, 1996), p. 33.

43. USDA Forest Service, *Forest Statistics for Clatsop County, Oregon*, p. 6.

44. Ibid., pp. 5.

45. Ibid., pp. 5–6.

46. Ibid., p. 11.

47. Gail Wells, *The Tillamook: A Created Forest Comes of Age* (Oregon State University Press: Corvallis, OR, 1999), p. 143.

48. Ibid., pp. 79–86.

49. Glen Kirkpatrick, "The Rediscovery of Clark's Point of View," *We Proceeded On* (publication of the Lewis and Clark Trail Heritage Foundation, Inc.) 25, no. 1 (1999), p. 29. In 1946 the site was converted to a branch of the McLaren School for delinquent boys. The boys at the school cleared land and built trails and roads as part of their rehabilitation. See "Buying a Dream," *Portland Oregonian*, 14 October 1990, L1.

50. The phrase "earthquake-throw" was coined by the forest ecologist James K. Agee, personal communication, August 2000.

51. "Spruce Division Camps 1918," *Seaside (Oregon) Signal*, 16 May 1991; and Johansen, *Empire of the Columbia*, pp. 477–478.

52. James K. Agee, personal communication, August 2000; and Crown Zellerbach Corp., "Press release on completion of company reforestation activities," dated 1954. Copy in possession of the authors; Scott Marlega, personal communication, May 2000; Crown Zellerbach Corp., "Clatsop County Tree Farm," unpublished report dated 1946. Information on West Coast tree farms for annual progress report to joint committee. Copy in possession of the authors; and E.P. Stamm, "Statement for Santa Barbara conference," unpublished information on

timber holdings, logging, and manufacturing by Crown Zellerbach Corp. in Oregon and Washington, dated 1957. Copy in possession of the authors.

53. "Buying a Dream," *Portland Oregonian*.

54. "One Family's Conservation Ideal Preserves some Tillamook Head Acreage," *Daily (Oregon) Astorian*, 17 June 1994.

55. Cannon, *Administrative History*, p. 129.

56. Ibid., p. 23.

57. "Fort Clatsop Official Map and Guide" (Fort Clatsop National Memorial, U.S. Department of the Interior, National Park Service, undated); James K. Agee, *A Conceptual Plan for the Forest Landscape of Fort Clatsop National Memorial, Report CPSU/UW 89-1* (Seattle, WA: U.S. Department of Interior, National Park Service and University of Washington, College of Forest Resources, 1989), p. 18; and Cannon, *Administrative History*, p. 133.

58. Cannon, *Administrative History*, p. 134; and Agee, *A Conceptual Plan for the Forest Landscape*.

59. Ibid., p. 4.

Chapter 6

The Lower Willamette and the West Slopes of the Cascades

Atmosphere filled with smoke consequently unable to see much of the surrounding country. Country much burnt.... Our route has been through what might be called a hilly prairie country, the grass mostly burnt off by recent fires, and the whole country sprinkled with oaks, so regularly dispersed as to have the appearance of a continued orchard of oak trees.

—Henry Eld, with the Wilkes Expedition, September 9, 1841, near present-day Independence, Oregon

Since the country has been in the possession of the whites it is found that the wood is growing up rapidly a stop having been put to the fires so extensively lighted throughout the country every year by the Indians.

—Charles Wilkes, journal entry of June 9, 1841

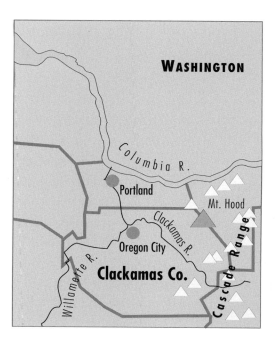

The lower Willamette River and the west slope of the northern Oregon Cascades.

The landscape of the Pacific Northwest has been shaped by human beings for longer than most people realize. After the first human inhabitants of this region crossed the Bering land bridge about 11,000 years ago[1] and settled along the Pacific Coast, they developed cultural practices designed to shape the environment from which they needed to make a living. They used the forests and prairies for food, clothing, and shelter. In the course their subsistence activities, the Indians modified large portions of landscape so that it better suited their needs.

The coming of European-Americans in the past 200 years has ushered in its own set of rapid and profound changes. Like the original inhabitants of the Northwest before them, settlers from the eastern states came and stayed because here they found a good living and a pleasant home. Lewis and Clark brought back the news that the Northwest was a desirable region to settle in, and the fur trade opened the country to white settlers. These settlers, mostly farmers, came because they wanted land. Settlement and the subsequent development of the cities and rural areas of Oregon have made profound changes on the prairies and forests of the lower Willamette and the western Cascades. Towns and roads, farming and ranching, harbors and railroads, logging and sawmilling—all have left their imprint.

Furs and Farming

It is hard to say exactly who was the first farmer in the Northwest, but the first large-scale farming began at the Hudson's Bay Company post at Fort Vancouver.

The Hudson's Bay Company's first toehold along the lower Columbia was Fort Astoria, which the company had appropriated after the outbreak of the War of 1812. The Astorians, employees of John Jacob Astor's American fur-trading venture, were fearful the British navy would seize the fort, and so they agreed to sell it to their British competitors. Before any money changed hands, however, a British naval vessel took possession of the post and ran up the Union Jack—technically an act of war that brought Fort Astoria into the peace negotiations after the war.[2] The fort was returned to the United States in the 1814 peace treaty, but the Hudson's Bay Company continued to operate it as a trading post. The company merged with its Montreal rival, the North West Company, in 1821. For several years afterward, a few dozen men were

Fort Vancouver in 1855, painted by the artist Richard Covington.

dispatched to this far-off outpost at the corner of the continent, enduring a lonely existence in a rainy climate.

The Hudson's Bay Company moved its headquarters upriver to Fort Vancouver in 1825 on the orders of Sir George Simpson, the company's London-based head of North American operations. At least part of his rationale was to find a better place, in the words of Chief Factor John McLoughlin, to "cultivate the soil and raise our own provisions."[3] Astoria provided a deep-water port and a convenient trading post, but its hilly, heavily timbered terrain did not suit it for farming. The question of the boundary between British and American territory was still open, and the company did not want to rely for its subsistence on American imports or British goods shipped halfway around the world.[4]

Fort Vancouver was established on March 19, 1825, and christened with a bottle of rum smashed across its flagpole. Its 300 acres spread across three large meadows opening on the Columbia about 6 miles above the mouth of the Willamette.[5] There were also five openings to the north and east. George Simpson, visiting the fort, described the site as ". . . beautifully situated on the top of a bank about 1¼ Miles from the Water side commanding an extensive view of the River the surrounding Country and the fine plain below which is watered by two very pretty small Lakes and studded as if artificially by clumps of Fine Timber."[6]

Some details on the tree species at the fort site were provided by John Scouler, who visited shortly after the fort was established: "The forests around the fort consists chiefly of *Pinus balsamea* and *P. canadensis* . . . " (probably Douglas-fir and western hemlock). Scouler found other interesting plants, including the camas lily: "The root of the *Phalangium esculentem* is much used by the natives as a substitute for bread. They grow abundantly in the moist prairies, the flower is usually blue, but sometimes white flowers are found."[7] Today the camas lily is known to scientists as *Camassia quamash*.

Another description of the site comes from Hudson's Bay Company doctor William Fraser Tolmie, who visited in 1833, after the establishment was moved nearer the river in 1829: "Below fort for some way it is covered with gigantic relics of the primeval forest, which form a broad belt of wood extending to river's edge. Proceeded along a rough road passing through the wood. The magnificence & grandeur of its colossal tenants was very impressive & the ground was beautifully carpeted with wild flowers & low creeping evergreen shrubs. Many of the pines were strip't of their bark for a few feet above root & the turpentine was profusely exuded in large pellucid drops." The stripping of the trees was undoubtedly the work of the Indians, who used pine pitch to seal baskets. If the "pines" were western redcedars, the bark may have been stripped and woven into baskets and mats or shredded for skirts and capes. Perhaps homesick for more cultivated surroundings, Tolmie exclaimed, "What an excellent cricket field this part of [the] plain would make."[8]

The fort's employees set to work planting potatoes, beans, and peas. By the next year, 1826, the Fort Vancouver farm had 1,420 acres under cultivation. The most important crop was wheat, which had value as both food and currency. The farm also produced peas, barley, oats, buckwheat, Indian corn, and potatoes for food, plus turnips, pumpkins, vetch, cole crops, and clover and timothy for hay. Scottish gardeners started a vineyard and an orchard. Apples grew so thick on the limbs of dwarfed trees that they looked like "onions fastened on a string."[9]

Chief factor McLoughlin imported cattle and hogs from California and the Hawaiian Islands, and sheep from England.[10] As the cattle multiplied and became too numerous for the farm's acreage to support, they were swum across the channel to Sauvie Island (or Wappato Island, as William Clark had named it because of the quantities of wapato roots growing there), or they were taken clear across the river and driven to the Tualatin Plains, southwest of present-day Portland.

Spring and summer flooding was a problem in the low fields next to the Columbia. The farm crew sometimes successfully raised a second round of crops after the flooding subsided in May or June. This flooding was "the greatest obstacle to [the fields'] cultivation, until the plan was adopted of waiting for the floods to subside, after which crops are found to flourish quite as well as if put in the ground earlier."[11] In 1828, chief trader James Douglas, in charge while McLoughlin was away, reported that the early rise of the river was followed by another in May, and an "irresistable flood" inundated the levees built to protect the fields, destroying 80 acres of crops. Undaunted, Douglas put in more peas, barley, buckwheat, and potatoes.[12]

Sir George Simpson was well satisfied with the productivity of the farm. He wrote McLoughlin in 1829: "The rapid progress you have already made in that object far surpasses the most sanguine expectations which could have been formed respecting it."[13] At its height, the Fort Vancouver farm was the agricultural center of the company's empire west of the Rockies. Its importance was captured in a statement by John McLoughlin in 1837: "During these Ten years in which the Farm has been in operation, it has supplied all the provisions required at this place, along the Coast, and for the Shipping in the country, which together generally amounts to about £2,000 annually."[14]

Spreading Settlement

In the late 1820s, a group of retired Hudson's Bay Company employees started their own farms at a settlement on the Willamette River that came to be called French Prairie, on the plain between the

Willamette and Pudding rivers. These men were mostly French Canadian, and under company policy they would have received a free passage to their original homes in the East. But they had worked a long time in the Northwest, and some had married Indian women and raised families. McLoughlin, ever alert to the expediency of moral principle, desired that their half-Indian children be brought up by both parents "as whites and Christians" and, not coincidentally, in a place "where they and their mothers would serve as hostages for the good behavior of their [Indian] relatives."[15]

The cemetery at St. Paul, Oregon, established by Bishop A.M.A. Blanchet in the late 1830s, is regarded as the oldest European-American burial ground in Oregon. Among those buried here are Étienne Lucier and André Picard, French-Canadian trappers who retired from the Hudson's Bay Company to settle and farm at French Prairie.

To encourage them to settle down and farm in the vicinity, McLoughlin lent each prospective settler livestock and seed and sold him supplies at reduced rates. Within several years French Prairie became a thriving agricultural community with its own Hudson's Bay Company receiving warehouse. Some of the men settled elsewhere; Sauvie Island received its present-day name from Laurent Sauvé, a Hudson's Bay Company employee who established a dairy farm there in 1838.[16]

In the early 1830s, the promise of riches again brought Americans to the Northwest. Nathaniel Wyeth, a New England ice merchant who like John Jacob Astor hoped to make his fortune in Northwest furs, came in 1832 and again in 1834. In his ship, the *May Dacre*, Wyeth brought with him the tools, supplies, and belongings of Methodist missionaries Jason Lee and his nephew, Daniel Lee. The men themselves traveled overland from Missouri, escorted and protected by Wyeth's employees. Wyeth's men started a farm at French Prairie, and another crew built a would-be fishing post, Fort William, on Sauvie Island, with a few storehouses, a blacksmith's and cooper's shop, and a distillery.[17] Wyeth had dreams of a fishing empire that would turn Columbia River salmon into gold.

Like most of the lower river lands at the time, Sauvie Island was well wooded with oak, ash, poplar, willow, and cottonwood, and also with large firs and cedars. In 1835 Wyeth built a canoe out of one of the cedars that was big enough to hold 25 barrels from his distillery. "The whole tree was 242 feet long and this by no means the largest tree on Wappatoo Island," Wyeth wrote.[18]

Like Astor, Wyeth failed in his attempt to become a fur magnate. He had entered the trade against stiff competition and at a time when the fur market was waning.[19] His scheme to develop a Columbia River fishery was premature. His company folded and his employees deserted within a year or two of his arrival. However, Wyeth left his mark on Oregon history by opening the road to Oregon. His other fort, the famous Fort Hall, would become in a few years an important way station for emigrants along the Oregon Trail.

The Missionaries

Jason and Daniel Lee established a mission and farm at French Prairie. The mission made few converts; Indian parents were reluctant to send their children to a place where they might catch white people's diseases. Moreover, the Indians "were neither humble nor grateful for Christian teachings, and they expected to be paid for attending worship." In November of 1843, watching an eruption of Mount St. Helens, the missionaries sang, with joyful reverence, the hymn, "How awful is our God." The Indians "failed to comprehend the

Jason Lee, the missionary and immigration booster.

Summit House on the Barlow Road in 1929, with Mount Hood in the background.

Modern-day photo of the Barlow Road, taken from Summit Meadows.

lessons their teachers read into such a phenomenon."[20]

The Lee mission's greater importance is that it widened channels of communication with the United States, encouraging increasing numbers of settlers to attempt the long journey to the Oregon Country. This indeed may have been Jason Lee's chief aim; from 1838 onward he "seems to have become increasingly a professional colonizer." A lecture tour he made that year through the Mississippi Valley and New England touted the benefits of Oregon settlement. Lee's persuasive words, along with those of the imaginative Hall Jackson Kelley, a Boston schoolteacher and booster extraordinaire with a self-imposed mission to propagate "Christianity in the dark and cruel places about the shores of the Pacific," increasingly found a receptive audience in the United States. Between 1840 and 1842, 162 people came to Oregon. The next year came the "Great Migration" of 1843: 875 people, three-quarters of them women and children, made the journey. In 1844 the emigrants numbered 1,475; in 1845, 2,500. The yearly influx of pioneers peaked with the migration of 1852, numbering almost 10,000 people. In all, 53,000 emigrants came to the Oregon Country between 1840 and 1860.[21]

The First Towns

Those who arrived in the 1842 emigration mostly settled around Oregon City, forming the nucleus of the territory's first town. They arrived destitute, and it was too late in the year to plant crops. The Hudson's Bay Company's John McLoughlin put some of the emigrants to work in his gristmill or his two sawmills at Willamette Falls.[22] He also gave them food and supplies and extended them credit. McLoughlin was compassionate, and he was also realistic: he had no wish to deal with the social unrest that would ensue if settlers' children starved during their first winter in Eden:

> *It was evident if there was not a proportionate increase of seed sown in 1843 and 1844, there would be a famine in the country in 1845, which would lead to trouble, as those that had families, to save them from starvation, would be obliged to have recourse to violence to get food for them.... In short I afforded every assistance to the immigrants so long as they required it, and by management I kept peace in the country.*[23]

By 1845 the population at the village at Willamette Falls numbered about 300. The fledgling Oregon City had become the first American settlement in the Oregon

An engraving of Willamette Falls in 1878.

Oregon City in 1848, as painted by Henry Warre.

Oregon City in 1857 (from the town's opposite end) in a photo taken by Lorenzo Lorain.

Modern-day photo of Oregon City, taken from the same perspective as the Lorain photo.

Territory. It had "one Roman Catholic and one Methodist chapel, about 100 dwelling houses, stores, etc.," wrote Lieutenants Henry Warre and Mervyn Vavasour, who had been dispatched by the British government to assess the strength of the Americans in Oregon Territory at the height of the tension over the British-American boundary question. "An excellent grist mill (the whole of the machinery, etc., having been exported from England by Dr. McLoughlin) and several saw mills."[24]

Other towns arose along the Willamette, and "houses and wharves appeared at forest clearings where speculators hoped the frontier's new metropolis would rise."[25] Linnton, 5 miles below Fort Vancouver on the Columbia, had been settled in the early 1840s and then apparently abandoned; by 1846 only one family lived there. In 1845, Francis Pettygrove platted 16 blocks of riverbank near his boat landing on the west bank of the Willamette, and a coin was flipped to give the new metropolis the name of Portland, after Portland, Maine, Pettygrove's home town.[26] "Twelve or fifteen new houses are already occupied, and others building; and, with a population of more than sixty souls, the heads of families generally industrious mechanics, its prospects of increase are favorable," wrote Lieutenant Howison in 1846. Settlements also arose at Milwaukie, West Linn, and Salem, "of which too little exists to be worthy of an attempt at description."[27]

The emigrants created a population boom in the Oregon Territory. A census in 1845 counted 2,019 people in the Champoeg, Clackamas, Tualatin, and Yamhill areas and 91 in Clatsop County.

Portland's Front Avenue and Stark Street in 1852.

Just four years later, the population, which then included settlers in Linn, Benton, and Polk counties, had more than quadrupled to 8,779, according to a special territorial census ordered by Governor Joseph Lane. The federal census of 1850 counted 11,873 persons south of the Columbia.[28]

Land Claims and Farms

The year 1850 also marked a milestone in the settlement of the Oregon Territory. In that year Congress passed the Donation Land Claim Act, granting 320 acres of land to white male settlers of Oregon who were U.S. citizens. Married couples could claim 640 acres—a whole square mile. An 1853 amendment extended the act to emigrants arriving as late as December of 1855 and permitted claimants to patent or "prove up" on their claim after two years' occupancy and payment of $1.25 an acre.[29]

Besides inducing a flurry of hasty marriages and propelling young girls suddenly into a marriageable status, the Donation Land Act hastened the settlement of the Willamette Valley, extensive acres of which were taken up within three or four years. When the original act expired in 1855, only the wooded hills along the valley margins were left unclaimed. Eventually 7,437 claims were patented under the law and its subsequent amendments, covering 2,500,000 acres within Oregon's boundaries.[30]

The settlers came to a land that seemed to them Edenic, a "wide, flat, green prairie swelling here and there into buttes, oak savannas, streams pouring from the two mountain ranges through slopes of hemlock, spruce, fir, and incense cedar to feed the river that meandered the whole of the Valley's length and gave the place its name."[31]

The 1846 description of Lieutenants Warre and Vavasour of the lower Willamette Valley makes it clear why the land-hungry emigrants found it so appealing:

> *The surrounding country is fertile, and the forests of pine and oak are interspersed by prairies on which the settlers build their houses, raise their crops and pasture their cattle.*
>
> *The settlement extends about sixty miles on either bank of the river, the country is comparatively level, that on the right [east] bank being frequently inundated during the spring freshets for a considerable distance into the interior; the soil yields an abundant return, with comparatively little labor; and the pasturage is excellent.*
>
> *To the eye the country, particularly the left bank of the river, is very beautiful. Wide extended, undulating prairies, scattered over with magnificent oak trees, and watered by numerous tributary streams (on which several saw mills are now in operation) reach far to the south....[32]*

Traveling up to Willamette Falls, Warre and Vavasour "proceeded through a thickly wooded country, with occasional patches of open prairie, watered by numerous streams." Like the Columbia, the Willamette was subject to spring flooding: "This road to the falls has been made with much care, but the rivers having overflown their

Interior valleys

The Willamette Valley and other interior valleys were once covered with grassland prairies and woodlands composed of Oregon white oak, a drought-tolerant, fire-resistant deciduous hardwood. Very little is known about the composition of presettlement grasslands because livestock grazing and other development have introduced numerous exotic plant species. Fire, especially fire set by Native American peoples as part of their cultural practices, was an integral influence on valley plant communities.[1] Some researchers believe the interior valleys would have been more forested with Douglas-fir when white settlers arrived if fire had been less frequent. Fires began to be suppressed shortly after that time, and the colonization by Douglas-fir of some Willamette Valley locations since then suggests this is correct.

Oregon white oak groves, called savannas, are characterized by widely spaced trees and an open canopy. Oak trees grow as tall as 40 to 80 feet, developing broad, rounded crowns.[2] Associated tree species include Douglas-fir, ponderosa pine, grand fir, Pacific madrone, bigleaf maple, and Oregon ash.

Oak savannas may have either grass or shrub understories. Shrub species include poison-oak, which may form a low shrub or a vine that climbs oak trunks to considerable heights, as well as serviceberry, snowberry, California hazel, hawthorn, and Indian plum. Along valley edges, the oak savannas grade into the Douglas-fir forests of the western hemlock zone.

The riparian forests of the interior valleys occupy the rivers' broad, flat margins. Rivers move slowly and meander, and seasonal floods are common. On riverbanks and islands, black cottonwood often forms pure stands. In swampy, seasonally flooded areas and alongside low-gradient streams, Oregon ash is most common. White alder and bigleaf maple are also found in these riparian areas.[3]

In the Puget Lowlands, large prairies are located south of Tacoma and Olympia on gravelly, dry soils. These areas support western white pine, lodgepole pine, and ponderosa pine.[4]

[1] Robert Boyd, ed., *Indians, Fire, and the Land in the Pacific Northwest* (Corvallis, OR: Oregon State University Press, 1999).

[2] Warren R. Randall, Robert F. Keniston, Dale N. Bever, and Edward C. Jensen, *Manual of Oregon Trees and Shrubs* (Corvallis, OR: OSU Book Stores, 1988).

[3] J.F. Franklin and C.T. Dyrness, *Natural Vegetation of Oregon and Washington,* USDA Forest Service General Technical Report PNW-8 (Portland, OR: USDA Forest Service Pacific Northwest Forest and Range Experiment Station, 1973).

[4] Ibid. See also H.P. Hansen, "Postglacial Forest Succession, Climate, and Chronology in the Pacific Northwest," *Transactions of the American Philosophical Society* 37(1947), pp. 1–130.

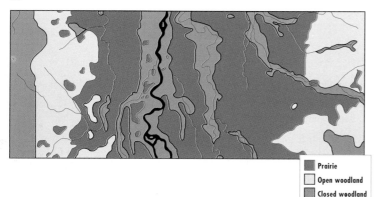

	Prairie
	Open woodland
	Closed woodland

B

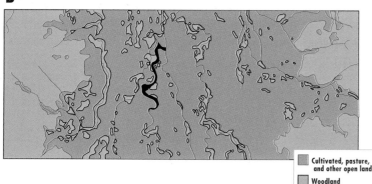

	Cultivated, pasture, and other open land
	Woodland

Vegetation in the Willamette Valley in (a) 1854 and (b) 1970. Native prairies have been replaced by pastures and cultivated fields, and open woodlands have been replaced either by fields, or, along the steeper valley margins, by forests. The gallery forests along the rivers are mostly gone.

banks and carried away the logs which had been placed across as a substitute for bridges, we had much difficulty in effecting our passage, swimming our horses and wading through numerous swamps and marshes."[33]

The two lieutenants also traveled downriver to the Multnomah Channel, opposite Sauvie Island, and thence over the ridge on the Columbia's south bank to the Tualatin Plains. "The country is densely covered with pine and cedar . . . The Tuality Plains are very beautiful, the ground rich and undulating, intersected by hills of fir and oak timber."[34]

The forests of the valley tended to occur in three places: in "gallery forests" of Douglas-fir, Oregon ash, cottonwood, willow, alder, and maple along the river; in scattered groves of fir and oak surrounded by prairie; and in dense thickets of maple, Douglas-fir, cedar, and hemlock in the foothills of the Coast Range and Cascades. The settlers were particularly drawn to the domesticated look of scatterings of trees interspersed across a rolling, grassy prairie.[35] J.G. Cooper, author of the 1853 botany report for the transcontinental railroad survey, said that from a distance the oak groves "look much like orchards, giving to the prairies . . . a rural and home-like aspect." The prairies "seem so much like old farms that it is hard to resist the illusion that we are in a land cultivated for hundreds of years. . . ."[36]

Perhaps Cooper did not think Indian burning amounted to cultivation, but he was aware that the region's native inhabitants regularly burned their prairie lands and that these firings kept trees from encroaching. Speaking of the prairies of southwestern Washington, Cooper noted, "The Indians, in order to preserve their open grounds for game, and for the production of their important root, the camas, soon found the advantage of burning, and when they began this it was only those trees already large that could withstand the fires."[37]

Settlers favored the prairie-woodland margin for practical as well as aesthetic reasons. In an October 1838 letter from Fort Vancouver to the head office of the Hudson's Bay Company, James Douglas wrote, "The intermixture of woods & fertile plains, peculiarly adapts it for the residence of civilized man, affording lands easily tilled, excellent pasture, fuel and building materials of the best quality."[38]

The settlers tended to avoid the deep woods, which were hard to clear. "Nearly all the prairie land is now taken up," wrote Lieutenants Warre and Vavasour in 1846-47, "and the immigrants are too indolent to clear the woods."[39] Settlers also avoided the treeless sweeps of prairie, which lacked the wood they needed for fences, houses, barns, and furniture.

Everywhere on the frontier the first lands claimed were those on the prairie margins adjacent to the forest. More often than not the farmsteads themselves were situated within a few hundred feet of the trees. Travelers passing through the central portions of the larger prairies encounter few habitations. They might come upon a fence, some livestock, a cultivated field and perhaps even a lone dwelling, but in most districts only the smokey gray plumes rising from cabins hidden in the shadows of the forest's edge and the forest fields along the prairies' margins indicated the settled condition of the country.[40]

Settlers also tended to prefer the upland margins of the Willamette River to the richer bottom lands, perhaps because of the river's habit of frequent flooding. In 1844, pioneer James Clyman recorded in his diary, "Considerable injury was done by late Freshet heard of 1000 or Twelv Hundred bushel of wheat being lost in the graneries on the low grounds of the Wilhamet Likewise large lots of fencing and in some instances hogs and other stock being drowned or carried away by the water." They also may have wanted to avoid the swampy, mosquito-infested bottoms because of their fear of malaria.[41]

Changes to the Landscape

Settlement wrought dramatic changes to the landscape of the prairies and wooded foothills. The rapid settlement of the Willamette Valley in the 1840s and the severe decline in Indian populations, owing mainly to several decades' depredation by disease and the relocating of Indians to reservations beginning in the mid-1850s, brought a stop to Indian burning, and thus began a slow but steady increase in forest cover. It may surprise some to realize that the pioneer period was one of expansion of woodland in the Willamette Valley, because the suppression of large-scale fires removed the most important barrier to tree growth. Protected from fire, young white oaks and conifers began to encroach on the grasslands. The open hills west of Salem, which Henry Eld in 1841 had described as "hilly prairie country," were covered with brushfields by the 1870s.[42]

The settlers themselves used fire to clear the land. Some prairie areas were covered with a dense growth of ferns reaching 8 or 10 feet high. Fire was the best way to rid the land of these troublesome weeds. However, the pioneers generally saw wildfire as a threat, not a blessing. Fire does far more damage in a culture where people live in settled dwellings and towns than it does among more nomadic peoples. By and large European-Americans did not regard fire kindly, and they suppressed wildfires as vigorously as they could.[43] Fires deliberately started for land-clearing purposes reached nowhere near the extent or frequency of those set by Indians.

Disease and the native population

One reason the landscape of the Northwest looked so appealingly untouched to the European-American settlers is that the population of its original inhabitants had been much reduced by introduced diseases before most settlers arrived. The native peoples' lack of resistance to Old World disease organisms made them extremely vulnerable to such illnesses as smallpox, measles, and malaria. As a result, native populations plummeted following white settlement.

Smallpox apparently arrived by ship in the 1770s, killing an estimated 30 percent of the native population. Smallpox was reintroduced in 1800–1801. When Lewis and Clark arrived five years later, they estimated a population of 9,000 Kalapuyas, the Willamette Valley people. In the early 1830s, the Hudson's Bay Company put the figure at either 7,785 or 8,870.[1]

Beginning in 1831, an attack of what was called intermittent fever—probably malaria—struck the Fort Vancouver area each summer. The disease was particularly hard on the Indians. John McLoughlin estimated that three-quarters of the Indian population in the Fort Vancouver area died during the first outbreak. In 1841, the surviving population of the Willamette and lower Columbia valleys was estimated at 600.[2]

The botanist John Kirk Townsend, who visited Fort Vancouver in 1835, offered this bleak observation: "Probably there does not now exist one, where, five years ago there were a hundred Indians; and in sailing up the [Columbia] river, from the cape to the cascades, the only evidence of the existence of the Indian, is an occasional miserable wigwam, with a few wretched, half-starved occupants."[3]

[1] Robert Reed Bunting, "Landscaping the Pacific Northwest: A Cultural and Ecological Mapping of the Douglas-fir Region, 1778-1900" (Ph.D. dissertation, University of California, Davis, 1993), pp. 104-5; and Robert Boyd, ed., *Indians, Fire, and the Land in the Pacific Northwest* (Corvallis, OR: Oregon State University Press, 1999), p. 99.

[2] Bunting, "Landscaping the Pacific Northwest," p. 105; and Boyd, *Indians, Fire, and the Land,* p. 99.

[3] John Kirk Townsend, *Narrative of a journey across the Rocky Mountains, to the Columbia River, and a visit to the Sandwich Islands, Chili &c., with a scientific appendix* (1839; reprint, Corvallis: Oregon State University Press, 1999), cited in Bunting, "Landscaping the Pacific Northwest," p. 106.

In consequence, the valley prairie land began to afforest itself. In 1878, T.L. Davidson was making rails out of trees that had sprouted since he arrived.[44] "Contemporary estimates of the extent of reforestation ran into the hundreds of thousands of acres," says Bowen.[45] The distribution pattern of woodlands in the valley has also changed. The gallery forest along the river is mostly gone, and open woodlands on the rolling valley floor have also mostly disappeared. The steep hillsides and foothills now have many more trees than they did in the 1850s.[46]

In contrast, the community of native grasses has almost disappeared since settlement. With less than 1 percent of the native-prairie plant community remaining, it is more endangered than old-growth forests. Native bunchgrasses and fescues and wildflowers like the Kincaid's lupine began to disappear as farmers plowed the prairies and planted wheat, oats, potatoes, peas and beans, corn, vegetables for market, and finally orchards.[47]

The grazing of livestock also has had a large impact on native valley vegetation. Sheep probably came into American settlers' possession around 1843 or 1844, and by 1850 there were slightly more than 4,000 head in the valley. Cattle were introduced in large numbers in 1836 when Ewing Young organized the Willamette Cattle Company. Young pulled together a party of settlers who sailed to San Francisco and bought several hundred head of longhorned Spanish cattle for $3 a head from the Mexican authorities at Sonoma. The 11-member crew of cowboys drove the cattle to Oregon, arriving safely with 630 head, which were distributed among those who had put up the capital for the venture.[48]

The livestock wandered freely over the grasslands, "and the valley began to earn a reputation as a great stock country."[49] The first woolen mill opened in Oregon City in 1857, and in time wool and garment manufacturing became one of Oregon's principal industries. Grazing also had an impact on the mountain valleys of the western Cascades. Grazing lands in these upland pastures were sometimes burned by stockmen seeking to "green up" the land. Some were damaged by overgrazing.[50]

The swampy, braided character of the river lowlands began to change when farmers began ditching and draining Willamette Valley lowlands by the 1870s. Settlers also drained beaver ponds to reclaim farmland.[51] The quantity of wetlands in Oregon declined by 38 percent between 1780s and the 1980s, according to a 1990 federal report.[52] The valley bottom became less hospitable to waterfowl, as Salem pioneer John Minto (who himself drained a beaver pond) noticed in 1908: "To me it seems easily unbelievable by a person coming here now, to state the quantity of waterfowl, cranes, curlew and snipe which wintered on the grasses and roots of the damp lands of the valleys and the sloughs, ponds and streams sixty-four years ago. . . . These damp-land and water fowls and animals, which once found here their breeding places, have gone forever."[53]

The Forests

Early settlers of the Oregon Territory appreciated more than the fertile soils and garden-like landscape of their new homes. Another element of their surroundings was less homey, more sublime. "What astonished the immigrants . . . was not so much the Valley, about as Edenic as they had expected, but something above it—that great white escarpment against the blue of the eastern sky—the mountains."[54] The forests on these mountain slopes were equally monumental. "Inexhaustible" was a word often used by early observers of the forests of the west side of the Cascades. Botanist J.G. Cooper referred to "the immense and inexhaustible timber on the mountains."[55]

Lieutenant Henry L. Abbot remarked in 1854 on the huge trees and the quantity of fallen logs on the Cascades' west slopes. Sent out by the U.S. Army to search for likely railroad routes, Abbot traveled from The Dalles to the Willamette Valley over the south flank of Mount Hood. His party had with them wheeled carts and about 60 head of livestock. Abbot's journal entry for October 7 reads, "To-day we had to struggle through a tangled forest of spruce, yew, fir, and pine, with many fallen logs crossing, and sometimes even piled up on the trail. . . . Driving about sixty loose animals through this forest was no easy task."[56]

The party camped that night in a muddy mountain meadow next to a lake. "Its banks were so miry that our animals could with difficulty drink. Here we were compelled to encamp; our mules had spent the day in jumping over or creeping under logs, and the men in struggling after them and repairing broken packs." Wryly, he observed, "We were all fully convinced that wandering amid 'forests primeval' in poetry, and among the Cascade mountains, are two essentially different things." The practical difficulties, however, did not quench Abbot's appreciation of the sublimity of the landscape: "Mount Hood towered high above us, and his huge, snow-capped head, now appearing and now disappearing among drifting masses of clouds, gave a wild grandeur to the little camping place, which will be long remembered."[57]

Abbot's admiration widened into awe when his party reached the summit of the trail. "A magnificent panorama burst upon our view. . . . For days we had been struggling blindly through dense forests, but now the surrounding country lay spread out before us for more than a hundred miles. The five grand snow peaks, Mount St. Helens, Mount Ranier [sic], Mount Adams, Mount Hood, and Mount Jefferson, rose majestically above a rolling sea of dark, fir-covered ridges, some of which the approaching winter had already begun to mark with white."[58]

Logging and Sawmills

The timber on the mountains remained standing for the next half-century while Oregon's first logging was taking place along the gentler slopes closer to tidewater. The first logs to be felled by Europeans in Oregon toppled at Astoria in 1811, as Astor's men with difficulty cut down the huge spruces and hemlocks to build their fort. In addition to his many other roles in Northwest history, the Hudson's Bay Company's John McLoughlin was the territory's first commercial lumberman. In 1828 he built a water-powered sawmill near the present-day site of Camas, Washington. The mill turned out 2,000 to 2,500 board feet of lumber a day and had a crew of 25 to 30 workers, mostly Hawaiians. In 1829 McLoughlin sent the first shipment of lumber to the Hawaiian Islands, and two years later Fort Vancouver lumber appeared in California markets.[59]

The main business of the Hudson's Bay Company remained furs, however, and the next sawmills in Oregon were built to meet primarily local needs. The first American mill was built by the Methodist missionaries in 1838. In 1843, Henry Hunt brought sawmill equipment overland from Indiana. The next year he built a mill 30 miles upstream from Astoria, on a bluff next to a 70-foot waterfall whose cascading water turned a wheel and powered a sash saw. By 1844 Oregon City had two sawmills powered by water tumbling over Willamette Falls, and lumber was selling for $2 a hundred board feet.[60] Portland got its first sawmill in 1849.

Hunt's lumber was exported as well as sold locally. The export market may not have been large, but it made a difference in local prices, according to an 1848 story in the Oregon City newspaper, the *Oregon Spectator*: "Oregon lumber is shipped to California and the Sandwich [Hawaiian] Islands—and its value for shipment controls its price at home."[61]

The nascent Northwest timber industry got a major boost when gold was discovered on the American River in California in 1849. That and subsequent gold discoveries at Yreka, California, in 1850–51, and at Jacksonville, Oregon, in 1851, opened markets for mine timbers and building lumber. Prices were "fabulous," according to Judge Matthew Deady. Currency began to be seen in the territory for the first time. In the spring of 1848 there were 18 water-powered sawmills operating on the Willamette and lower Columbia rivers. Within a year there were about 30. Three years later Oregon had about 100 sawmills.[62]

The region's first steam sawmill was built in Portland in 1850. In 1851, Captain Lewis Love rafted 300,000 feet of logs to Portland from his claim on the Columbia Slough. He said there were "quite a number of other fools" doing the same thing. By the 1880s, Oregon's timber industry was "the wheel which sets all other wheels in motion," said the *Portland Oregonian* in 1888.[63] Six or seven large sawmills on the lower Columbia sent overseas a combined 75 to 100 million board feet yearly during the 1880s and 1890s. But Oregon's lumber production was dominated by smaller mills selling mostly to local markets.

The Railroads

Early boosters were convinced that Oregon's abundant natural resources merited her a place among industrial giants. Railroads, they believed, would work their magic to realize Oregon's vision of "agrarian paradise and industrial potential." In the tones of a latter-day Ezekiel, Washington Territory's J.W. Goodell wrote in 1856 of his vision of "large cities, with their numerous spires, glistening in the rays of the morning sun, their streets teeming with busy thousands, and their numerous wharves crowded with immense steamers and ships from all parts of the world, receiving and discharging their immense cargoes. I turn my eyes eastward, and behold an immense train of rail road cars thundering down the inclined plain of the Cascades."[64] Frances Fuller Victor, writing in 1872 of Oregon City's disadvantages as a river port, was confident that railroads "will ultimately remove any disabilities of that kind, and with its splendid water-power, backed by a country productive in soil, timber, and mineral deposits, its future seems as well assured as that of any town in Oregon."[65]

In the 1860s, the federal government began to offer land grants to finance the construction of railroads. The railroad companies were supposed to sell the land to settlers, furthering the government's goal of developing the agricultural and industrial potential of the West. But the railroad companies did not always comply with the rules, and millions of acres ended up in the hands of commercial interests that were acquiring large blocks of timber.[66]

The first transcontinental line was completed in 1869. Ben Holladay's Oregon and California Railroad linked Portland with Salem, Eugene, and Roseburg by 1872. Henry Villard's Oregon Railway and Navigation Company had a line up the Columbia as far as Walla Walla by 1882, and over the next year Villard's crews pushed the line through Idaho to Helena, Montana, where it joined Northern Pacific's route to St. Paul, Minnesota, and linked the Pacific Northwest to the East for the first time.[67]

Not all Oregon communities had the blessings of rail immediately. "Transverse feeder lines which cut across the Willamette Valley proved disappointing," wrote the historian Dorothy Johansen. The Oregon and Southeastern, affectionately called "Old Slow and Easy," was "a homely short line that meanders up the valley of the Row River [near Cottage Grove] a matter of twenty miles and finally bogs down in the middle of

The land-grant checkerboard

To finance the railroads that would open the West to settlement and development, the federal government offered grants of public land to railroad companies, beginning in the 1860s. The companies were supposed to sell the land to settlers to finance the railroad construction. But many companies did not follow through on the deal, and much of the grant land ended up in the possession of large companies that wanted to build up timber empires.

One railroad company, the Oregon and California (called the O&C), was granted 12,800 acres for every mile of railroad it built. The land lay in alternating square-mile sections of land along the railroad right-of-way. After the company reneged on its commitment to sell the land to settlers, the government reclaimed about 2 million acres of the grant land. Grant lands of another company in southwestern Oregon, the Coos Bay Wagon Road, also were retaken. Today these lands and the remaining public-domain lands are managed by the Bureau of Land Management. Because of the alternating pattern of the original land grants, the BLM and neighboring lands show up on a map as a distinctive checkerboard pattern of federal and private holdings.[1]

[1] John H. Beuter, *Legacy and Promise: Oregon's Forests and Wood Products Industry* (Portland, OR: Oregon Business Council and Oregon Forest Resources Institute, 1998), pp. 10–11.

nowhere." Nevertheless, the railroads brought the Pacific Northwest a large influx of new citizens—the population grew by 132,000 between 1870 and 1880, and almost half a million more between 1880 and 1890. The railroads also ushered in a two-decade economic boom and a period of sustained optimism that ended only with the nationwide depression of 1893.[68]

Railroads encouraged the rapid expansion of the lumbering industry that took place at the end of the nineteenth century. They not only opened previously untapped timber lands, but they also created an unprecedented demand for railroad ties and bridge timbers. Until railroads came along, the forests on the high ridges of the Coast Range and Cascades had remained virtually untouched. Short stretches of rail made it possible for lumbermen to get at these

A logging train negotiating a curvy trestle.

stands and profitably haul the big trees out of the woods. In 1884 the Oregon-Pacific Railroad penetrated the Santiam Canyon, making Cascades timber available to Willamette Valley and California markets. By 1889, Oregon had seven logging railroads (compared to Washington's 22 and California's 37), and more were "being introduced everywhere."[69]

Still, up until the 1890s the impact of logging on Oregon's vast forests was "hardly noticeable, except along the drainages of the major rivers that provided the primary transportation routes," says the forest economist John Beuter. Beuter estimates that accumulated logging between 1811 and 1891 probably did not exceed 15 or 16 billion board feet. To put that number into perspective, the timber logged in 1952, Oregon's highest year ever, was almost 10 billion board feet.[70]

Along with the railroads, improvements in logging and milling technology began to spread throughout the Pacific Slope beginning in the 1880s. Teams of horses and oxen that were used to haul the logs out of the woods began to be replaced by John Dolbeer's steam-powered donkey, used for the first time on Dolbeer's logging operation near Eureka, California, in 1881. Subsequent improvements were made by him and others, and steam yarding quickly spread up and down the Pacific Coast. By the turn of the century there were 293 donkey engines in use in Washington, 35 in Oregon, and 61 in California.[71]

The donkey engine was not only cheaper to use than draft animals and a bullwhacker, but it could log when the ground was too muddy for bull teams to work. The efficiency of the steam donkey also made it easier to take more logs off a site. Bull-team loggers had of necessity selected only the finest-grained, most marketable trees. With the advent of steam and steel in the woods, clearcutting increasingly supplanted the selective logging of the old days. Harvests rose dramatically in the early years of the century, and lumber output almost doubled every decade. In 1904, 987 million board feet of lumber was produced in Oregon. In 1914 the figure was 1.8 billion board feet; in 1924 it was 3.7 billion board feet.[72]

Equally revolutionary changes were happening in the sawmills. More and more steps in the lumber manufacturing process were becoming mechanized, with improved headrigs (the saws that do the initial breaking down of the log), circular saws, replaceable saw teeth, and finally band saws, as well as many other improvements. Mill owners diversified their products, acquiring specialized equip-

Concentration of timber ownership in the Pacific Northwest, c. 1913, by size of holding.

Group	Group size (million board feet)	Number of owners	Billion board feet owned	Percent of total	Percent cumulatively
1	Over 25,000	3	237.4	23.5	23.5
2	13,000–25,000	5	101.4	10.4	33.5
3	5,000–13,000	15	97.4	9.6	43.1
4	3,500–5000	18	71.0	7.0	50.1
5	2,000–3,500	26	64.6	6.4	56.5
6	1,000–2,000	67	91.9	9.1	65.6
7	500–1,000	86	59.2	5.8	71.4
8	250–500	96	34.3	3.4	74.8
9	125–250	176	31.9	3.1	77.9
10	60–125	222	18.3	1.8	79.7
11	Less than 60	?	205.6	20.3	100.0
Total		**714**	**1,013.0**		**100.0**

Source: U.S. Bureau of Corporations, *The Lumber Industry*, 1, pt. 1:29.

ment to make box shooks (the pieces used in assembling boxes), molding, sashes, doors, and other kinds of finished goods.[73]

The effect of these changes was to increase both the operating costs and the potential rewards of the lumber business. They ushered in a transformation of the Pacific Northwest timber industry from a largely unorganized group of local, independent operators to a big business dominated by players from other regions, principally the Midwest, with large amounts of capital at their disposal.

During the 1880s, fortunes that had accumulated in the hands of Lake States timber companies, the fruits of heavy logging there, were being invested in the rising timber industry of the West. "Newspapers and journals carried frequent reports of firms that were moving, or contemplating moving, to the West Coast. Enough new mills appeared on the Pacific shore to lend credence to the wildest rumors."[74] In addition, many midwestern lumbermen were buying up large tracts of West Coast timber land. In January of 1900, Frederick Weyerhaeuser and a group of St. Paul businessmen bought 900,000 acres of former grant land from the Northern Pacific Railway Co. Weyerhaeuser and his group paid $6 an acre for enough prime timber land to last Weyerhaeuser's company for decades. In the next few years Weyerhaeuser added to his holdings, and by 1902 the company had almost 2 million acres in Oregon and Washington, most of it former railroad grant land.[75]

The Progressive Movement

In the 1890s, there arose a nationwide ferment of political and social ideology that came to be called the Progressive Movement. Arising in part from a popular repugnance at the capitalist excesses of the Gilded Age, the Progressive Movement carried a conviction that forests ought to be protected from the depredations of big timber companies. The forests of New England, the Lake States, and the South had been heavily cut over, and people were nervous about the way timbermen were eyeing the rich forests of the West.[76]

Flooding in the East in the late 1870s had renewed debate about the link between deforestation and flooding. In 1873, a committee from the American Association for the Advancement of Science petitioned Congress to protect the United States' disappearing forests. In 1879, Charles Sprague Sargent, a Harvard professor of arboriculture, called for the federal government to preserve forest land from settlement.[77]

In 1891, arising out of the Progressive agenda, came a land reform law that changed the course of history with respect to the Northwest's forest lands.[78] The law enabled the President of the United States to create forest reserves on federal lands still in the public domain. The General Revision Act authorized the President to "set apart and reserve … any part of the public lands wholly or in part covered with timber or undergrowth, whether of commercial value or not, as public reservations." The Organic Act of 1897 spelled out the purpose of those reserves: "to improve and protect the forest within the reservation, or for the purpose of securing favorable conditions of water flows, and to furnish a continuous supply of timber for the use and necessities of citizens of the United States… ."[79]

In 1892, President Benjamin Harrison created Oregon's first forest reserve, the 142,000-acre Bull Run Reserve on the western slopes of Mount Hood. The next year, President Grover Cleveland designated another 4.5 million acres as the Oregon Cascade and Ashland Reserves. Over the next 65 years, the reserves were expanded and organized into 12 national forests covering 15.5 million acres—a quarter of Oregon's total land area, encompassing about half its forest land.[80]

In a 1905 letter to Gifford Pinchot, the first Chief of the Forest Service, Roosevelt's secretary of agriculture spelled out the purpose of the national forests: they were to be "devoted to … the permanent good of the whole people and not for the temporary benefit of individuals or companies." Where interests conflicted, questions "will always be decided from the standpoint of the greatest good to the greatest number in the long run"—a succinct summary of Pinchot's Progressive creed.[81]

The national forests were never intended to be preserves. Logging was permitted—in fact, securing "a continuous supply of timber" was one justification for their existence. As it turned out, however, very little logging took place on the national forests from the time of their creation up until World War II. Private lands still had

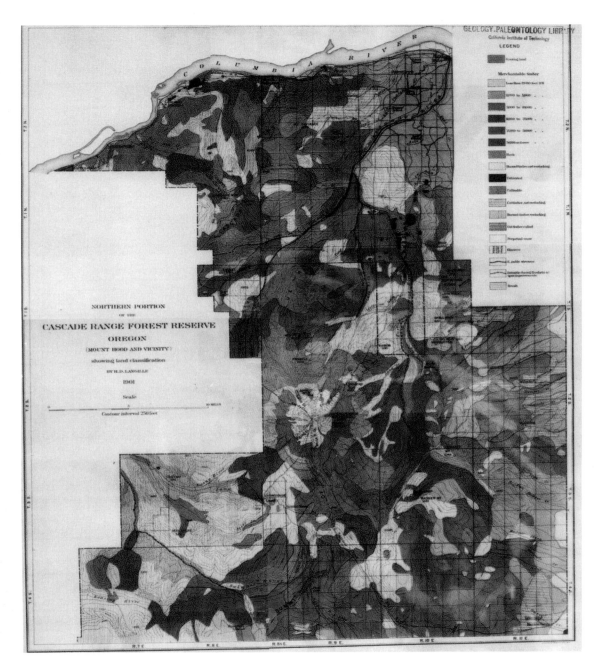

A 1901 map of the northern portion of Cascade Range Forest Reserve (now Mount Hood National Forest). Bright yellow (top box in key) is grazing land. The next six boxes in the key denote areas of merchantable timber ranging from less than 2,000 board feet/acre (the lightest green) to 50,000 and over (the darkest green). Solid red patches are denoted "cultivable" for farmland. Red horizontal stripes denote "cut timber, not restocking".

plenty of timber to harvest, and there was little demand for federal timber before World War II and its booming aftermath. "In fact, until the 1940s, private timberland owners feared that timber from the federal lands might be dumped on the market and drive down the market value of their timber."[82] The main effect of the creation of forest reserves in the Northwest was to keep the timber in the Cascades virtually untouched from harvesting for 50 years.

Fire, however, had not spared the western Cascades. Henry Gannett, in a 1902 report for the U.S. Geological Survey, estimated that out of Oregon's total acreage of once-timbered land, "not less than 18 percent . . . has been destroyed by fire." About half the forest land in Clackamas County, on the slopes of the Cascades east of Oregon City, had been recently burned, Gannett reported. However, because the land west of the Cascade crest is "abundantly watered, and in all other respects extremely favorable for tree growth," Gannett was optimistic that the land would reforest itself. "All these burns are in some stage of reforesting, and in most of them reforesting has gone forward rapidly and very favorably. Much of this burned country is now covered with a dense stand of young trees."[83]

Wind River Experiment Station and nursery in southern Washington in 1914, 1925, and 1954, showing regrowth of forest in the background.

Clark-Wilson Lumber Company sawmill in Portland, 1937.

Thirty years later, the Forest Service issued a report that was, if anything, even more sanguine. Despite "comparatively small bodies of second growth and old burns, small deforested areas, and cut-over areas," they reported that "almost unbroken stands of old-growth Douglas-fir cover the lower slopes and foothills of the Cascade Range practically the length of the State."[84]

Stepped-up Harvests

Harvests from all Oregon's forests rose dramatically from the 1940s through the 1970s in response to the booming market in wood products after World War II. Timber from federal forests—the national forests and BLM lands—began to be a larger part of the mix by the mid-1950s, and in 1963, harvests from federal forests exceeded those from nonfederal lands for the first time. Overall harvest levels peaked in 1952 with an all-time high of 10.4 billion board feet.[85]

In Clackamas County, which includes Oregon City, the west slopes of the Cascades, and some of the Mount Hood National Forest, the patterns of harvest generally followed those of the state as a whole, but the pace was a little slower. During the immediate postwar years, harvests rose from 262 million board feet to 410 million board feet. After a slight decline, harvests hit 416 million board feet in 1956 and an all-time high of 448 million in 1959.

A New Era

As harvests were reaching their peak, however, the attitudes of the American people toward forests and the natural environment as a whole were undergoing a profound change. A heightened public concern about the state of the environment was embodied in a series of federal laws that significantly changed the policy for managing federal forests like the Mount Hood National Forest.[86]

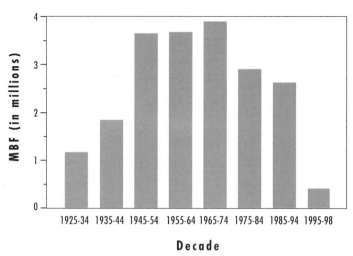

Sawlog production and timber harvest by decade in Clackamas County from 1925 to 1998.

The Multiple Use-Sustained Yield Act of 1960 made multiple use an explicit principle for federal forest management. The Wilderness Act of 1964 articulated a policy for setting aside wilderness areas and preserving them from any sort of commodity use. The National Environmental Policy Act (NEPA) of 1969 required federal land managers to conduct environmental-impact assessments of any major proposal; the public may comment on these proposals, and citizens may appeal land management decisions, or, if not satisfied, sue in federal courts.[87]

Four laws passed in the 1970s further expanded the scope and responsibilities of federal forest management. The 1973 Endangered Species Act made the protection of plant and animal species a federal responsibility. The 1974 Forest and Rangeland Renewable Resources Planning Act (RPA) required the Forest Service to assess the status of the nation's renewable natural resources and to determine national needs for these resources. Two laws passed in 1976, the Federal Land Policy and Management Act (FLPMA) and the National Forest Management Act (NFMA), require that management planning on federal lands consider both biological diversity and economic feasibility.[88]

Also during the 1970s and 1980s, states were enacting their own environmental laws. In 1971 came Oregon's Forest Practices Act, regulating forestry practices on nonfederal lands, including road construction, logging practices, and reforestation. As amended in 1987, the law requires landowners to better protect areas near streams and requires the state Board of Forestry to protect threatened and endangered species sites and other ecologically sensitive areas, including significant wetlands. Further amendments in 1991 limited the size of clearcuts, set standards for leaving snags and large pieces of wood on logging sites, and strengthened reforestation provisions.[89]

Since NEPA, the federal courts have assumed an ever larger role in management of federal forests. "The agencies have struggled to meet the requirements of all the new laws. At the same time, they have been besieged by intense pressure from traditional resource use constituents and an increasingly influential environmental movement. Given these polarities and the ambiguities in portions of the new laws, it was inevitable that disputes would end up in the courts."[90]

After the northern spotted owl was listed as threatened in 1990, a federal judge issued an injunction effectively halting timber sales on national forests and BLM lands in western Oregon. President Bill Clinton convened a team of biologists, economists, and social scientists that came to be called the Forest Ecosystem Management Assessment Team, or FEMAT. It was the FEMAT team that devised the Northwest Forest Plan, under which Northwest federal forests are now being managed.

Federal Judge William Dwyer lifted the logging injunction in 1994 after finding that the Northwest Forest Plan satisfies the habitat requirements for spotted owls and other species. The plan protects up to 80 percent of remaining old-growth forests—setting harvest levels at 1.2 billion board feet, down 70 percent from the levels of the 1970s. Actual harvest levels have been well below 1.2 billion board feet.[91]

The president's plan was supposed to be a compromise between traditional resource-use interests and the environmental community. It was supposed to halt the lawsuits and let timber harvesting proceed, although at much-reduced levels, on the federal forests. But the compromise was never an easy one, and the plan is still the focus of legal challenges.

A Balancing Act

Because of its situation, close to heavily populated Portland and the Willamette Valley, the western Cascades have been a playground as well as a timber basket. Mount Hood is the second most climbed mountain in the world, after Fujiyama in Japan. The mountain has five ski areas, one of which, Timberline Lodge, is open year-round. Timberline Lodge, built in 1937 by the Works Progress Administration and the Civilian Conservation Corps, attracts thousands of guests and visitors each year.

The forest has 1,230 miles of trails used for hiking, skiing, and snowmobiling. On the slopes of the mountain are huckleberry patches cherished by Indians as traditional food-gathering sites. The Bull Run watershed, the nation's first forest reserve, is Portland's source of drinking water.

Visitors to the mountain enjoy fishing, camping, boating, hiking, berry-picking and mushroom collecting. In the National Forest's six wilderness areas, rangers count 47,000 visitor-days per year. The forest as a whole receives about 5 million visitors per year.[92]

Of the forest's 1.06 million acres, just under one-third have been designated as late-successional reserves, which are exempt from harvest under the Northwest Forest Plan. Withdrawn from harvest by congressional or administrative order are another 257,450 acres. There are 484,350 acres of "matrix lands," the lands available for timber harvest. After riparian reserves and nonforested areas are subtracted from these, about 204,000 acres remain for timber harvest.

In 1998, 41.2 million board feet of timber were harvested from 3,344 acres. That figure is down slightly from 1997, when

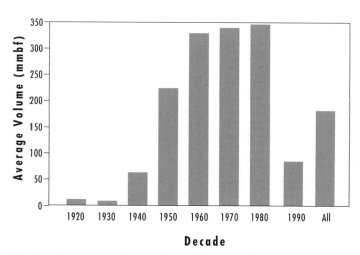

Timber harvest on Mount Hood National Forest from 1920s to present.

Panoramic photos taken from Kinney Ridge in the Willamette National Forest in 1937.

The same sites rephotographed from about the same vantage points in 1987. The lake in the second and third photos is Detroit Lake, formed when Detroit Dam was built on the Santiam River in 1953.

just under 50 million board feet were cut, but up from 1996, when about 26 million board feet were cut. Harvesting was mostly by selective cutting, thinning, or "sanitation cutting" of trees killed by bark beetles. Only 2 percent of the timber was clearcut in 1998.[93]

Management planning on the national forests, including the Mount Hood National Forest, requires a balancing act among the varied demands for the rich resources of the forest—its timber, its recreational opportunities, its Native American cultural heritage, its scenic beauty, its watersheds, and the many other values that Oregonians want their forests to provide.[94]

Notes to Chapter 6

1   Or perhaps longer. The points in history when people first arrived on the West Coast of North America, and by what routes they traveled, are still being debated by anthropologists. See Kenneth M. Ames and Herbert D.G. Maschner, *Peoples of the Northwest Coast: Their Archaeology and Prehistory* (London: Thames and Hudson, 1999), p. 63–64.

2.   Patricia C. Erigero, *Cultural Landscape Report: Fort Vancouver National Historic Site*, vol. 2 (Seattle, WA: U.S. Department of Interior, National Park Service, 1992), p. 6; and Dorothy O. Johansen, *Empire of the Columbia*, 2d ed. (New York: Harper & Row, 1967), p. 105.

3.   R.M. Waite, "Copy of a document found among the private papers of the late Dr. John McLoughlin," in *Transactions of the Eighth Annual Re-Union of the Oregon Pioneer Association for 1880*. Cited in Erigero, *Cultural Landscape Report*, p. 46.

4.   William Adrian Bowen, "Migration and Settlement on a Far Western Frontier: Oregon to 1850" (Ph.D. dissertation, University of California, Berkeley, 1972), p. 16; and Erigero, *Cultural Landscape Report*, p. 59.

5.   Ibid., p. 14.

6.   Frederick Merk, *Fur trade and Empire: George Simpson's Journal: Remarks connected with the fur trade in the course of a voyage from*

York Factory to Fort George and back to York Factory, 1825–25; together with accompanying documents (New Haven, CT: Harvard University Press, 1931), cited in Erigero, *Cultural Landscape Report*, p. 19.

7. John Scouler, "Dr. John Scouler's journal of a voyage to N.W. America," *Oregon Historical Quarterly* VI (June 1905), cited in Erigero, *Cultural Landscape Report*, p. 19; and James K. Agee, personal communication, July 2000.

8. R.G. Large, ed., *The Journals of William Fraser Tolmie: Physician and Fur Trader* (Vancouver, BC: Mitchell Press, 1963), pp. 173–175, cited in Erigero, *Cultural Landscape Report*, p. 20; and Cliff Snider, personal communication, May 2000.

9. Terri A. Taylor and Patricia C. Erigero, *Cultural Landscape Report: Fort Vancouver National Historic Site*, vol. 1 (Seattle, WA: U.S. Department of Interior, National Park Service, 1992), p. 62; and Johansen, *Empire of the Columbia*, p. 127.

10. Johansen, *Empire of the Columbia*, p. 127.

11. J.G. Cooper, "Report Upon the Botany of the Route," in *Reports of explorations and surveys to ascertain the most practicable and economical route for a railroad from the Mississippi River to the Pacific Ocean*, vol. XII, book II, part II (36th Cong., 2d Sess., United States Senate. Washington, DC, 1860), p. 20.

12. Erigero, *Cultural Landscape Report*, p. 61.

13. Ibid., p. 59.

14. John McLoughlin, Private Papers 1825-1856 (Bancroft Library mss. P-A 155:2, University of California, Berkeley), cited in Bowen, "Migration and Settlement on a Far Western Frontier," p. 17.

15. Ibid., p. 18a.

16. Ibid., p. 18; and Terence O'Donnell, *That Balance So Rare: The Story of Oregon* (Portland, OR: Oregon Historical Society Press, 1988), p. 40.

17. Bowen, "Migration and Settlement on a Far Western Frontier," p. 19; Robert Reed Bunting, "Landscaping the Pacific Northwest: A Cultural and Ecological Mapping of the Douglas-fir Region, 1778–1900" (Ph.D.

dissertation, University of California, Davis, 1993), p. 146; Johansen, *Empire of the Columbia*, pp. 147–148; and H.E. Tobie, "The Willamette Valley Before the Great Immigrations" (master's thesis, University of Oregon, Eugene, OR, 1927), p. 4.

18. Tobie, "The Willamette Valley," p. 4.

19. Johansen, *Empire of the Columbia*, p. 147.

20. Bowen, "Migration and Settlement on a Far Western Frontier," p. 20; and Johansen, *Empire of the Columbia*, p. 163.

21. Bowen, "Migration and Settlement on a Far Western Frontier," p. 20–21; Johansen, *Empire of the Columbia*, p. 144; William E. Hill, *The Oregon Trail: Yesterday and Today* (Caldwell, ID: The Caxton Printers, Ltd., 1992), p. xxv; and O'Donnell, *That Balance So Rare*, p. 35.

22. Bowen, "Migration and Settlement on a Far Western Frontier," p. 30; and Chester Leonard Tunnell, "History of Oregon City to 1870" (master's thesis, University of Oregon, Eugene, OR, 1940), p. 9.

23. McLoughlin, Private Papers, pp. 19–20, cited in Bowen, "Migration and Settlement on a Far Western Frontier," p. 137.

24. Henry Warre and Mervyn Vavasour, "Documents relative to Warre and Vavasour's military reconnoissance in Oregon, 1845-6," in *Oregon Historical Quarterly* X, vol. I (1996), p.51.

25. Bowen, "Migration and Settlement on a Far Western Frontier," p. 40; and O'Donnell, *That Balance So Rare*, p. 53.

26. Warre and Vavasour, "Documents," p. 46; and O'Donnell, *That Balance So Rare*, p. 53.

27. Neil Howison, "Report of Lieut. Neil M. Howison, United States Navy, to the commander of the Pacific Squadron; being the result of an examination in the year 1846 of the coast, harbors, rivers, soil, productions, climate, and population of the Territory of Oregon" (30th Cong., 1st Sess., United States House of Representatives, 1848; reprint, Portland, OR: *Oregon Historical Quarterly* XIV, no. I, 1913), p. 42.

28. Bowen, "Migration and Settlement on a Far Western Frontier," pp. 34, 37, 39. Emigrants arriving in the 1848 and 1849 migrations were not

counted very carefully, says Bowen, and the out-migration of as many as 2,000 fortune-seekers to the California gold fields makes it probable that Oregon had a net decline in population for at least one of those years.

29. Johansen, *Empire of the Columbia*, p. 231.

30. John H. Beuter, *Legacy and Promise: Oregon's Forests and Wood Products Industry* (Portland, OR: Oregon Business Council and Oregon Forest Resources Institute, 1998), p. 10; Johansen, *Empire of the Columbia*, pp. 232, 234; and Jerry C. Towle, "Changing Geography of Willamette Valley Woodlands," *Oregon Historical Quarterly* LXXXIII, no. I (spring 1982), p. 75.

31. O'Donnell, *That Balance So Rare*, p. 35.

32. Warre and Vavasour, "Documents," p. 52.

33. Ibid., p. 76.

34. Ibid., pp. 75–76.

35. Towle, "Changing Geography," pp. 68–69; and Bunting, "Landscaping the Pacific Northwest," p. 185.

36. Cooper, "Report Upon the Botany of the Route," pp. 28, 39.

37. Ibid., p. 23.

38. James Douglas, "Letter to the Govr. Deputy Govr. & Committee Honble Hudsons Bay Company from James Douglas at Ft Vancouver, Oct. 18, 1838," in E.E. Rich, ed., *The Letters of John McLoughlin from Fort Vancouver to the Governor and Committee, First Series, 1825-38* (London: The Champlain Society for The Hudson's Bay Record Society, 1941), cited in Bunting, "Landscaping the Pacific Northwest," p. 187.

39. Warre and Vavasour, "Documents," p. 77.

40. Bowen, "Migration and Settlement on a Far Western Frontier," p. 130.

41. Ibid., pp. 131–132.

42. William A. Slacum 1837, "Slacum's Report on Oregon 1836-7," *Oregon Historical Quarterly* XIII, vol. 2 (June 1912), p. 201; Towle, "Changing

Geography," p. 77; and Bowen, "Migration and Settlement on a Far Western Frontier," p. 128.

43. Cooper, "Report Upon the Botany of the Route," p. 22; and Bunting, "Landscaping the Pacific Northwest," pp. 284, 290.

44. T.L. Davidson, "By the Southern Route into Oregon" (Salem, Oregon, 1878) (Bancroft Library mss. P-A 23, p. 1, University of California, Berkeley, CA), cited in Bowen, "Migration and Settlement on a Far Western Frontier," p. 128.

45. Matthew P. Deady, "History and Progress of Oregon after 1845" (Portland, Oregon, 1878) (Bancroft Library mss. P-A 24, p. 59, University of California, Berkeley), cited in Bowen, "Migration and Settlement on a Far Western Frontier," p. 128.

46. Towle, "Changing Geography," p. 71.

47. Mark Wilson, personal communication, September 1995; and Bowen, "Migration and Settlement on a Far Western Frontier," pp. 193–206.

48. Bowen, "Migration and Settlement on a Far Western Frontier," pp. 188. Authorities differ on the number of cattle purchased in California. Bowen (p. 174) says "approximately 700"; Johansen, *Empire of the Columbia*, (pp. 180–181), says 830.

49. O'Donnell, *That Balance So Rare*, p. 60.

50. Michael Williams, *Americans and Their Forests: A Historical Geography* (Cambridge: Cambridge University Press, 1989), p. 307.

51. Bunting, "Landscaping the Pacific Northwest," p. 277.

52. Thomas E. Dahl, *Wetland Losses in the United States 1780's to 1980's* (Washington, DC: U.S. Department of the Interior, Fish and Wildlife Service, 1990), cited in Bunting, "Landscaping the Pacific Northwest," p. 279.

53. John Minto, "From Youth to Age as an American," *Oregon Historical Quarterly* IX, no. 1 (March 1908), pp. 131–132.

54. O'Donnell, *That Balance So Rare*, p. 35.

55. Cooper, "Report Upon the Botany of the Route," p. 18.

56. Henry L. Abbot, "Report of Lieut. Henry L. Abbot, Corps of Topographical Engineers. Explorations for a railroad route from the Sacramento Valley to the Columbia River," in *Reports of explorations and surveys to ascertain the most practicable and economical route for a railroad from the Mississippi River to the Pacific Ocean*, vol. VI, chapter V (33d Cong., 2d Sess, United States Senate, 1855), pp. 97-98.

57. Ibid., pp. 98-99.

58. Ibid., p. 99.

59. Beuter, *Legacy and Promise*, p. 9; and Bunting, "Landscaping the Pacific Northwest," pp. 416-417.

60. Bunting, "Landscaping the Pacific Northwest," pp. 418-419.

61. Ibid., p. 423.

62. Deady, "History and Progress of Oregon," p. 15; and Bunting, "Landscaping the Pacific Northwest," pp. 427, 432.

63. Bunting, "Landscaping the Pacific Northwest," pp. 428, 434, 452-453.

64. William G. Robbins, *Landscapes of Promise: The Oregon Story, 1800-1940* (Seattle: University of Washington Press, 1997), pp. 182-183.

65. Frances Fuller Victor, *All over Oregon and Washington: Observations on the Country, its Scenery, Soil, Climate, Resources, and Improvements* (San Francisco, CA: John G. Carmany & Co., 1872), pp. 164-165.

66. Beuter, *Legacy and Promise*, p. 10.

67. Johansen, *Empire of the Columbia*, pp. 309, 311; and Thomas R. Cox, *Mills and Markets: A History of the Pacific Coast Lumber Industry to 1900* (Seattle: University of Washington Press, 1974), p. 199.

68. Johansen, *Empire of the Columbia*, pp. 302, 314.

69. Cox, *Mills and Markets,* pp. 200, 211; and Emily W.B. Russell, *People and the Land through Time: Linking Ecology and History* (New Haven, CT: Yale University Press, 1997), p. 168.

70. Beuter, *Legacy and Promise*, p. 13.

71. Cox, *Mills and Markets*, p. 227, 231, 233.

72. Ibid., p. 233; Bunting, "Landscaping the Pacific Northwest," p. 501; and Bob Bourhill, *History of Oregon's Timber Harvests and/or Lumber Production* (Salem, OR: Oregon Department of Forestry, 1994).

73. Cox, *Mills and Markets*, pp. 233–237.

74. Ibid., p. 239.

75. Williams, *Americans and Their Forests*, pp. 310–311.

76. Ibid., p. 298.

77. Bunting, "Landscaping the Pacific Northwest," p. 512.

78. Beuter, *Legacy and Promise*, p. 13.

79. Jan M. Prior, "Kinship, Environment, and the Forest Service: Homesteading in Oregon's Coast Range" (master's thesis, Oregon State University, Corvallis, OR, 1998), p. 35.

80. Beuter, *Legacy and Promise*, p. 13.

81. Ibid., p. 16.

82. Ibid., p. 17.

83. Henry Gannett, *The Forests of Oregon* (Washington, DC: U.S. Department of Interior, U.S. Geological Survey, 1902), pp. 11–12.

84. H. J. Andrews and R. W. Cowlin, *Forest Resources of the Douglas-fir Region, USDA Forest Service Misc. Pub. 389* (USDA Forest Service, 1940), cited in USDA Forest Service, *Log Production in Washington and Oregon: An Historical Perspective, Resource Bulletin PNW-42* (Portland, OR: USDA Forest Service, Pacific Northwest Forest and Range Experiment Station, 1972).

85. Beuter says 9.8 billion board feet. See Beuter, *Legacy and Promise*, p. 19; and USDA Forest Service, *Log Production in Washington and Oregon*.

86. Beuter, *Legacy and Promise*, p. 21.

87. As of 1992, 2.3 million acres in Oregon have been designated as wilderness. See Beuter, *Legacy and Promise*, p. 21.

88. Beuter, *Legacy and Promise*, p. 22.

89. Ibid., pp. 22–23.

90. Ibid., p. 23.

91. James K. Agee, personal communication, July 2000.

92. USDA Forest Service, *Monitoring and Evaluation Report, Fiscal Year 1998* (Mount Hood National Forest: USDA Forest Service, 1998).

93. Ibid.

94. Ibid.

Chapter 7

The Alsea Basin and the Central Coast Range

Light Showers of Rain, proceeded forwarded [sic] entered the Mountain and followed a small stream which as we went forward encreased to 30 Yards in width this stream flows into the Ocean we had to cross it no less than ten times when we reach'd a small plain where we erected our Camp some very steep hills to ascend: underwood very thick....

—From the journal of Alexander McLeod, traveling down the Nestucca River to the Oregon Coast, May 30, 1826

The Indians at Alsea and Yaquina bays told him there were no trails up either the Yaquina or Alsea rivers, because the forest was impenetrable. The Indians had tried to cut a trail from the Willamette Valley across the Coast Range and down the Alsea River, but had abandoned the project because of the roughness of the country.

—William Morris, referring to the 1849 journey of Lieutenant Theodore Talbot.

The central Oregon Coast Range.

The long, narrow valley of the Alsea River bisects Oregon's Coast Range at about the north-south midpoint. It is one of a dozen or so valleys incised into the western slope of the Coast Range. Because of its rugged terrain and its remoteness from more favorable areas in the Willamette Valley and along the coast, it was not much frequented by the Alsea Indians who lived along the shores of the bay and ocean. The Indians traveled inland along the river to dig camas bulbs and cut yew branches, from which they crafted their bows.[1] But they did not live along the Alsea's rugged upper banks, so far as we know.

The Alsea River near Clemens Park.

White settlers also found the forests of the central Coast Range a remote and forbidding place. This was a hard land from which to wrestle a living.[2] The central Coast Range was slower to be populated by European-Americans than the more hospitable pioneer settlement locations of Oregon City and Astoria. Indeed, the coastal valleys remain rural and isolated even today. Because of this relatively late and sparse development, the forests along the Alsea River and its upland tributaries were slower to be changed by human activities such as homesteading and logging. These forests give us a good opportunity to look back in time, peel off layers of natural and human-caused disturbances, and get a glimpse of what the forests of the central Coast Range looked like when Lewis and Clark arrived.

Early Impressions

Unlike Astoria and Oregon City, the Alsea Basin was not visited by early explorers and traders who recorded their observations of the landscape for posterity. However, we do have general descriptions of vegetation along another coastal stream farther to the north, the Nestucca, and also of the central coast and the Yaquina and Alsea estuaries. In May of 1826, Alexander Roderick McLeod led a Hudson's Bay Company trapping party from Fort Vancouver through Champoeg and down the Nestucca River to where it empties into the ocean, north of Cascade Head. On this trip, McLeod's party traveled south as far as the Siuslaw River.

McLeod was a trapper, not a botanist, and it is clear from his journals that his main preoccupations were trapping beaver for profit and hunting deer for food. But his terse, practical prose offers glimpses of the countryside here and there. Early in their journey the party passed the base of Chehalem Mountain and reached the south branch of the North Yamhill River, in present-day Yamhill County. This is the skirt of the Coast Range, where the Willamette Valley begins to fold into foothills. McLeod noted, "the face of the Country continues fine and open, Groupes of Oak Trees dispersed in every direction beautifies the senery very much."[3]

At the mouth of the Big Nestucca, McLeod and his men turned south and traveled two or three miles, "and put up for the night nigh a Rivelet coming out of a Lake which led us to imagine that Beaver might be in the neighbourhood search was made but to no purpose…the face of the Country as far as we can see in the direction we are going is hilly and except a short distance covered with thick woods to the Beach."[4]

The next day they walked along the beach for 3 miles and came to a river "about a hundred and fifty yards wide there being good feeding for our horses at the entrance." The next day, June 4, the party crossed that river and proceeded to another one about 3 miles farther down—perhaps the Neskowin, which enters the ocean just north of Cascade Head. They tried to borrow a canoe from the Indians, but the Indians had nothing to lend. "These people are poorly provided with Craft and no wood fit for the purpose can be found in this vicinity nothing but dwarf Trees covers the Banks bordering on the Coast."[5]

Looking southwest from Cascade Head.

They had an arduous climb over Cascade Head, beginning on June 8. "Rainy weather proceeded about four miles over a very hilly Country, had to cut our way through as we went forward, tho' lightly loaded our horses were much fagged, some of our late visitors [their Indian guides] proved serviceable and volontarily assisted—two Elks were killed." It had rained most days since the party left Fort Vancouver in early May, and the going was not only steep and brushy but slippery: "Very bad road and much underwood to cut which employed two of us regularly, horses much harrassed owing partly to the softness of the ground in which they frequently sunk very deep, and the steepness of the Hills, not uncommonly throws them over and they roll to the Base, so far fortunately without any serious accident. We have got through a rough piece of Country within these few days."[6]

On the 18th they camped on the south shore of the Yaquina River—the "Econne"—where, McLeod said, "great hopes exist of taking some Beaver in this vicinity." They succeeded in trapping about 40 beavers and a couple of otters during their 11-day encampment. They moved 6 miles south to present-day Beaver Creek and trapped a few more. Early in June, McLeod sent two of the men south "for the purpose of Trapping in the next River, call'd by the Natives Alciyieh." McLeod left no description of the countryside around Alsea Bay, but he did remark that "in every little Stream Vestiges of Beaver is to be seen . . . to revive our hopes."[7]

Beavers—ecological engineers

Beaver at work on a forest stream in the Coast Range.

Beavers can be a major cause of forest disturbance along the waterways in Coast Range forests. Sometimes called "ecological engineers," beavers are considered by wildlife biologists to be a "keystone" species because they have a great deal of influence on forest riparian areas.[1] Their foraging and dam-building activities affect habitat for other wildlife that live along and in streams, including salmon species. Beavers are generally regarded as a favorable influence on salmon habitat because their dams add woody debris to streams and create pools for salmon spawning and rearing.

Not much is known about the size of beaver populations in the Coast Range before European-American settlement. The earliest historical record comes from the journals kept by Alexander McLeod during his two trapping expeditions for the Hudson's Bay Company in 1826. The company had a policy of "keeping the country closely hunted" in order to stay ahead of their competition and strengthen British territorial claims. As the company's governor, George Simpson, put it in a letter to John McLoughlin: "The first step that the American Government will take toward Colonization is through their Indian Traders and if the country becomes exhausted in Fur bearing animals they can have no inducement to proceed thither."[2] The main trapping activities of the Hudson's Bay Company were concentrated north and east of the Columbia, in the Snake River country, and not in the Coast Range.

McLeod found fewer beaver than he expected on his first expedition down the Oregon Coast, from May through August of 1826. The second trip was more successful; McLeod returned to Fort Vancouver in March of 1827 with 663 skins. His boss, John McLoughlin, was not satisfied, however: "it is certain had he started in proper time and only come back when the rainy Season set in, and had common able active men he would have brought Twelve hundred made [sic] Beaver." Some researchers interpret McLoughlin's reaction to mean the Coast Range had an abundance of beavers and that McLeod's party had simply been incompetent in trapping them. Others, noting the general paucity of information in the company's records about beaver in the Coast Range, and the fact that the company did not dispatch any subsequent trapping expeditions there, believe beaver were common but not as abundant as they were in other locations in the Northwest.[3]

Beavers thrive along meandering rivers and lake shores bordered by deciduous trees and shrubs, especially cottonwood, aspen, alder, and maple. In a recent study of streams emptying into Drift Creek, a tributary of the Alsea, wildlife researchers found that beaver activity was noted most in shallow, narrow streams in narrow valleys. Dams were found most frequently on streams 13 to 17 feet wide, with less than 3 percent gradient, flowing through valleys 80 to 100 feet wide. Beavers feed on a wide variety of plants, but they seem to prefer aspen and willow. Coast Range beavers also forage on red alder, salmonberry, vine maple, and bigleaf maple. Beavers feed on the inner bark of trees, and they nibble shrubby vegetation fairly indiscriminately.[4]

Beaver activity on a Coast Range stream.

In areas where beavers are abundant, they make a considerable impact on the shape of the waterway and the composition of the surrounding vegetation. Beavers build lodges in small streams and along lake shores, and they also dig burrows into streambanks, adding large quantities of mud to the bottom of the river. Beavers chew through the boles of streamside trees, denuding patches of riverbank in the process. Their dams back up stream flows, and the resulting flood can cover areas of up to several acres.[5] Flooding from beaver dams creates large patches of wetlands in the riparian forest. These wetlands, dominated by willow, cattails, rushes, duckweed, and a diverse community of grasses, herbs, and sedges, provide habitat to a variety of wildlife.

The heavy trapping of beavers early in the nineteenth century led to major declines in their populations all over the Northwest. In 1825, the Scottish botanist David Douglas noted that beavers in the Willamette Valley were scarce, although the valley was once "looked on as the finest place for hunting west of the Rocky Mountains." A Hudson's Bay trapper observed in 1838 that the area between Fort Vancouver and northern

California had been "closely hunted and is now greatly impoverished." In 1843, Oregon settlers noted that beavers "had become nearly extinct in the lower valley of the Columbia."[6]

After the trappers had done their work, subsequent settlement, farming, and logging altered northwestern river landscapes dramatically. As a result, say some researchers, beaver are nowhere near as numerous as they once were. The reduction in their numbers has lessened an important agent in the creation of forest wetlands, and has thus "considerably modified riparian areas of the Oregon Coast Range."[7]

On the other hand, beaver populations today seem to be up considerably from the recent past. "My understanding is that beavers are present in greater numbers now than they have been in a long time," says Dale L. Nolte, wildlife biologist with the Olympia Wildlife Research Center. "Whether their numbers are beyond those encountered prior to settlement is difficult to assess because of the lack of data on animal numbers at that time. However, it would be incorrect to infer that beaver numbers are low" at present.[8]

Some experts speculate that, owing in part to historical timber harvesting, beavers may be more abundant in the Coast Range now than they were before European-Americans arrived. Bob Gilman, a professional trapper of beavers, believes that past timber harvesting extended beaver habitat by clearing away large mature conifers and opening riparian areas to invasion by red alder and other deciduous trees and shrubs. On the other hand, red alder was a major component of the plant community along Coast Range streams even before European-American settlement, and it is not clear that postsettlement logging has caused a significant increase in riparian alder. Researchers on a study now in progress are reporting more beavers in clearcuts than in forested reaches of the Coast Range. This may be a sign of expanding populations, but it could also result from migration.[9]

[1]John P. Hayes and Joan Hagar, "Ecology and Management of Wildlife and Their Habitats in the Oregon Coast Range," in *Forest and Stream Management in the Oregon Coast Range* (in press).

[2]E.E. Rich, ed., *The Letters of John McLoughlin from Fort Vancouver to the Governor and Committee, First Series, 1825-38* (London: The Champlain Society, 1941), cited in Robert Reed Bunting, "Landscaping the Pacific Northwest: A Cultural and Ecological Mapping of the Douglas-fir Region, 1778-1900" (Ph.D. dissertation, University of California, Davis, 1993).

[3]K.G. Davies, *Peter Skene Ogden's Snake Country Journal 1826–27* (The Hudson's Bay Record Society, London, 1961), pp. lix, 219; D. Guthrie and J. Sedell, "Primeval Beaver Stumped Oregon Coast Trapper," *News & Views* (Department of Fisheries and Wildlife, Oregon State University, June 1988), p. 15, cited in Raymond E. Rainbolt, "Historic Beaver Populations in the Oregon Coast Range," unpublished paper dated Dec. 15, 1999. Copy in possession of the authors.

[4]Hayes and Hagar, "Ecology and Management of Wildlife"; S.H. Jenkins and P.E. Busher, "Castor canadensis," *Mammalian Species* 120 (1979), pp. 1–8, cited in Rainbolt, "Historic Beaver Populations"; N. Suzuki and W.C. McComb, "Habitat Classification Models for Beaver (*Castor canadensis*) in the Streams of the Central Oregon Coast Range," *Northwest Science* 72, no 2 (1998), pp. 102–110,

cited in Rainbolt, "Historic Beaver Populations"; and Karen Leidholt-Bruner, David E. Hibbs, and William C. McComb, "Beaver Dam Locations and Their Effects on Distribution and Abundance of Coho Salmon Fry in Two Coastal Oregon Streams," *Northwest Science* 4 (1992), 218–223.

[5]Bob Gilman, personal communication, August 2000; and David Hibbs, personal communication, October 2000.

[6]Davies, *Peter Skene Ogden's Snake Country Journal*, p. 46; Rich, ed., *The Letters of John McLoughlin*, p. 279; and O. Johnson and W.H. Winter, "Route across the Rocky Mountains with a description of Oregon and California: their geographical features, their resources, soils, climate, productions, etc., etc.," *Oregon Historical Quarterly* 7 (1906), p. 102, cited in Rainbolt, "Historic Beaver Populations."

[7]Tara Nierenberg and David E. Hibbs, "A Characterization of Unmanaged Riparian Areas in the Central Coast Range of Western Oregon," *Forest Ecology and Management* 129 (2000); and Tara R. Nierenberg, "A Characterization of Unmanaged Riparian Overstories in the Central Oregon Coast Range" (master's thesis, Oregon State University, Corvallis, OR, 1996).

[8]Dale L. Nolte, personal communication, August 2000.

[9]Bob Gilman, personal communication, August 2000; David Hibbs, personal communication, October 2000; and Thais Perkins, personal communication, October 2000.

McLeod's party turned around at the Siuslaw River, having found disappointingly few beaver.[8] They returned to Fort Vancouver in August, and set out on their second journey in September. This time McLeod was accompanied by the Scottish botanist David Douglas, who was seeking the habitat of the sugar pine (*Pinus lambertiana*) among the hills of the Umpqua. The party traveled up the Willamette and crossed into the Umpqua Valley via Elk Creek, near present-day Elkton. The Umpqua's Valley mouth lies about 55 miles south of the Alsea's.

On the first of October the party turned west toward the mountains. David Douglas noted that "Deer were scarce, and the [Indian] custom of burning the soil is highly unfavourable to botanizing. This plan prevails every where, though the natives vary in their accounts of the reason for which it is done, some saying that it is in order to compel the deer to feed in the unburnt spots, where they are easily detected and killed; others, that the object is, to enable them to find wild honey and grasshoppers, both of which serve for their winter food."[9]

McLeod noted, more laconically, "Pasture is rarely found . . . the fire destroyed all the grass." Somewhat querulously, he added, "Obichons woman was delivered of a female child, in consequence of her indisposition we had to stop in the rear."[10]

The trip down the Umpqua took the party across hilly, timbered country. David Douglas described the scene in this passage from his journal entry of October 9, 1826:

> *I ascended a low hill, about two thousand five hundred feet above its platform, the lower part covered with trees of enormous size, and the same sorts as on the Columbia. On the summit are only low shrubs, small oaks, and a species of* Castanea *[chinkapin]. This fine species I first took for a* Shepherdia, *as it was only shrubby in growth, but I shortly found it on the mountains, growing sixty to one hundred feet high, and with a diameter of three to five feet. The leaves of this tree, (*Castanea chrysophylla*) [golden chinkapin] give quite a peculiar and lovely tint to the landscape. . . . Here, too,* Pinus resinosa *[red pine] grows immensely large, two hundred and fifty feet high, and fifty-five feet in circumference. . . . My feet are very sore with walking over the burnt and decayed stumps, and struggling through the thick under-growth of* Pteris Aquilina *[bracken fern] and* Rubus suberectus *[a blackberry species], which are bound together with several decayed species of* Vicia *[vetch].[11]*

Both McLeod and Douglas were commenting on the effects of what was then the most important influence on the landscape of both the Willamette Valley and the Coast Range: fire. As we have already noted, burning by Indians shaped the landscape of the Willamette Valley, perhaps for several millennia. However, deliberate burning by Indians probably did not play a major role in the broad-scale development of Coast Range forests.[12]

Natural wildfire, however, has been a periodic visitor to these forests for thousands of years.[13] In 1934, forester William G. Morris wrote about the impact of wildfires on the landscapes of the Cascades, Willamette Valley, and Coast Range during the previous century: "From evidence present in the forest today, we know that forest fires during the past century have devastated hundreds of thousands of acres." He cited a survey of forest lands in western Oregon and western Washington that found many acres of even-aged stands of trees 40, 50, 60, and 70 years of age. In the Coast Range, young stands of even-aged Douglas-fir trees typically get started when the previous stand is destroyed by a major disturbance: "The cutting done in the early days for

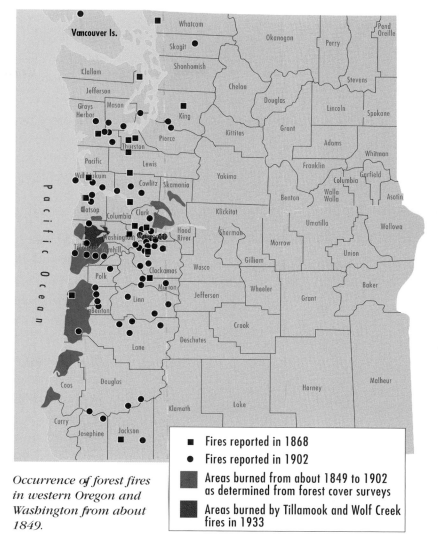

Occurrence of forest fires in western Oregon and Washington from about 1849.

- ■ Fires reported in 1868
- ● Fires reported in 1902
- Areas burned from about 1849 to 1902 as determined from forest cover surveys
- Areas burned by Tillamook and Wolf Creek fires in 1933

lumbering and land clearing was entirely inadequate to account for the large acreage of timber now 80 to 90 years old, and it is concluded that most of this acreage represents land reforested after burning."[14]

At least two and possibly three great fires swept across the central Coast Range in the mid-1800s, before the country was much settled by European-Americans. An article in the *Portland Oregonian* in August of 1894 describes a great fire around Nestucca Bay in 1845. According to the reporter's informant, Pierre Belleque of

Fire raged across the ridges of Tillamook County in 1933, leaving a bleak aftermath of ash and snags. Fire is the predominant natural force shaping the development of Coast Range forests.

French Prairie, the fire spread from a slash fire on a ranch near Champoeg. Belleque quoted Dick Harna, a chief of the Nestuccas whom he had talked to several years previously. Harna and his people had been camped near Woods, in Tillamook County. When the fire came, they retreated north to Sand Lake, leaving all their belongings. There were yet no white people living in that part of the country.[15]

Another Indian story tells of a big fire that devastated the countryside from Tillamook to Coos Bay in 1846. John B. Horner later recorded the story in *Oregon, Her History, Her Great Men, Her Literature.* He quoted Chief Cutlip, who said many people and animals died in the blaze: "the heat was so intense at Coos Bay that many people were driven into the water for protection." Salmon River John, "an Indian who was accustomed to weigh his words carefully" said the fire was so great in the Yaquina Bay region that "the flames leaped across the river, that many of the Indians perished and that only those were saved who took refuge in the water."[16]

Another account came from William Smith, an Alsea Indian, in 1910. The fire raged along the coast north of the mouth of the Siuslaw when Smith was a child. The year was about 1850, as near as he could

Table 7-1. Historical fires in Oregon over the past 150 years.

Year	Location	Estimated acres burned
1848	Nestucca	290,000
1849	Siletz	800,000
1853	Yaquina	482,000
1865	Silverton	988,000
1868	Coos Bay	296,000
1933	Tillamook	240,000
1936	Bandon	143,000
1939	Saddle Mountain	190,000
1945	Wilson River/Salmonberry	180,000
1951	North Fork/Elkhorn	33,000
1966	Oxbow	44,000

remember. He and his family had been visiting at the villages near the mouth of the Siuslaw, and were returning home when the fire came upon them. "The people did not remain near the woods. Everybody was staying near the ocean on the beach. The fire was flying around just like the birds. It was just dark all over. The sun had disappeared. All the hills were on fire." [17]

After the fire cooled off, some members of the group went back along the beach from Heceta toward the Siuslaw to see the damage. "Everywhere, even the blossoms of the highest trees had been burned down, . . . even the trees (that) lay in the water caught fire." Smith remembered the terrified reactions of his family: "My grandmother was crying all the time. She was crying for her people: 'All my people must have perished in the flames.'" [18]

In August of 1849, Lieutenant Theodore Talbot, exploring the Siletz River, Yaquina Bay, Alsea Bay, and surrounding countryside, noted that a fire was burning somewhere south of the Yaquina River when he was there: "The mountains were enveloped with such a dense mass of smoke, occasioned by some large fires to the south of

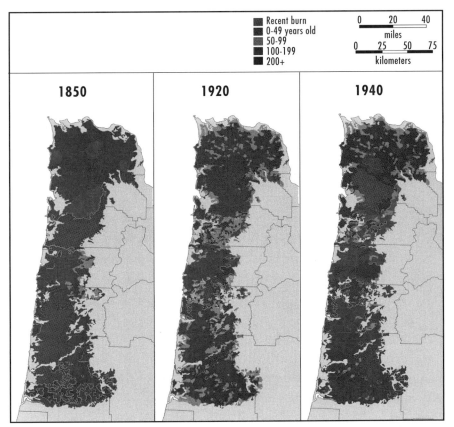

Maps showing burned areas of the Coast Range and ages of surrounding forest in 1850, 1920, and 1940. From Bureau of Land Management data.

us, that we could see but little of the surrounding country. These fires are of frequent occurrence in the forests of Oregon, raging with violence for months, until quelled by the continued rains of the winter season." Talbot also passed through a large swath of burned forest, "several miles in extent, where the little trail which we followed, indifferent at best, was often completely broken up, and we were compelled to have recourse to our axes to make a way through the heaps of charred logs."[19]

Talbot may have been seeing smoke from the fire that William Smith remembered 60 years later. However, his observations of the landscape around Yaquina Bay do not mention any burned areas, and he noted heavy stands of timber along the lower Yaquina, Alsea, Siletz, and Salmon rivers. It may be that the fire in the Yaquina Bay area struck after Talbot was there, or that the men who remembered the fire years later got their dates slightly wrong. Or it may be that the fire burned in different locations from those which the informants remembered. However, the young age of the forest stands along the southern bend of the Siletz River and through Lincoln County to the Siuslaw River indicate that it was established after a fire in the 1840s. The evidence, Morris says, shows that "a great fire of the period 1845-1849, probably of the year 1849, burned 500,000 or more acres of forest between the Siuslaw and Siletz rivers."[20]

The flush of fire in the 1800s coincided roughly with white settlement, which suggests that European-American settlers touched off some of the forest fires. In addition, according to tree-ring studies the 1840s were a drier-than-normal decade. Several years of dry weather might be expected to increase the frequency and severity of forest wildfires. Some researchers estimate that more than one-third of the forests of the northern Coast Range burned in the late 1840s. They also estimate that almost all the remaining unburned forest—96.5 percent—was 100 years old or older in 1850.[21]

The year 1868 was a bad year for fire all over the Northwest. That summer was the driest for almost 60 years. Early in September the Coast Range was afire in several places, especially around Yaquina Bay. For three days, said the *Oregonian* (quoting the *Corvallis Gazette*) on September 1, "the fire has been sweeping both sides of the Bay and all its tributaries. People eat their noonday meals by candle light, so intensely thick is the smoke that the sun has been lost for some time, and nervous folks are getting very anxious about Old Sol. Reports are coming in daily of persons making narrow escapes, and many houses have been destroyed."[22]

Fires recorded in tree rings

Researchers who have analyzed tree rings from 10 areas west of the Cascade crest, including two areas in the Coast Range, have found evidence that corroborates reports of widespread fires during the 1800s. They hypothesize that a period of widespread fire occurred from about 1400 to 1650. This was followed by a cooler period with fewer fires. Fire again became widespread after 1800 and continued until the early twentieth century. The latest fire period, say the researchers, was associated with European settlement, a warming climate, and the presence of large tracts of forest older than 300 years.[1]

[1] Peter J. Weisberg and Frederick J. Swanson, "Regional Synchronicity in Changing Fire Regime Patterns of the Western Cascades, U.S.A." (paper in review), copy in possession of the authors.

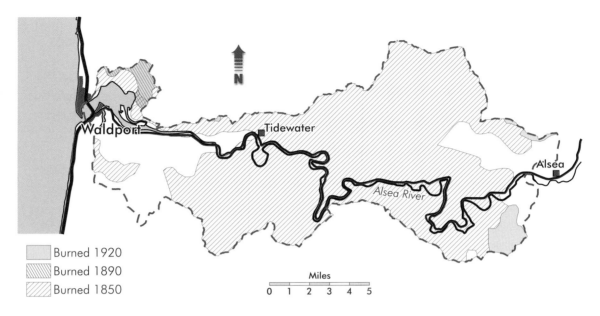

Fire history of the lower Alsea Basin.

Burned 1920
Burned 1890
Burned 1850

Large areas around Coos Bay were burned that year. Fire struck the forests northeast of the bay in Douglas County and south around the Sixes and Elk rivers near Port Orford, in Curry County. "The entire coast has suffered greatly from the fires," wrote an observer, "and it is feared that most of the cedar near Port Orford is burned or badly damaged."[23]

Homesteading in the Woods

Because of subsequent fires and logging, it is impossible to know exactly where the boundaries of the great Coast Range fires were. It is certain that a fire, or more than one, partially cleared some of the dense forest around Drift Creek, a tributary of the Alsea River, in the latter part of the nineteenth century, immediately before homesteaders began claiming sections of the valley for their own.[24]

The clearing by fire of these heavily wooded drainages may have been part of the inducement for the Alsea Basin's first homesteaders, who moved into the area in the 1870s. Instead of thick, tall timber, much of the land was probably covered with fallen logs, snags, brush, and young Douglas-fir and alder seedlings small enough for a settler to fell with an axe. "One or more major fires before this settlement period opened up the land and may have given it a more hospitable appearance," wrote Jan Prior in her extensive study of the environmental and cultural history of the Drift Creek area.[25]

The first settlers of the Alsea Basin and other coastal river valleys were the latecomers, those who were not lucky enough to grab a piece of the prime farmland of the Willamette Valley. The Oregon Country may have seemed vast and inexhaustible to pioneers' eyes, but under the generous provisions of the 1850 Donation Land Claim Act, most of the Willamette Valley was claimed by 1853.

Behind the land-claim laws was a conviction that the West's public land ought to be turned over to private citizens who would farm it. This conviction had its roots in Thomas Jefferson's vision of a nation of prosperous, independent small farmers who would stand as a bulwark against the tyranny of big government. But the laws, conceived in the environment of the settled eastern seaboard, often did not deal well with the realities of the vast and rugged western landscape.[26]

To be sure, the Donation Land Act was highly successful in conveying into private hands the rich farmlands of the Willamette Valley, a landscape that was perhaps the West's closest cousin to the gentle, farmstead-studded river valleys of the East. With the best Willamette Valley lands quickly taken, latecomers began to make their way into the valleys of the Coast Range in search of promising homestead sites. The earliest homesteaders came to the Alsea Valley in the 1850s. The newcomers raised grain, vegetables, and flax along the narrow bottoms of the Alsea and its tributaries. They ran hogs, sheep, goats, and dairy cattle in the hillsides, cursing the young trees and shrubs that kept springing up on their arduously cleared pastures.[27]

They were settling on lands that, for the most part, were inhospitable for farming. The earliest arrivals took the valley bottoms,[28] most of which were cleared for grazing: "Probably 90% of the primary riverine environments and many of the lower reaches of tributary creeks [of the Coast Range] were . . . logged and transformed into pasture for cattle and sheep."[29] Later settlers were relegated to the steeper, more forested uplands. One surveyor described the landscape east of Drift Creek, near present-day Harlan, as "exceedingly rich, but terribly rough. The mountains are very steep and covered with a dense growth of fern, salal, cherry & other brush. Thousands of large logs lying in all directions. The large timber is dead, having been killed years ago. There is however, much valuable timber dead cedar & fir of which the settlers build houses and fence fields. . . .[30]

Dead or burned trees are mentioned in many of the survey notes of the Alsea area, another indication of recent forest fires. Settlers regarded downed dead trees as a gift—not only were the men spared the effort of felling them, but if the logs were not too burned or rotted, they could be split into boards where they lay.[31] A descendent of one of the earliest settlers wrote:

> *Building materials were very scarce so the fire was a boon to the pioneers. Most of the huge trees were killed and since much of the timber had been several hundred years old it was very fine grained, also straight; therefore when the trees were cut in the desired lengths it could be split in to some of the finest lumber to construct some nice buildings. Red cedar was the most desirable wood, followed by fir. This writer has seen many of these buildings and they were very comfortable and well constructed.[32]*

The settlers, no doubt believing the lands were better for farming than they actually were, encountered an immediate and vexing problem: the rapid regrowth of trees and brush. "Many of the homesteaders had to continue to burn off the constantly emerging saplings, ferns and other undergrowth on the portions of their claims that they intended to cultivate. At the time of 'proving up' to receive their final patent certificate, most homesteads had only a few acres under cultivation. The remaining portions of the claims, unless they were used for grazing, were often left to return to forested conditions."[33]

Enduring long hours of astonishingly hard work, isolated from neighbors by steep, muddy trails and miserable winter weather, the Alsea homesteaders lived hard lives. "It must have been a very lonesome winter for mother," wrote the daughter of an early settler. "The nearest neighbor woman lived eight or nine miles away over those trails, but she came to visit us, and her boys and girls came to see us quite often. They were surely always welcome at our house. . . ."[34]

To brighten their spare existence, the homesteaders made time to get together and socialize. One pioneer descendent remembered stories about barn dances, ". . . the building reverberating to the strains of Red Wing, Gooseberry Pie, Cotton-eyed Joe, and the Irish Washer Woman." Another recalled the day, sometime in the 1910s, when her family acquired a phonograph, the first in the neighborhood. They and some of their neighbors had telephones by then—they'd hooked up to the Forest Service line that ran to the Table Rock lookout station. "What fun we had," the author remembered, "listen-

Charles W. Brown's homestead in the Alsea drainage, about 1910.

Site of the Charles W. Brown homestead, taken in 1993. It was impossible to take a picture from the original vantage point because trees had regrown to cover it.

A cut-over Douglas-fir stand that was burned and seeded for pasture, near Grand Ronde, Oregon, 1944.

ing to everything from 'Madame Butterfly,' 'Over the Waves,' and 'Uncle Josh.' Father would play these records over the party line, and phone after phone would click as they all were listening."[35]

In the end, the homesteaders in the Alsea Valley mostly failed at farming. Fewer than half of the original claimants in the township Prior studied actually patented their claims. and of those who did, most eventually sold out or rented to other prospective farmers. The most successful homesteaders made a living raising goats, but they had to supplement their income with county road building, work in the sawmills, or as farm laborers in the Willamette Valley.[36]

The Forest Reserves

The establishment of forest reserves toward the end of the century signaled a shift away from the federal government's initiative to privatize public lands. There was a growing conviction, prompted by a nationwide conservation movement, that some lands ought to be held and managed by the federal government for the common good. Opposition to the forest reserves was fierce, both from timber companies desirous of acquiring the lands for themselves, and from homesteaders, sheep grazers, and other citizens who did not approve of the federal government's being in the land and timber business.[37]

In a letter written around the turn of the century to the Oregon Board of Horticulture, Salem-area pioneer and sheep rancher John Minto took strong exception to the American Forestry Association's endorsement of forest reserves. Not only did their report falsely

Western hemlock zone

Forests in the western hemlock zone are the most common forest type in western Washington and Oregon. They occur throughout the Coast Range, on the western slopes of the Cascades at elevations of 1,800–4,000 feet, and in many parts of the Puget Lowland region. These forests are usually composed of Douglas-fir, a very long-lived conifer species. However, because Douglas-fir seedlings do not germinate and grow well under the shade of mature forest canopies in western Oregon, shade-tolerant trees such as western hemlock and western redcedar will eventually dominate, unless disturbance intervenes.

The climate in the western hemlock zone varies considerably according to latitude, elevation, aspect, and position in relation to mountain ranges. Annual precipitation is generally between 60 and 120 inches, most of which falls during the winter months. Winter temperatures are mild, with temperatures seldom dipping below freezing. Summers are warm and dry.

Western redcedar is a common component of forests in the western hemlock zone. It is particularly abundant in the cool, wet forests of southern Washington. Sitka spruce is also a component; it grows on the western slopes of the Coast Range. Incense-cedar, ponderosa pine, and western white pine are found in the zone's drier environments, such as along the Willamette Valley margin. Grand fir grows in low-elevation forests, while Pacific silver fir becomes increasingly abundant at higher elevations of the Cascades and northern Coast Range. Pacific yew, a small understory conifer, is widespread in mature forests throughout the western hemlock zone, although it is usually not abundant.

Broad-leaved hardwood trees grow predominantly in disturbed, riparian, and dry environments within the western hemlock zone. Red alder, bigleaf maple, and golden chinkapin are most common. Riparian forests growing along rivers and streams are composed of red alder, black cottonwood, Oregon ash, and bigleaf maple. Dry, low-elevation sites may support evergreen hardwoods such as Pacific madrone and golden chinkapin. Oregon white oak, an extremely drought-tolerant deciduous hardwood, grows on dry ridges and south-facing slopes. Moist locations in the Coast Range support dense stands of red alder.

Numerous shrub species grow under forest canopies in the western hemlock zone. California hazel, oceanspray, and rhododendron are found in the drier places. Moist forests support vine maple, salal, Oregongrape, and several species of huckleberry. Extremely wet forests, like those located on the western slopes of the Coast Range, may have few shrubs. Rather, swordfern and other herbaceous species typically comprise the understory. Mosses, liverworts, and other bryophytes often cover the branches of live trees and downed logs.[1]

[1]See J.F. Franklin and C.T. Dyrness, *Natural Vegetation of Oregon and Washington,* USDA Forest Service General Technical Report PNW-8 (Portland, OR: USDA Forest Service Pacific Northwest Forest and Range Experiment Station,1973).

denigrate sheepmen for destroying the forest and range, he said, but the whole idea of forest reserves, sequestering millions of acres away from private enterprise, was a hindrance to economic development, and antidemocratic besides: "Is there any reason for the people of other states to interfere with the people of Oregon harvesting their timber wealth in their own way. . . ?" wrote Minto.[38] It was not the last time an Oregonian would express such a sentiment.

In 1897 there were 29 forest reserves nationwide, totaling almost 39 million acres. By 1905, 83 reserves embracing almost 86 million acres had been designated.[39] Most of these were established after 1901 by President Theodore Roosevelt. In 1907, an amendment

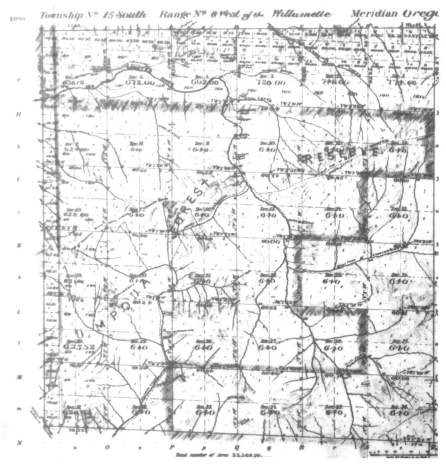

General Land Office survey map showing portions of the Umpqua Forest Reserve, later renamed the Siuslaw National Forest.

to an agricultural appropriations bill threatened to take away the President's authority to establish forest reserves. The amendment was introduced by Oregon's Senator Charles Fulton, whose fierce opposition to the idea of forest reserves spoke for John Minto and a good many others.

Gifford Pinchot, Chief of the newly created Forest Service, had his staff "working feverishly at mapping all possible remaining forested public lands." President Roosevelt quickly added another 16 million acres two days before he signed the appropriations bill. These "midnight reserves," as they became known, included the Umpqua and Tillamook Forest Reserves, which were later combined and renamed the Siuslaw National Forest.[40]

Some agricultural land was caught within the hastily drawn boundaries of the "midnight reserves." These lands were supposed to be returned to private ownership, but there were complaints that the Forest Service wasn't moving fast enough. So in June of 1906, the Forest Homestead Act was passed, making it possible to claim lands within the forest reserves. To be available for homesteading, lands had to be "chiefly valuable for agriculture" and capable of being farmed "without injury to the forest reserves," in the judgment of the local Forest Service rangers whose job it was to make such determinations.[41]

Claimants filed 1,079 applications for homesteads within the Siuslaw National Forest under the Forest Homestead Act between 1907 and 1917. As under all the homestead laws, settlers were required to cultivate the land—something that had already proven difficult for many Alsea Basin settlers. Those who felt they had particularly hard circumstances could petition for relief from some of the cultivation requirements.

One such petitioner's claim was denied in 1919 by the local forest supervisor because "the applicant's sole reason . . . seems to be that the land is rough and difficult to clear"—not a good enough excuse, evidently. However, the request was ultimately granted by the General Land Office's assistant commissioner in Washington, D.C., who ruled that the cultivation requirements could be reduced "where the presence of stumps, brush, lodge pole pine, or other valueless or non-merchantable timber prevents the clearing and cultivation of the prescribed area."[42] The official may have been trying to make it easier for homesteaders to patent their claims—perhaps still clinging to the principle that the best use of former public-domain lands was private agriculture.

In the Alsea country, 60 years had passed since the first homesteaders had settled. Many of the burned lands now had good-sized Douglas-firs growing on them. After 10 years of classifying the suitability of lands for farming on behalf of prospective homesteaders, the Siuslaw National Forest began classifying the remaining lands as to their chief value. Based on general summaries, most of the lands were classified, unsurprisingly, as chiefly valuable for forests.[43] Forest Assistant Lawrence B. Pagter described the land in one township thus:

> *The agricultural value of the patented [already homesteaded] lands are [sic] quite low, and the public lands, containing little or no arable lands, have consequently no value for agricultural purposes. The patented lands include as much, if not more land of a bench-like character than any other township within the Forest, but little has been done to develop such lands, although they would have a high value for grazing, were more intensive methods applied to them. The hill lands ... would also have a grazing value, even though their agricultural values were nil, but it would not exceed the value for forest purposes.... The Douglas fir type is the virtual type for this township, but the big fires of the past have practically destroyed the old growth trees....[44]*

Buying Back the Homesteads

In the 1930s, the federal government invited homesteaders to sell their land back to the government under a New Deal plan called the Submarginal Land Program. The program's very name implied what most Alsea Basin homesteaders had learned the hard way. The Alsea homesteads returned to the government under this program were absorbed into the Siuslaw National Forest. The foresters tore down the buildings on most of the properties and planted Douglas-fir on the land.[45] Today those trees are big enough to be merchantable, and the few vestiges of the former homesteads are decaying into the earth. Scattered old fruit trees and a few naturalized exotic perennials are virtually the only physical evidence remaining about a community, a way of life, and a slice of history.

The Alsea Indian Reservation

Some of the Coast Range's most marginal land, from an agricultural point of view, was reserved for another use—resettling Indian people who had been evicted from their homes along the Siuslaw, Umpqua, and Rogue rivers and around Coos Bay. The Siletz Indian Reservation, created in 1856, encompassed the whole west side of the central Coast Range, more than a million acres stretching from Cape Lookout to the mouth of the Siltcoos River.[46]

There the Indians lived bleak lives in unfamiliar surroundings. Their intimate acquaintance with their several homelands did them little good in this strange environment. Indian Agent R.B. Metcalfe wrote of their lamentable situation in 1858: "The country assigned to these people is poorly adapted to stock raising, there being little or no grass, except on the small prairies, which will be required for cultivation, and the wild game, which was tolerably abundant last year, have all been driven back to the high mountains. As the spring salmon do not run up any of these streams, it leaves us entirely

Coquille Thompson's family lived originally on the upper Coquille River. He is 87 years old in this 1937 photo, taken on the Siletz Reservation.

destitute of food during the spring and summer, except as has been provided by the government."[47]

It wasn't long before pressure for development on Yaquina Bay prompted calls from white settlers to take back some of the reservation land. Oyster beds had been discovered in the bay by a sea captain with customers in San Francisco, but they lay in waters that belonged to the Indians. Yaquina Bay also showed promise as a deep-water harbor. By 1864, settlers in the Willamette Valley had begun building a wagon road from Corvallis to Yaquina Bay, preparing to take advantage of this potential seaport.[48]

In the end, the settlers won. In December of 1865, President Andrew Johnson signed an executive order taking a 25-mile-long strip of land out of the middle of the reservation, splitting it into two pieces, the Alsea and the Siletz. Further lobbying by white settlers resulted in the closure of the Alsea subagency in 1875; the Siletz subagency was reduced in size at the same time. Additional bites were taken out of the reservation over the next century, and in 1956 the remaining 3,200 acres of reservation land were taken from the Indians and opened to white settlement.[49]

The Timber Economy

Lumbering was ultimately more successful than farming in the Alsea, and changes to the landscape in this century have come mostly from the cutting of timber. In 1948, almost 90 percent of the 288,000-acre Alsea Basin was classed as forest land. The forests were predominantly composed of Douglas-fir 90 to 100 years old.[50]

During the decade between 1943 and 1953, between 450 and 500 million board feet of timber were cut in the basin. The first sawmill had been built on the Alsea River in the late 1880s. By the mid-1950s there were about 30 sawmills in the whole drainage basin, and about 160 logging operations. In contrast to the lower-lying, more accessible areas around the lower Columbia and Willamette rivers, the steep hillsides of the Coast Range were slow to be logged. The amount of old-growth in the Coast Range as a whole was estimated to have been about 43 percent in 1933, based on a forest survey conducted in that year, down from about 61 percent before the great fires of the late 1840s.[51] A glance at the harvest patterns over the decades of the twentieth century gives an idea of how the basin's dense, patchy cover of old-growth and even-aged second-growth forest has been altered, and how young second- and third-growth stands have sprung up in the wake of the chainsaw.

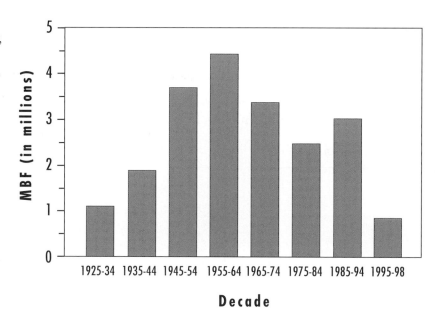

Sawlog production and timber harvest by decade in Lincoln County from 1925 to present. Tillamook County figures were added to Lincoln County's for 1932 and 1940.

About 70 percent of the timber land in the Alsea Basin is federally managed. This is a higher percentage of public ownership than is the case in the Coast Range as a whole, where the figure is 46 percent. The Siuslaw National Forest lies to the west, and a checkerboard of BLM and timber-industry lands lies to the east, in Benton County, along the river's north bank. Because the Alsea drains parts of three counties—Lincoln, Benton, and Lane—there are no easily accessible data for historic harvests there. However, the Lincoln County figures from the Oregon Department of Forestry give an approximation of the area's logging patterns since the 1920s.[52]

In 1925, the earliest year for which there is a record, 175 million board feet of timber were cut in Lincoln County. Harvests immediately declined, except for a spike in 1929. In 1933, at the depth of the Depression, only 80 million board feet were harvested. Harvests in Lincoln County rose gradually through the 1930s and early '40s, peaking in 1943 at 361 million board feet. After a year's wartime hiatus, the cutting resumed at almost the same level and, after a brief lapse in the early '50s, it spiked to 610 million board feet in 1955. Harvests declined in the early '60s, but bounced up to 453 million board feet in 1968, the last peak year. During the '70s, harvests hovered between about 209 and 340 million board feet, took a plunge during the recession of the early '80s, and climbed back up to 357 million board feet in 1992.

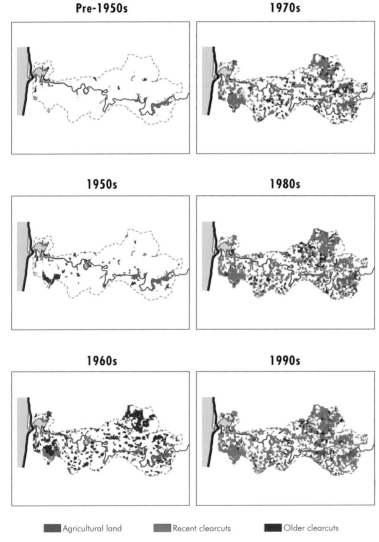

Pre-1950s **1970s**

1950s **1980s**

1960s **1990s**

■ Agricultural land   ■ Recent clearcuts   ■ Older clearcuts

Land cover (agricultural lands, recent clearcuts, and older clearcuts) in the lower Alsea Basin from before the 1950s to the 1990s.

This pattern generally mirrors that of western Oregon as a whole. Log production in western Oregon peaked in 1929, with 4.18 billion board feet, but then dropped sharply during the Depression. In 1932 only 1.29 billion board feet were harvested. As the economy improved during the mid-1930s, log production increased in western Oregon, and in 1952 it reached an all-time high of 10.4 billion board feet.[53] The harvest continued to be generally high, in the neighborhood of 8.3 to 9.7 billion board feet, until the recession year of 1961, when it dipped to 7.4 billion board feet. Then levels edged up again, peaking at 9.7 billion board feet in 1968, hovering between 7.6 and 9.6 through the 1970s, and declining to around 6 billion board feet during the recession of the early 1980s. There was

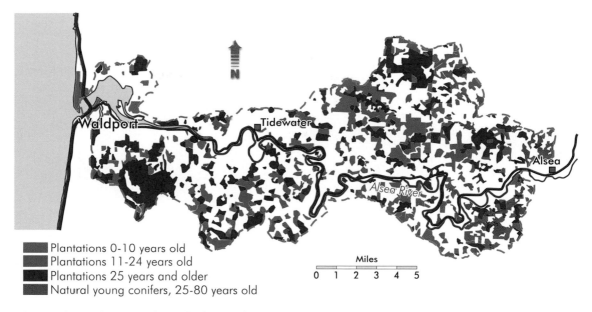

Plantations 0-10 years old
Plantations 11-24 years old
Plantations 25 years and older
Natural young conifers, 25-80 years old

Managed stands currently in the lower Alsea Basin.

another surge of harvest between 1985 and 1989, peaking in 1986 at 8.7 billion board feet.

Before World War II, most Oregon logs came from private lands. Only a small share of timber was harvested from national forests or Bureau of Land Management forests. In the late '40s and early '50s, however, demand for wood products boomed as Europe was rebuilt after the devastation of the war. At that time, mature timber on private lands was beginning to be depleted. Forest Service and BLM lands began contributing more and more timber to the total harvest. In the whole of Oregon, public-land harvests surpassed those from private lands in 1962.[54]

In 1970, the national forests were the largest single log-producing ownership in western Oregon, accounting for 30 percent of the total log harvest. From the 1970s until a few years ago, federal and nonfederal harvests in western Oregon have been about equal.[55] Since the late 1980s, however, federal harvests have declined dramatically in response to public concern about environmental issues.

As a leisurely drive to the coast from Corvallis over Highway 34 reveals, the Alsea Basin today is a patchwork of mostly young second-

Panoramic photos taken from Saddle Mountain in the Siuslaw National Forest in 1934 (above). The same sites re-photographed from similar vantage points in 1988 (right).

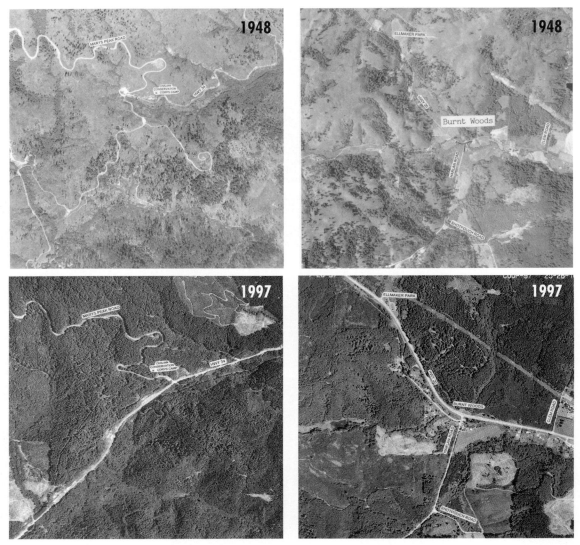

Aerial photos showing regrowth of forest cover near Marys Peak between 1948 and 1997.

Aerial photos showing regrowth of forest cover near Burnt Woods between 1948 and 1997.

and third-growth forests. Its condition is fairly typical of that of the central Coast Range as a whole. Much of the forest 40 years old and older was probably regenerated naturally, with seedlings germinating from seeds blown in from still-standing mature trees. Forests younger than 30 years most likely grew from planted seedlings. The 1971 Oregon Forest Practices Act and its attendant forest-practice rules require prompt and successful reforestation after logging. Coast Range forests regenerated themselves through natural seeding over many thousands of years, but today, the great majority of harvested areas in the Alsea country and across western Oregon are reforested with planted seedlings.

Notes to Chapter 7

1. Ray M. Northam, "Rural settlement and resources of the Alsea Valley" (master's thesis, Oregon State College, Corvallis, OR, 1955), p. 1; and Stephen Dow Beckham, *The Indians of Western Oregon: This Land was Theirs* (Coos Bay, OR: Arago Books, 1977), pp. 70-71.

2. Jan M. Prior, "Kinship, Environment, and the Forest Service: Homesteading in Oregon's Coast Range" (master's thesis, Oregon State University, Corvallis, OR, 1998), p. 1; and Northam, "Rural settlement," p. 13.

3. K.G. Davies, *Peter Skene Ogden's Snake Country Journal 1826-27* (London: The Hudson's Bay Record Society, 1961), p. 151.

4. Ibid., p. 152.

5. Ibid., p. 153.

6. Ibid., pp. 154-155.

7. Ibid., pp. 158-162.

8. Ibid., p. lix.

9. Ibid., p. 179, citing David Douglas, *A sketch of a journey to the north-western parts of the continent of North America, during the years 1824, 5, 6, and 7* (1836; reprint, Portland, OR: *Oregon Historical Quarterly* 04 (1904), pp. V, VI.

10. Davies, *Peter Skene Ogden's Snake Country Journal*, p. 179.

11. Ibid., p. 181, citing Douglas, *A sketch of a journey.*

12. William J. Ripple, "Historic Spatial Patterns of Old Forests in Western

Oregon," *Journal of Forestry* 92, no. 11 (1994), p. 48, citing James K. Agee, *Fire History of Douglas-fir Forests in the Pacific Northwest*, USDA Forest Service General Technical Report PNW-285 (Portland, OR: USDA Forest Service, Pacific Northwest Research Station, 1991), pp. 25–33.

13. J.K. Agee, *Fire Ecology of Pacific Northwest Forests* (Covelo, CA: Island Press, 1993); Colin J. Long, Cathy Whitlock, Patrick J. Bartlein, and Sarah H. Millspaugh, "A 9000-year Fire History from the Oregon Coast Range, Based on a High-resolution Charcoal Study," *Canadian Journal of Forest Research* 28 (1998), pp. 774–787; and many others.

14. William G. Morris, "Forest Fires in Western Oregon and Western Washington," *Oregon Historical Quarterly* 35, no. 4 (1934), p. 314.

15. Ibid., p. 318.

16. Morris, "Forest Fires," p. 319, citing John B. Horner, *Oregon, Her History, Her Great Men, Her Literature* (Portland, OR: The J.K. Gill Co., c. 1921).

17. Morris, "Forest Fires," p. 320; and Beckham, *The Indians of Western Oregon*, pp. 96–97.

18. Morris, "Forest Fires," p. 320; and Beckham, *The Indians of Western Oregon*, pp. 96–97.

19. Morris, "Forest Fires," p. 321.

20. Ibid., p. 322.

21. Ibid., p. 314. See also Ripple, "Historic Spatial Patterns of Old Forests," p. 48, citing L. Graumlich, "Long-term Records of Temperature and Precipitation in the Pacific Northwest Derived from Tree Rings" (Ph.D. dissertation, University of Washington, Seattle, 1985; and Peter D.A. Teensma, John T. Reinstra, and Mark A. Yeiter, *Preliminary Reconstruction and Analysis of Change in Forest Stand Age Classes of the Oregon Coast Range from 1850 to 1940, BLM Technical Note T/N OR-9* (Portland, OR: USDI Bureau of Land Management, 1991).

22. Morris, "Forest Fires," p. 328, citing the *Portland Oregonian*, September 1, 1868. See also Morris, p. 332.

23. Morris, "Forest Fires," p. 329.

24. Ibid., p. 332; and Prior, "Kinship, Environment, and the Forest Service," p. 46.

25. Ibid., p. 1.

26. Paul Hirt, *A Conspiracy of Optimism: Management of the National Forests since World War Two* (Lincoln, NB: University of Nebraska Press, 1994). Not until 1878 was a land-claim law enacted that was designed for logging and mining rather than agriculture—the Timber and Stone Act.

27. Northam, "Rural settlement," pp. 12–13; and Ed Hendrix, personal communication, April 18, 2000.

28. Prior, "Kinship, Environment, and the Forest Service," p. 68.

29. Stephen Dow Beckham, personal communication, December 6, 1999.

30. United States Department of Interior, General Land Office. Survey notes, 1875a:451–2, cited in Prior, "Kinship, Environment, and the Forest Service," pp. 44, 49. That survey was conducted in 1875. Even by 1917, there were still areas of the Alsea Basin that had not yet been surveyed because the topography was so rugged.

31. Prior, "Kinship, Environment, and the Forest Service," pp. 49, 69.

32. C. Frank Grant, unpublished family memoirs, 1990, p. 18, cited in Prior, "Kinship, Environment, and the Forest Service," p. 69.

33. Prior, "Kinship, Environment, and the Forest Service," p. 61.

34. Hazel Crooks [Shelby] Horlin, "The Life Story of Leora Watkins Crooks Anderson (and Her Family)," unpublished manuscript dated 1975, p. 1, cited in Prior, "Kinship, Environment, and the Forest Service," p. 72.

35. Grant, unpublished family memoirs, p. 39, cited in Prior, "Kinship, Environment, and the Forest Service," p. 70; and Horlin, "The Life Story of Leora Watkins Crooks Anderson," p. 33, cited in Prior, p. 81.

36. Prior, "Kinship, Environment, and the Forest Service," p. 2.

37. Ibid., p. 36.

38. John Minto, "Forestry interests," letter published in *Report of the Secretary, Oregon State Board of Horticulture* (Oregon State Board of Horticulture: Salem, OR, undated, c. 1900), pp. 5, 16–17.

39. E. Louise Peffer, *The Closing of the Public Domain: Disposal and Reservation Policies, 1900-50* (Stanford, CA: Stanford University Press, 1951), cited in Prior, "Kinship, Environment, and the Forest Service," p. 36.

40. Prior, "Kinship, Environment, and the Forest Service," pp. 36-37.

41. Ibid., p. 38.

42. Ibid., p. 42; and USDA Forest Service, Loyd Drorbaugh LAC case file (USDA Forest Service, Siuslaw National Forest, August 2, 1919), cited in Prior, p. 43.

43. Prior, "Kinship, Environment, and the Forest Service," p. 60.

44. Lawrence B. Pagter, *Land Classification of Siuslaw National Forest, Oregon* (Corvallis, OR: USDA Forest Service, Siuslaw National Forest, July 31, 1917), cited in Prior, "Kinship, Environment, and the Forest Service," p. 60.

45. Prior, "Kinship, Environment, and the Forest Service," p. 65.

46. Beckham, *The Indians of Western Oregon*, pp. 145, 147-149.

47. Ibid., p. 150.

48. Ibid., p. 161.

49. Prior, "Kinship, Environment, and the Forest Service," p. 66; Beckham, *The Indians of Western Oregon*, p. 162. During the 1950s, in an effort to bring Indians into the mainstream culture, the federal government terminated the trust relationship with 109 tribes and bands, including 62 in Oregon. Recently, vigorous efforts have been made to restore the trust relationship. In 1997, the Confederated Tribes of Siletz won restoration, making them a federally recognized tribal confederation. The Siletz confederation now has a reservation of 3,666 acres. See *Oregon Blue Book*, Office of the Secretary of State, Salem, pp. 268-9.

50. Northam, "Rural settlement," pp. 24-25.

51. Ibid., p. 26; and Ripple, "Historic Spatial Patterns of Old Forests," p. 48.

52. William J. Ripple, K.T. Hershey, and Robert G. Anthony, "Historical forest patterns of Oregon's central Coast Range," *Biological Conservation* 93

(2000), p. 131. The checkerboard pattern resulted when land granted to the Oregon and California Railroad in 1866 was taken back by the federal government after the railroad company was found guilty of fraud. The land grants, lying in alternating sections (a section is a square mile, $\frac{1}{36}$ of a township) along the railroad right of way, are now managed by the Bureau of Land Management along with the remaining public-domain lands. See John H. Beuter, *Legacy and Promise: Oregon's Forests and Wood Products Industry* (Portland, OR: Oregon Business Council and Oregon Forest Resources Institute, 1998), p. 11; and Bob Bourhill, *History of Oregon's Timber Harvests and/or Lumber Production* (Salem, OR: Oregon Department of Forestry, 1994).

53. USDA Forest Service, *Log Production in Washington and Oregon: An Historical Perspective, Resource Bulletin PNW-42* (Portland, OR: USDA Forest Service, Pacific Northwest Forest and Range Experiment Station, 1972, p. 6. Authorities differ on the exact board footage logged in 1952. The Forest Service says 10.4 billion board feet; Beuter and Bourhill say 9.8 billion board feet. See Beuter, *Legacy and Promise*; and Bourhill, *History of Oregon's Timber Harvests.*

54. Beuter, *Legacy and Promise*, p. vi; and Bourhill, *History of Oregon's Timber Harvests*, p. 4.

55. USDA Forest Service, *Log Production in Washington and Oregon*, pp. 11–12; and Beuter, *Legacy and Promise*, p. vi.

Chapter 8

The Meaning of Dynamic Nature

As we approach the bicentennial of the visit of the Corps of Discovery, there is a rising interest in all things connected with Lewis and Clark. A public television series a few years ago fascinated millions of viewers with the story of the arduous journey and its successful completion. The historian Stephen Ambrose's highly readable 1996 book about the Lewis and Clark journey, *Undaunted Courage,* was a bestseller among the general public and was well received by historians. Ambrose and his family and friends have reenacted the journey of the Corps of Discovery every year for a quarter-century, and many others follow in their footsteps. The trail of Lewis and Clark has become a well-worn path.

People seem drawn to the Lewis and Clark experience. The story resonates irresistibly with heroism—readers thrill to the account of Lewis escaping a wounded grizzly bear; of Sacajawea trekking 2,500 miles with a baby in tow. The journey also offers an opportunity for people to encounter, if only in imagination, a landscape that existed before Europeans colonized the West—a landscape that in many people's minds was pure, pristine, untarnished, and eternal. In the civilized, urbanized, globalized culture of America in the early twenty-first century, Lewis and Clark have come to stand for an enlightened ecological consciousness, a sensitivity to the cultures of native peoples, and an appreciation for unaltered, undeveloped nature.[1]

Lewis and Clark might be surprised to hear themselves commemorated in this way, nearly 200 years after they made their journey.[2] They came on a fact-finding mission prompted by geopolitical circumstances and ordained by a President bent on economic domination of western North America. They were practical men, diligent and objective journal-keepers, keen observers of their natural surroundings, and candid (and not always approving) commentators on Indian ways.

They knew very well the dynamic character of the western landscape. Their journals are full of observations about it—the meandering waters of the Missouri that constantly undercut its banks, sending down slumps of earth that threatened to swamp the pirogues; the sandbars that formed in a few hours in the bed of the Platte and just as quickly disappeared; the muddy Marias riverbank that abruptly caved and nearly carried one of the men over a cliff. Camped with the Corps on a narrow ledge along the lower Columbia, Clark wrote about being slammed by drift logs, pelted from above by boulders, and hammered by rain and wind.[3]

Many people today seem to assume that the landscape Lewis and Clark saw was somehow more "natural" than any that existed before or since. Our cultural ideal of the

Oak Creek, in Oregon State University's McDonald Research Forest.

"natural" landscape is strongly conditioned by what we believe the land looked like immediately before European settlement. Our aesthetic sensibility draws us to a landscape that we perceive as "wilderness," untouched by humans and existing in a timeless state.[4]

These assumptions are based on an ideal that bears little resemblance to reality. Human influences since white settlement have been significant, but as we have seen, natural and prehistoric Native American influences had been at work on the land long before European-Americans arrived. The forests we see today along the lower Columbia certainly look different from the ones Lewis and Clark saw. But the forests also looked different 500 years before they arrived, and 2,000 years before they arrived. They will look different when our grandchildren are old. The dynamic character of natural processes forces us to rethink some of our assumptions about what nature is like apart from human influences, how we affect nature, how nature affects us, and what our proper place in nature should be.[5]

The "Balance" of "Nature"?

Dynamic nature is a hard idea to get the mind around. It represents a change in how society views the world—a paradigm shift, in the words of the philosopher Thomas Kuhn.[6] Our own culture's attitude toward nature is influenced by, among others, a vision of nature as having an intrinsic order, a balance among its parts and dynamics. Such a vision fosters an assumption, accepted by many without too much thought, that if you leave nature alone it will achieve and maintain an equilibrium that is both true to its own processes and favorable to human needs and interests. This book's sketch of the many influences at work on Oregon's forests makes it clear that there is no one point of equilibrium, no one set of conditions that constitute "the balance of nature."

On the other hand, the absence of an identifiable equilibrium point does not mean natural systems are chaotic. The ecologist Daniel Botkin's book *Discordant Harmonies* (1990) captures in its very title the reality of dynamic natural systems—biological processes occurring in a geophysical context, keyed to climate, characterized by recurring though irregular patterns of events, and subject to seemingly random disturbances. Just because a system has elements of chance does not mean everything is unpredictable. With the help of such tools as statistics and computer models, we can use our knowledge of past and current processes to help us arrive at probabilities of various kinds and degrees of change.

The dynamic nature of forests, and of all natural systems, is driven by processes at work both within the system and outside of it. As we learned in Chapter 2, forests, like all plant communities, follow more or less predictable pathways of succession. Certain communities of plants, animals, and microbes successively occupy and are replaced by other communities over time, with accompanying changes in soil and microclimate conditions.[7] These pathways are interrupted unpredictably by disturbances, such as fire and windstorms, of varying frequency, size, and intensity. Other processes, such as fluctuations in populations of insects or disease-causing organisms within a system, also complicate the pathways of succession.

These dynamics take place within a context of climate, which itself is always in a state of flux. Warmer, drier climatic conditions favor certain species over others, and they also are associated with different patterns of disturbance. Forest fires, for instance, were more widespread west of the Cascades during the warmer periods of the last 600 years than during the cooler periods.[8] As we have seen in Chapter 1, past swings in climatic conditions have produced major shifts in the kinds of trees and other plants that occupied forested sites at different points in the past.

Where is "Normal"?

What does it mean for us to understand nature as fundamentally dynamic, rather than fundamentally static? How do we approach an understanding of processes that go on in the absence of an identifiable equilibrium? Without an obvious baseline, how is it possible to know what is "normal" and what is out of kilter at any moment?

Finally, and most importantly, how are we to know what we are supposed to *do* with nature? What should we manipulate, and how much? What should we leave alone?

We did not consider it our job to answer these questions in this brief chapter, but only to raise them. Many good minds have wrestled at length with such questions. A good place to explore further the implications of dynamic nature is in the works of Daniel Botkin, especially his *Discordant Harmonies* (1990) and *Our Natural History: The Lessons of Lewis and Clark* (1995).[9] Based on a reading of Botkin and others, the stories about Oregon's dynamic forest landscape in the preceding chapters, and the research of scientists who are trying to grab hold of dynamic forests long enough to study them, we offer a few thoughts.

Fires and Floods are Good?

An understanding of dynamic nature challenges cherished and persistent assumptions. It makes us think in hard, unfamiliar, even distasteful ways. Take, for example, the conventional attitude toward natural disturbance. Fires, floods, landslides, earthquakes, volcanoes, and windstorms are awesome, fearsome events. Nature's life-threatening qualities inspire a mingled fascination and dread in us, a response that seems to be hard-wired into our limbic systems.

An understanding of dynamic nature forces us to confront and challenge this most basic of instinctive responses. It forces us to stretch our imaginations past the comfort level and think of these events instead as a vital source of renewal for natural communities. For example, it was forest fires in the Cascades and Coast Range during the thirteenth, fourteenth, and fifteenth centuries that set the stage for the large expanses of old-growth forests Lewis and Clark and other early explorers found when they arrived five centuries later.

Floods—such as the devastating floods that prompted many Missourians to find a new life at the end of the Oregon Trail—are also a source of renewal. Daniel Botkin writes of the "Faustian bargain" engineers made with the Missouri River when they built levees to tame its meanders. This policy traded "short-time stability, a chance to build and live on the floodplain, to farm that floodplain year after year, without worrying about the dreadful floods, ... for a loss of the renewing sediments that had created the fertile farmland in the first place." Despite all the engineers' best attempts, the river went ahead and flooded anyway, causing billions of dollars in damage.[10]

Oregon's wet winters of the recent past have brought flood and landslide issues into sharp public focus. For people, landslides and floods are inconvenient and sometimes tragic, as when a hillside in Douglas County slumped after a heavy rain in November of 1996, destroying a house and killing four people. The rainstorm, considered to be between a 50- and a 100-year event, also triggered a mudslide that crossed Highway 38 (also in Douglas County), burying a car and killing its driver.[11] Because the slopes from which the landslides originated had been logged within the previous decade, the state legislature, in response to public concern, gave the Oregon Department of Forestry authority to temporarily ban logging on areas identified as high risk for slides, or where a slide might endanger human life.

Most researchers agree that logging increases the risk of landslides in wet, steep areas such as Coast Range forests, but the risk is there to start with. Landslides are irregular, unpredictable, and occur frequently in the absence of human activities. Besides being a hazard to humans, landslides and floods can thoroughly disrupt habitat functions for fish and wildlife in some locations.

Yet in the wet forests of the Coast Range, these disturbances are part of the natural landscape dynamic, and the fish and wildlife have adapted to the periodic, localized occurrence of these events over time. Research by fish biologists has shown that some of the woody debris and gravel in coastal forest streams, believed to be essential components of fish habitat, may have come from landslides originating some distance away from the stream.[12] These slides may disrupt habitat in the short term, but they probably create habitat in the long term, as the debris and gravel settle. Landslides seem to be one of the essential catastrophic disturbances that make the coastal forest what it is.

An understanding of dynamic nature, then, makes us confront our deepest anxieties. Instead of fearing fires and floods as "bad" and

Riparian restoration project in Salmon Creek, a tributary of the Yaquina River. The conifer logs on the ground, now anchored by alder trees, will rise with rising creek waters.

going to great length to avert them, we are challenged to acknowledge that, first, they will always be with us, and, second, their continued irregular recurrence is an essential dynamic of nature. These disturbances are woven into the very fabric of our landscape. We cannot eliminate them no matter how hard we try.

What is the alternative? It is to embrace disturbance and, within socially acceptable limits, invite it into our relationship with the landscape, including our management strategies for forests. It is not easy to act against survival instinct. The incentive to try comes from acknowledging that many of our past attempts to mold nature to our narrow ideas of "good" have ultimately failed to meet our objectives.

Which Nature?

An understanding of dynamic nature forces us to reexamine other assumptions. One is the notion that nature is completely malleable. This assumption rests on the metaphor of nature as a machine—predictable, understandable, and dependent on humans to keep its goods and services flowing. The notion of malleable nature assumes that "we can manage wildlife, forests, and other living resources to a point of maximum yield," and that "we can change [nature] and improve it in any way we like" to achieve whatever economic or social goals we may choose.[13]

The notion of a completely malleable nature has informed much of the past century's policy toward natural resource management. It assumes that there is one best way for a landscape to be, and that human effort can make it be that way forever. This is the vision that drove the construction of 18 major dams along the

Columbia and Snake river systems in the mid-twentieth century. It is the vision that drove the philosophy of sustained yield in the days when "management" meant replacing "decadent" old-growth forests with young, "thrifty" planted stands, in the days when objectives were simple and the tools to meet them well developed.

None of this is to say that old-growth forests are inherently "better" than young stands—a dynamic forest landscape has both, in varying quantities, at different times and places—or that dams are never a good idea. The point is that these policies, in trying to pin a particular set of human-induced conditions on the landscape at all times and in all places, were not in harmony with the ever-changing character of the land.

In the context of forests, an understanding of dynamic nature challenges the assumption that there is an obvious target for management—whether it be to cover the ridgetops with tree farms, or cultivate a blanket of old-growth forest over the whole region, or shoot for some eternal combination of forests of different ages and sizes in between. If forests have existed in a variety of conditions through time, then there is no obvious reference point. An understanding of dynamic nature would encourage us to decide for ourselves what set of conditions on the forest landscape best meets our needs, while observing the limits of what is ecologically possible. To embrace the many values humans hold about their forests, it might be wise to define "human need" in the broadest possible way—to include, for one, the need to know that salmon will be swimming up the rivers of the Northwest after we are dead.

On the other hand, an understanding of dynamic nature also challenges the notion that "Nature knows best"—that in the absence of human impacts nature will assume and maintain some eternal golden mean. The conflict between those who would manage the forests for human use and those who would preserve them often comes down to an argument about whether humans are doing too much to nature, or doing too little.[14] The "Nature knows best" argument says we should do as little as we can get by with. The "Nature is malleable" argument says we should do as much as we want. An understanding of dynamic nature reframes the question—

it says we should do a lot in some places and not much in others, depending on our objectives and the limits posed by the natural system. It reinforces the wisdom of adaptive management—watching to see what happens when we do something to the land, and making changes according to whether our activities seem to be having the desired effect.

In this way, an understanding of dynamic nature reinforces the old-fashioned idea of *stewardship*. In a dynamic landscape, humans must be good stewards of their environment, having both the authority to make significant changes in natural patterns when and where they see fit, and the responsibility to make those changes in light of the best available knowledge about how the land will likely respond.

Determining what this sort of stewardship will look like at the level of policy and practice is the task that faces policymakers and the public today. It is beyond the scope of this book, and beyond the expertise of either of the authors, to speculate on what policy directions or management strategies might ensue from a broad understanding of dynamic nature. But it seems to us that Botkin is right when he says natural-resource policy must be based on how nature really works, or it will fail.[15]

Which Frame of Reference?

A knowledge of the land's history, such as we have tried to sketch in this book, is essential for achieving an understanding of dynamic nature. Knowing the variety of forest conditions that existed at various points in the past can give an idea of the nature of the processes that produced them. A deeper knowledge of natural processes can in turn help us emulate the effects of these processes on the landscapes of the present and the future.

The historical range of landscape conditions is only beginning to be known. Landscape reconstruction is not an exact science. There is not a lot of paleoecological evidence from which to reconstruct past forest conditions, and what there is tends to be localized in space and time. The events recorded in pollen or charcoal layers and tree rings were only a few of the many that occurred. Pollen and charcoal records go back several millennia, but events are hard to pinpoint precisely in time and harder to extrapolate to a wider area. Pollen records tend to exist only in wet places; the drier uplands lack them. Studies of tree rings allow a more recent, more comprehensive look at fires and climate conditions, but the evidence is limited to living or undecomposed dead trees—not a very long record when considered against the sweep of time since the last Ice Age.

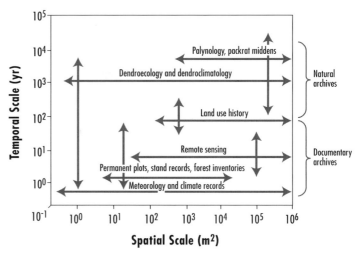

The range of spatial and temporal scales addressed by varying approaches to historical ecology.

Historical records, such as explorers' journals and pioneers' diaries, also have their limitations. They are obviously very recent. People noted only some of what they saw (and some of that inaccurately, no doubt), and they saw only a small fraction of what was there. The natural features of the landscape channeled the European newcomers in familiar pathways—up and down rivers, through valleys, along Indian trails. There is little direct observation of certain landscape features, such as undisturbed forests along the higher reaches of the Cascades and the Coast Range, that are of great interest today. Nevertheless, these findings augment an ever-developing body of general knowledge about landscape functions to help us better understand the dynamic character of natural systems.

The science of landscape reconstruction is also aided by such technology as GIS (geographic information systems), which offers various techniques to combine information from aerial and satellite images into deep, "layered" maps of a landscape. Scientists have also devised computer models that, through multiple runs, can simulate forest conditions as they might have existed far back in time, or as they might exist at some point in the future.[16]

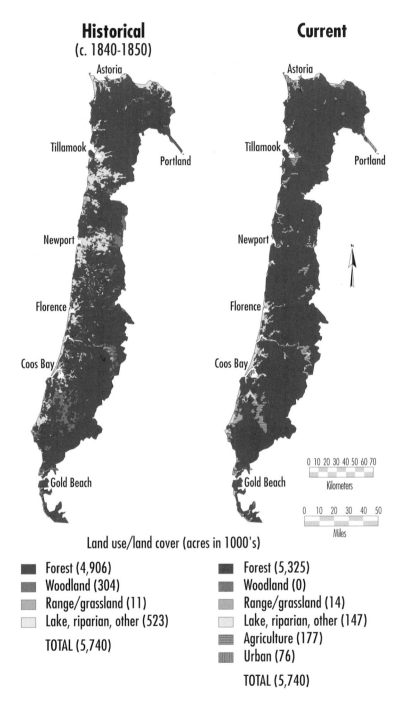

Historical
(c. 1840-1850)

Astoria
Tillamook
Portland
Newport
Florence
Coos Bay
Gold Beach

Current

Astoria
Tillamook
Portland
Newport
Florence
Coos Bay
Gold Beach

N

0 10 20 30 40 50 60 70
Kilometers

0 10 20 30 40 50
Miles

Land use/land cover (acres in 1000's)

Forest (4,906)
Woodland (304)
Range/grassland (11)
Lake, riparian, other (523)

TOTAL (5,740)

Forest (5,325)
Woodland (0)
Range/grassland (14)
Lake, riparian, other (147)
Agriculture (177)
Urban (76)

TOTAL (5,740)

Historical and current land use and cover in the Oregon Coast Range. From the State of Environment Report (Oregon Progress Board), 2000.

In recent studies, scientists have used paleoecological evidence and computer models to estimate the range of forest conditions that have existed across the landscape in the past. This *historical range of variability*, as it has been termed, is one key to managing in a dynamic context, because it can an offer a set of boundaries, "a frame of reference for evaluating potential future management scenarios."[17]

The concept of historical range of variability would seem to admit a broad range of management strategies across the landscape. The complexity of forest ecosystems makes any single, simple management approach problematic. For example, reserving large blocks of old forest from management may be appropriate in many places, but alone, it is not enough to conserve wildlife habitat. Forests of all ages, not just old-growth forests, are important for wildlife.[18] There will never be "a simple set of prescriptions for multiple-use, multiple-value management of complex ecosystems."[19] Indeed, the high degree of historical variability across the landscape over time indicates that Northwest forests can accommodate a diversity of management objectives and approaches.

That said, it is important to realize that the forests of the Northwest as they stand today are most likely outside the historical range of variability in terms of the amount of old forest left standing.[20] Wimberly's and his colleagues' model estimated that the coverage of old-growth forests (more than 200 years old) in the Coast Range cycled between 39 percent 1,500 to 3,000 years ago, to 55 percent 1,500 to 2,000 years ago. Over the past 1,000 years, average coverage of old-growth declined to about 45 percent.

Estimates of the extent of old-growth forests in the Coast Range during the last century have ranged from 61 percent, before the fires of the mid-1800s, to a little over 40 percent by the end of the century.[21] Today only about 5 percent of Coast Range forest is old growth, and 11 percent is late-successional (80 to 200 years old).

Wimberly's findings and those of others suggest that if society's objective is to pull forests closer to a semblance of what they were in the past, then the extent of older forest needs to be increased.[22] The science does not determine whether that should be the objec-

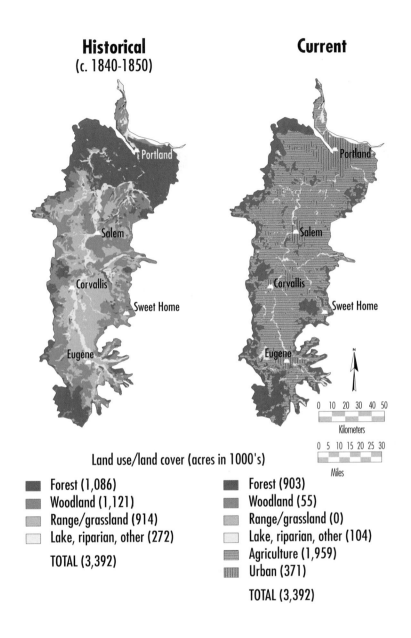

Historical
(c. 1840-1850)

Current

Portland

Portland

Salem

Salem

Corvallis

Corvallis

Sweet Home

Sweet Home

Eugene

Eugene

0 10 20 30 40 50
Kilometers

0 5 10 15 20 25 30
Miles

Land use/land cover (acres in 1000's)

Forest (1,086)
Woodland (1,121)
Range/grassland (914)
Lake, riparian, other (272)

TOTAL (3,392)

Forest (903)
Woodland (55)
Range/grassland (0)
Lake, riparian, other (104)
Agriculture (1,959)
Urban (371)

TOTAL (3,392)

Historical and current land use and cover in the Willamette Valley. From the State of Environment Report (Oregon Progress Board), 2000.

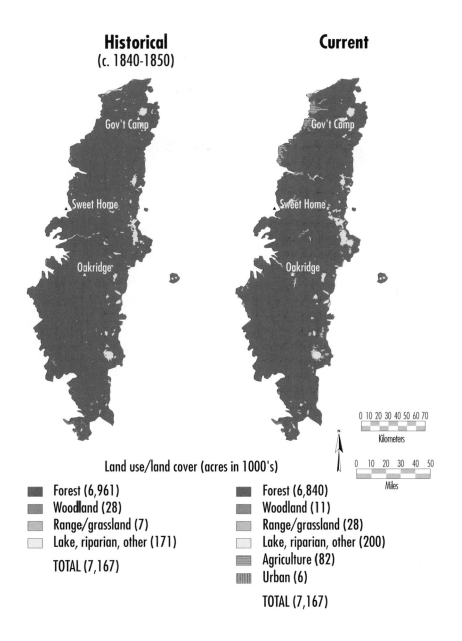

Historical
(c. 1840-1850)

Current

Gov't Camp

Sweet Home

Oakridge

0 10 20 30 40 50 60 70
Kilometers

0 10 20 30 40 50
Miles

Land use/land cover (acres in 1000's)

Forest (6,961)
Woodland (28)
Range/grassland (7)
Lake, riparian, other (171)

TOTAL (7,167)

Forest (6,840)
Woodland (11)
Range/grassland (28)
Lake, riparian, other (200)
Agriculture (82)
Urban (6)

TOTAL (7,167)

Historical and current land use and cover in the Oregon Cascades. From the State of Environment Report (Oregon Progress Board), 2000.

187

tive—it only offers a framework for weighing the benefits and risks of choosing such an objective in various places.

There are other choices. According to the forest ecologist J.P. Kimmins, a landscape does not have to be within the range of historical conditions to be considered healthy from an ecological point of view, as long as the ecosystem functions are intact:

> *Where natural or human-caused disturbance has taken the landscape out of its historical range, but the resulting condition is not a threat to the existence of any species or important local genetic populations of a species, and has not impaired the function of any key ecological processes, it is society and not science that must define whether the new landscape condition is more or less healthy, and has more or less integrity, than some former condition that was within the historical range.[23]*

A sense of the appropriateness of the mix of values we seek from our forests is something we cannot derive from the forest itself.

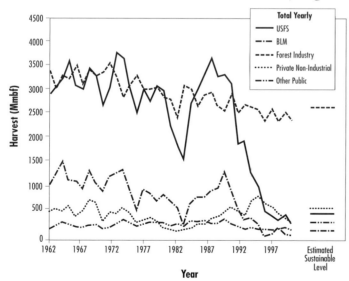

Historical timber harvest and estimated sustainable harvest level in the wetter ecoregions of the Northwest, such as the Coast Range and the western Cascades. From the State of Environment Report (Oregon Progress Board), 2000.

We have to decide that for ourselves, mindful of the forest's processes and ecological limits. Knowing something about the range of historical conditions in a given place allows managers to evaluate strategies in light of "wild" processes and patterns. It also allows society to determine what is gained and what is lost, in the way of both commodity production and ecosystem function, by deviating from historical patterns. How "natural" can the management be and still meet the objective? Would a given strategy be likely to push the landscape outside its historical range? What might that mean for the plant and animal community? Might it result in local elimination of certain wildlife populations? How high is the risk of such local extirpations? If they happen, are there other populations in other places that would remain self-sustaining? Knowing the historical range of variability can help managers, and society, make such choices with better knowledge of the likely consequences.

We have barely begun to capture the data we need to make such decisions. "We lack not only information about the state of nature," says Botkin, "but also an adequate understanding of how ecological systems function. . . ." Such detailed knowledge was not so critical within a "balance-of-nature" perspective, he says, because "we believed that nature simply knew best and our understanding was irrelevant to management."[24] Understanding nature as dynamic means fully appreciating the need for detailed knowledge of baseline conditions—how nature works apart from people—and also for knowledge of the complexities of how natural systems respond to human influences:

> *Prudent and wise management of nature requires a large effort. There is a great need for educational programs on the management of the environment, but such curricula currently have very little support and little academic status, and there are few appropriate interdisciplinary educational programs. An increase in funding for education in the management of the environment is necessary.[25]*

Thinking Things Through

A better understanding of dynamic nature can help us think through policy proposals more competently. As a case in point, there is a recent proposal to ban new roads on certain roadless areas of federal forests. A "Nature-is-malleable" position on this proposal might simply reject it out of hand on the grounds that we have plenty of roadless reserves and we don't need any more. A "Nature-knows-best" position might embrace it uncritically, reasoning that if some forest reserves are good, more are better. Indeed, the opinions voiced at the Forest Service's public hearings have fallen more or less into one of these two camps.[26]

Approaching the proposal from an understanding of dynamic nature might prompt some clarifying questions. First, the basic geography of the lands: Where are they on the ground? Where do they stand in relation to one another? What kinds of forests are growing on them? What kinds of natural or human-caused disturbances have influenced their development? What forest communities and habitat elements distinguish them one from another? What kinds and conditions of lands surround them? What values—ecological, economic, or social—do they offer to adjacent communities?

Second, the policy questions. Is there an articulated objective for reserving more forest land? Will the objective, however it be defined, be met equally on all the proposed lands? Is the criterion of roadlessness the only one we should consider, or are there other lands, perhaps with roads, that may be better candidates for reserves? If the objective is to preserve or restore habitat for certain wildlife species, or to absorb natural disturbances without loss of life or property, will the tracts of land be big enough? (The proposal in question mentions tracts of 5,000 acres or more. That is equal to 7.8 square miles, roughly a block of land 2 miles wide and 4 miles long.) If the objective is to preserve old-growth forests on the land, will there be enough younger forests elsewhere that will be spared to grow into old-growth condition when a disturbance shifts these reserved forests back to an earlier seral stage?

Finally, the practical questions: Might commodity extraction at some level be a better objective for some of the lands, say, those closer to communities that have the harvesting infrastructure in place? If so, could harvesting be managed profitably without roads? (Maybe it could.) If some roads are needed for profitable harvesting, might roads be built that tread lightly on the landscape in these areas? And then, might we consider taking out some older, less environmentally sensitive roads in more fragile areas?

By the time this book is published, this particular issue may have been resolved. However, any proposal of this kind raises an opportunity for citizens to ask these kinds of questions. An understanding of dynamic nature does not force a judgment one way or the other, to reserve or not to reserve. But it does force us to recognize that whatever values we are trying to preserve will not stay in the same place on the landscape forever. It encourages us to rethink our strategies for preserving older forest and all its values, and perhaps expand our repertoire beyond merely pinning existing old forests to the ground in certain locations and then walking away.

Political and Social Reality

An understanding of dynamic nature is necessary for good policy, but it is not sufficient. Good policy also needs to be based on political and social reality. For example, large-scale forest fires have been integral to the successional dynamic of Northwest forests. A policy encouraging the return of such fires might make sense ecologically, but not socially or politically.[27] Organized fire suppression was begun early in the twentieth century to protect landowners' investments in their timber. Today's landowners are no more likely than yesterday's to tolerate wildfires on their land if these fires can be prevented or suppressed.

Researchers have examined various approaches to emulate the effects of fire on forest land. One approach is to create "mortality patches" through clearcutting that are similar to those created by the smaller fires of the past, leaving dead logs and snags to keep nutrients and habitat elements on the site.[28] Using clearcutting to emulate fire does not assume that the two are perfectly analogous (they are not), but some researchers believe clearcutting can be conducted in a way that fulfills some of the renewing function of fires and enables the forest's successional development to go on without loss of ecological functions.

Another approach may be to reserve tracts of public forest land big enough and remote enough to absorb large natural disturbances without danger to life or private property. Some of the late-succes-

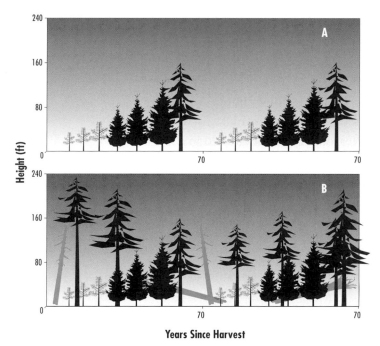

Height (ft)

240 — 160 — 80 — 0

A

70   70

240 — 160 — 80 — 0

B

70   70

Years Since Harvest

An idealized comparison of forest practices designed to maximize wood production (a) with those designed to both produce wood and enhance wildlife habitat (b). Plantations (a) are relatively simple in structure and are not very diverse in habitat qualities. Practices are now required that better emulate natural forest patterns, with the dual aim of producing wood for commodity use and maintaining a wider diversity of forest structures for wildlife habitat.

sional reserves on the national forests fall into this category.[29]

An understanding of dynamic nature would push managers to go beyond merely emulating or tolerating natural events. It would encourage them to manage so as to complement the effects of these disturbances—to welcome nature's uncertainties right into the management plan. Exactly how to do this is unclear. The rough rhythm of natural processes can be made partly tractable through statistics and computer modeling, but beyond that, managers will have to face the fact that they will never know the comfort of absolutely

predictable outcomes—not that they ever did, but an understanding of dynamic nature takes away even the illusion of certainty.

Will People Support it?

The best natural-resource policy based on the best scientific understanding of dynamic nature will fail if it does not have the support of the public. To propose strategies that will work in a dynamic context, policymakers will have to answer tough questions from citizens. What kinds of disturbance should we encourage or tolerate in a given landscape, and how much disturbance is too much? How do we cope with the rights of multiple owners and their multiple objectives across a forest landscape? Why should we trust that reserving forest lands from management is not always the safest bet?

We citizens are more likely to support forest management based on a dynamic understanding of nature if our own understanding is accurate. There is a need for public education and information on the dynamic nature of landscapes. This learning could be offered in a variety of ways—in books such as this one, in public-television programs, in educational materials that present scientific information in lay terms, in talks and seminars given by scientists to audiences of interested lay people. Informational materials could be prepared for or by voluntary groups of citizens, such as watershed councils or conservation groups, who come together because of a shared interest in good land stewardship. In whatever forum public education takes place, scientists have an obligation to reach out to citizens and convey their knowledge in accessible, user-friendly ways.

Freedom and Responsibility

Botkin says, "Nature in the twenty-first century will be a nature that we make." The question is whether this molding will be intentional or unintentional, desirable or undesirable.[30]

Nature does not tell us how to manage forests. It is up to us to decide that for ourselves, and that is perhaps the most difficult part of coping with dynamic nature. We are confronted with a landscape that is not only characterized by dynamic natural processes but overlain with a web of social and economic meanings, a landscape that, in our free-enterprise culture, represents a myriad of ownerships with sometimes conflicting objectives. And so it is a good thing for us that nature is not rigidly deterministic. A forest can develop along a number of pathways, some of which may be better for meeting human needs and desires than others. Within ecological constraints, we have a fair degree of freedom in manipulating forests to achieve those conditions that best suit us.

With this freedom comes responsibility for making wise choices. The wisdom of these choices will depend on scientific knowledge, but it will also depend on well-articulated economic, aesthetic, and moral reasoning. An understanding of dynamic nature suggests that forests are neither completely malleable nor completely beyond our beneficial influence. Understanding dynamic nature encourages us to take our stewardship responsibilities seriously, managing actively, but in the fullest possible awareness of the land's history and the likely consequences of our actions.

Another Voyage of Discovery

And so we close our book on the forests of Oregon as they were encountered by Lewis and Clark and their Corps of Discovery. Today, almost 200 years later, we have a valuable legacy of that journey captured in their journals—a keen-eyed, detailed, and unsentimental look at dynamic nature. Lewis and Clark's voyage is a fitting place for us to start on our own twenty-first-century voyage of discovery, a discovery of how the ever-changing processes of nature and the historical patterns of human use have influenced the landscape we have inherited. If we are willing to listen to the land and to one another, if we are willing to be moderate, humble, and patient with the land and with one another, such a voyage might also lead us to discover something good about ourselves. It might lead us to discover how our own wise stewardship can work in harmony with these processes to help us shape and tend a forested landscape that will both sustain its own processes and meet the needs and desires of its human inhabitants.

Two hundred years from now, our great-great-grandchildren will thank us for embarking on this voyage.

Notes to Chapter 8

1. Mark Spence, personal communication, April 2000.

2. Ibid.

3. Daniel Botkin, *Our Natural History: The Lessons of Lewis and Clark* (New York: Grosset/Putnam, 1995), p. 25; Stephen E. Ambrose, *Undaunted Courage: Meriwether Lewis, Thomas Jefferson, and the Opening of the American West* (New York: Simon & Schuster, 1996), p. 308; and Gary E. Moulton, ed., *The Journals of the Lewis & Clark Expedition*, vol. 6 (Lincoln: University of Nebraska Press, 1990).

4. Peter J. Weisberg and Frederick J. Swanson, "Regional Synchronicity in Changing Fire Regime Patterns of the Western Cascades, U.S.A." Paper in review. Copy in possession of the authors; and Daniel Botkin, *Discordant Harmonies: A New Ecology for the Twenty-first Century* (New York and Oxford: Oxford University Press, 1990), p. 195.

5. Botkin, *Discordant Harmonies*, p. vii.

6. Thomas Kuhn, *The Structure of Scientific Revolutions* (1970; reprint, University of Chicago Press, 1996).

7. J.P. Kimmins, *Forest Ecology: A Foundation for Sustainable Management,* 2d ed. (Upper Saddle River, NJ: Prentice Hall, 1997), p. 30.

8. Weisberg and Swanson, "Regional Synchronicity."

9. Botkin, *Discordant Harmonies*; and Botkin, *Our Natural History*.

10. Botkin, *Our Natural History*, pp. 33–34.

11. Oregon Department of Forestry, *Report on Rock Creek and Highway 38 (M.P. 13) Debris Flows November,* 1996, report from Squier Associates, Inc. (Salem, OR: Oregon Department of Forestry, 1998), pp. 3–4.

12. G.H. Reeves, L.E. Benda, K.M. Burnett, P.A. Bisson, and J.R. Sedell, "A Disturbance-based Ecosystem Approach to Maintaining and Restoring Freshwater Habitats of Evolutionarily Significant Units of Anadromous

Salmonids in the Pacific Northwest," *American Fisheries Society Symposium* 17 (1995), pp. 334–349, cited in John C. Tappeiner, II, David Hibbs, and William H. Emmingham, "Silviculture of Coast Range forests," in *Forest and Stream Management in the Oregon Coast Range* (in press).

13. Botkin, *Our Natural History*, p. 4.

14. Ibid., p. 12.

15. Ibid., p. xiv.

16. Michael C. Wimberly, Thomas A. Spies, Colin J. Long, and Cathy Whitlock, "Simulating Historical Variability in the Amount of Old Forests in the Oregon Coast Range," *Conservation Biology* 14, vol. 1 (2000), pp. 1–15.

17. Ibid.; Thomas W. Swetnam, Craig D. Allen, and Julio L. Betancourt, "Applied Historical Ecology: Using the Past to Manage for the Future," *Ecological Applications* 9, no. 4 (1999), pp. 1189–1206; and David O. Wallin, Frederick J. Swanson, Barbara Marks, John H. Cissel, and Jane Kertis, "Comparison of Managed and Pre-settlement Landscape Dynamics in Forests of the Pacific Northwest, USA," *Forest Ecology and Management* 85 (1996), pp. 291–309.

18. A.J. Hansen, "Conserving Biodiversity in Managed Forests: Lessons from Natural Forests," *BioScience* 41 (1991), p. 6.

19. F.J. Swanson and J.F. Franklin, "New Forestry Principles from Ecosystem Analysis of Pacific Northwest Forests," *Ecological Applications* 2, no. 3 (1992), p. 271.

20. Wimberly et al., "Simulating Historical Variability." p. 12.

21. Ibid., p. 10.

22. Hansen, "Conserving Biodiversity"; and Wallin et al., "Comparison of Managed and Pre-settlement Landscape Dynamics."

23. Kimmins, *Forest Ecology*, p. 509). Kimmins also maintains that "a comprehensive network of ecological reserves is a fundamental requirement for sustainable forest management" (p. 503).

24. Botkin, *Discordant Harmonies*, p. 197.

25. Ibid., p. 200.

26. "Views on road ban to pour in," *Salem (Oregon) Statesman-Journal*, 16 July 2000, pp. 1, 3.

27. Wallin et al., "Comparison of Managed and Pre-settlement Landscape Dynamics."

28. John H. Cissel, Frederick J. Swanson, and Peter J. Weisberg, "Landscape Management Using Historical Fire Regimes: Blue River, Oregon," *Ecological Applications* 9, no. 4 (1999), pp. 1217–1231.

29. K. Norman Johnson, personal communication, July 2000.

30. Botkin, *Discordant Harmonies*, p. 193.

Bibliography

Published Sources

Abbot, Henry L., "Report of Lieut. Henry L. Abbot, Corps of Topographical Engineers. Explorations for a railroad route from the Sacramento Valley to the Columbia River," in *Reports of explorations and surveys to ascertain the most practicable and economical route for a railroad from the Mississippi River to the Pacific Ocean,* vol. VI, chapter V (33d Cong., 2d Sess, United States Senate, 1855).

Agee, J.K., *Fire Ecology of Pacific Northwest Forests* (Covelo, CA: Island Press, 1993).

Agee, James K., *Fire History of Douglas-fir Forests in the Pacific Northwest.* USDA Forest Service General Technical Report PNW-285 (Portland, OR: USDA Forest Service Pacific Northwest Research Station, 1991).

Agee, James K., *A Conceptual Plan for the Forest Landscape of Fort Clatsop National Memorial.* Report CPSU/UW 89-1 (Seattle, WA: U.S. Department of Interior, National Park Service and University of Washington, College of Forest Resources, 1989).

Agee, James K., *Wildfire in the Pacific West: A Brief History and Implications for the Future.* USDA Forest Service General Technical Report PSW-109 (Berkeley, CA: Pacific Southwest Research Station, 1989).

Ambrose, Stephen E., *Undaunted Courage: Meriwether Lewis, Thomas Jefferson, and the Opening of the American West* (New York, NY: Simon & Schuster, 1996).

Ames, Kenneth M., and Herbert D.G. Maschner, *Peoples of the Northwest Coast: Their Archaeology and Prehistory* (London: Thames and Hudson, 1999).

Andrews, H.J., and R.W. Cowlin, *Forest Resources of the Douglas-fir Region* (USDA Misc. Pub. 389, 1940). Cited in USDA Forest Service, *Log Production in Washington and Oregon.* Resource Bulletin PNW-42 (Portland, OR: Pacific Northwest Forest and Range Experiment Station, 1972).

Atwater, B.F., and D.K. Yamaguchi, "Sudden, Probably Coseismic Submergence of Holocene Trees and Grass in Coastal Washington State," *Geology* 19 (1991): 706–709.

Bancroft, Hubert Howe, *History of the Northwest Coast,* Vol. 1: 1543–1800 (San Francisco: A.L. Bancroft & Company, 1884).

Barnosky, Cathy W., "Late Quaternary Vegetation in the Southwestern Columbia Basin, Washington," *Quaternary Research* 23 (1985): 109–122.

Barry, J. Nielson, ed., "Columbia River Exploration, 1792," *Oregon Historical Quarterly* (March 1932). Cited in Johansen 1967.

Beals, Herbert K., "The Last Temperate Coast: Maritime Exploration of Northwest America, 1542–1794" (annotated poster) (Portland, OR: Oregon Historical Society, 1990).

Beckham, Stephen Dow. *The Indians of Western Oregon: This Land Was Theirs* (Coos Bay, OR: Arago Books, 1977).

Beuter, John H., *Legacy and Promise: Oregon's Forests and Wood Products Industry* (Portland, OR: Oregon Business Council and Oregon Forest Resources Institute, 1998).

Bogart, L., "Geological and Exploration Associates," on the Web at http://ewu63562.ewu.edu/map.htm, 3/24/2000.

Bonnicksen, Thomas M., *America's Ancient Forests: From the Ice Age to the Age of Discovery* (New York: John Wiley & Sons, Inc., 2000).

Booth, D.E., "Estimating Prelogging Old-growth in the Pacific Northwest," *Journal of Forestry* 89 (1991): 25–29.

Botkin, Daniel, *Discordant Harmonies: A New Ecology for the Twenty-first Century* (New York and Oxford: Oxford University Press, 1990).

Botkin, Daniel, *Our Natural History: The Lessons of Lewis and Clark* (New York: Grosset/Putnam, 1995).

Bourhill, Bob, *History of Oregon's Timber Harvests and/or Lumber Production* (Salem, OR: Oregon Department of Forestry, 1994).

Boyd, Robert, ed., *Indians, Fire, and the Land in the Pacific Northwest* (Corvallis, OR: Oregon State University Press, 1999).

"Buying a dream," *Portland Oregonian,* 14 October 1990, L1.

Cannon, Kelly, *Administrative History: Fort Clatsop National Memorial* (U.S. Department of Interior, National Park Service, Seattle, WA, 1995).

Cissel, John H., Frederick J. Swanson, and Peter J. Weisberg, "Landscape Management using Historical Fire Regimes: Blue River, Oregon," *Ecological Applications* 9, no. 4 (1999): 1217–1231.

Cooper, J.G. "Report upon the botany of the route," in *Reports of explorations and surveys to ascertain the most practicable and economical route for a railroad from the Mississippi River to the Pacific Ocean,* vol. XII, book II, part II (36th Cong., 2d Sess., United States Senate. Washington, DC, 1860).

Cox, Thomas R., *Mills and Markets: A History of the Pacific Coast Lumber Industry to 1900* (Seattle, WA: University of Washington Press, 1974).

Crespi, Juan. *Missionary Explorer on the Pacific Coast: 1769–1774* (Berkeley, CA: University of California Press, 1927).

Dahl, Thomas E., *Wetland Losses in the United States 1780's to 1980's* (Washington, DC: U.S. Department of the Interior, Fish and Wildlife Service, 1990). Cited in Bunting 1993.

Davies, K.G., *Peter Skene Ogden's Snake Country Journal 1826–27* (London: The Hudson's Bay Record Society, 1961).

Douglas, David, *A sketch of a journey to the north-western parts of the continent of North America, during the years 1824, 5, 6, and 7* (1836; reprint, Portland, OR: *Oregon Historical Quarterly* IV, V (1904). Cited in Davies 1961.

Douglas, James, "Letter to the Govr. Deputy Govr. & Committee Honble Hudsons Bay Company from James Douglas at Ft Vancouver, Oct. 18, 1838," in E.E. Rich, ed., *The letters of John McLoughlin from Fort Vancouver to the Governor and Committee, First Series, 1825–38* (London: The Champlain Society for The Hudson's Bay Record Society, 1941). Cited in Bunting 1993.

Erigero, Patricia C., *Cultural Landscape Report: Fort Vancouver National Historic Site,* vol. 2 (Seattle, WA: U.S. Department of Interior, National Park Service, 1992).

Ficken, Robert E., *This Forested Land: Lumbering in Washington* (Seattle, WA: University of Washington Press, 1987).

Fort Clatsop Official Map and Guide (Fort Clatsop National Memorial, U.S. Department of the Interior, National Park Service, undated).

Franchere, Gabriel, *Adventure at Astoria, 1810–1814,* Hoyt C. Franchere, tr. and ed. (Norman, OK: University of Oklahoma Press, 1967).

Franklin, J.F., and C.T. Dyrness, *Natural Vegetation of Oregon and Washington* (Portland, OR: USDA Forest Service General Technical Report PNW-8, Pacific Northwest Forest and Range Experiment Station, 1973).

Gannett, Henry, *The Forests of Oregon* (Washington, DC: U.S. Department of Interior, U.S. Geological Survey, 1902).

Grigg, L.D. and C. Whitlock, "Late-glacial Vegetation and Climate Change in Western Oregon," *Quaternary Research* 49, no. 3 (1997): 287–298.

Guthrie, D. and J. Sedell, "Primeval Beaver Stumped Oregon Coast Trapper," *News & Views,* June 1988: 14–16 (Department of Fisheries and Wildlife, Oregon State University). Cited in Rainbolt, unpublished report.

Hansen, H.P., "Postglacial Forest Succession, Climate, and Chronology in the Pacific Northwest," *Transactions of the American Philosophical Society* 37 (1947): 1–130.

Hansen, A.J., "Conserving Biodiversity in Managed Forests: Lessons from Natural Forests," *BioScience* 41(1991):6.

Harcombe, P.A., "Stand Development in a 130-year-old Spruce-Hemlock Forest Based on Age Structure and 50 Years of Mortality Data," *Forest Ecology and Management* 14 (1986):41–58. Cited in Agee, *A Conceptual Plan,* 1989.

Harlow, W.M., and E.S. Harrar, *Textbook of Dendrology* (New York: McGraw-Hill Book Company, Inc., 1941).

Haswell, Robert, *Voyages of the Columbia to the Northwest Coast, 1787–1790 and 1790–1793,* Frederic W. Howay, ed. (Portland, OR: Oregon Historical Society and Massachusetts Historical Society, 1990).

Hayes, John P., and Joan Hagar, "Ecology and Management of Wildlife and Their Habitats in the Oregon Coast Range," in *Forest and Stream Management in the Oregon Coast Range* (in press).

Hemstrom, M.H., and S.E. Logan, *Plant Association and Management Guide, Siuslaw National Forest,* R6 Ecol 220-1986 (Portland, OR: USDA Forest Service, 1986).

Heusser, C.J., "Quaternary Palynology of the Pacific Slope of Washington," *Quaternary Research* 8 (1977): 282–306.

Hewson, E.W., J.E. Wade, and R.W. Baker, *Vegetation as an Indicator of High Wind Velocity. Phase I Final Report* (Oregon State University, Department of Atmospheric Sciences, prepared for the U.S. Department of Energy, DOE Contract EY-76-226, 1977).

Hibbs, D.E., and P.A. Giordano, "Vegetation Characteristics of Alder-dominated Riparian Buffer Strips in the Oregon Coast Range," *Northwest Science* 70 (1996): 213–222.

Hill, William E., *The Oregon Trail: Yesterday and Today* (Caldwell, ID: The Caxton Printers, Ltd., 1992).

Hirt, Paul, *A Conspiracy of Optimism: Management of the National Forests since World War Two* (Lincoln, NB: University of Nebraska Press, 1994).

Hitchman, James H., *Maritime History of the Pacific Coast, 1540–1980* (Lanham, MD: University Press of America, 1990).

Horner, John B., *Oregon, Her History, Her Great Men, Her Literature* (Portland, OR: The J.K. Gill Co., c. 1921).

Howison, Neil, *Report of Lieut. Neil M. Howison, United States Navy, to the commander of the Pacific Squadron; being the result of an examination in the year 1846 of the coast, harbors, rivers, soil, productions, climate, and population of the Territory of Oregon* (30th Cong., 1st Sess., United States House of Representatives, 1848; reprint, Portland, OR: *Oregon Historical Quarterly* XIV, no. 1, 1913).

Jacoby, G.C., "Tree-ring Dating of Coseismic Coastal Subsidence in the Pacific Northwest Region," Tree-ring Laboratory, Lamont-Doherty Earth Observatory, on the Web at http://erp.er.usgs.gov/reports/VOL37/PN/g2451.htm, 5/17/2000.

Jenkins, S.H., and P.E. Busher, "*Castor canadensis,*" *Mammalian Species* 120 (1979): 1–8. Cited in Rainbolt, unpublished report.

Johansen, Dorothy O., *Empire of the Columbia,* 2d ed. (New York: Harper & Row, 1967).

Johnson, O., and W.H. Winter, "Route across the Rocky Mountains with a description of Oregon and California: their geographical features, their resources, soils, climate, productions, etc., etc.," *Oregon Historical Quarterly* VII (1906): 62–104. Cited in Rainbolt, unpublished report.

Jumpponen, Ari, Kim Mattson, James M. Trappe, and Rauni Ohtonen, "Effects of Established Willows on Primary Succession on Lyman Glacier Forefront, North Cascades Range, Washington, U.S.A.: Evidence for Simultaneous Canopy Inhibition and Soil Facilitation," *Arctic, Antarctic, and Alpine Research* 30, no. 1 (February 1998): 31–39.

Kerr, R.A., "Faraway Tsunami Hints at a Really Big Northwest Quake," *Science* 267 (1995): 962.

Kimmins, J.P., *Forest Ecology: A Foundation for Sustainable Management*, 2d ed. (Upper Saddle River, NJ: Prentice Hall, 1997).

Kirkpatrick, Glen, "The Rediscovery of Clark's Point of View," *We Proceeded On* (publication of the Lewis and Clark Trail Heritage Foundation, Inc.), 25, no. 1 (1999): 28–31, 39.

Kuhn, Thomas, *The Structure of Scientific Revolutions* (1970; reprint, University of Chicago Press, 1996).

Large, R.G., Ed., *The Journals of William Fraser Tolmie: Physician and Fur Trader* (Vancouver, BC: Mitchell Press, 1963). Cited in Erigero 1992.

Leidholt-Bruner, Karen, David E. Hibbs, and William C. McComb, "Beaver Dam Locations and Their Effects on Distribution and Abundance of Coho Salmon Fry in Two Coastal Oregon Streams," *Northwest Science* 4 (1992): 218–223.

Little, Elbert L., Jr., *Atlas of United States Trees,* v. 1, *Conifers and Important Hardwoods* (Washington, DC: USDA Forest Service, 1971). Cited in Moulton 1990.

Long, Colin J., Cathy Whitlock, Patrick J. Bartlein, and Sarah H. Millspaugh, "A 9000-year Fire History from the Oregon Coast

Range, Based on a High-Resolution Charcoal Study," *Canadian Journal of Forest Research* 28 (1998): 774–787.

Meany, Edmund S., *Vancouver's Discovery of Puget Sound* (New York: The Macmillan Company, 1915).

Merk, Frederick, *Fur Trade and Empire: George Simpson's Journal: Remarks connected with the fur trade in the course of a voyage from York Factory to Fort George and back to York Factory, 1825–25; together with accompanying documents* (New Haven, CT: Harvard University Press, 1931). Cited in Erigero 1992.

Minore, D., and H.G. Weatherly, "Riparian Trees, Shrubs, and Forest Regeneration in the Coastal Mountains of Oregon," *New Forests* 8, no. 3 (1994): 249.

Minto, John, "From Youth to Age as an American," *Oregon Historical Quarterly,* IX, no. 1 (March 1908): 73–172.

Minto, John, "Forestry interests," letter published in *Report of the Secretary, Oregon State Board of Horticulture,* Salem, OR, undated.

Morris, William G., "Forest Fires in Western Oregon and Western Washington," *Oregon Historical Quarterly* XXXV, no. 4 (1934): 313–339.

Moulton, Gary E., ed., *The Journals of the Lewis & Clark Expedition, November 2, 1805-March 22, 1806,* vol. 6. (Lincoln, NB: University of Nebraska Press, 1990).

Newman, J., producer, "The Missoula Flood" (television program) (Oregon Field Guide #1001. Portland, OR: Oregon Public Broadcasting, Oct. 4, 1998).

Nierenberg, Tara, and David E. Hibbs, "A Characterization of Unmanaged Riparian Areas in the Central Coast Range of Western Oregon," *Forest Ecology and Management* 129 (2000): 195–206.

Nokes, Richard J., *Columbia's River: The Voyages of Robert Gray, 1787-93* (Seattle, WA: Washington State Historical Society, 1991).

Norton, Helen H., Robert Boyd, and Eugene Hunn, "The Klikitat Trail of South-central Washington: A Reconstruction of Seasonally

Used Resource Sites," in *Indians, Fire, and the Land,* ed. Robert Boyd (Corvallis, OR: Oregon State University Press, 1999).

O'Donnell, Terence, *That Balance So Rare: The Story of Oregon* (Portland, OR: Oregon Historical Society Press, 1988).

"One family's conservation ideal preserves some Tillamook Head acreage," *Daily (Oregon) Astorian,* 17 June 1994.

Oregon Council for the Humanities, *The First Oregonians: An Illustrated Collection of Essays on Traditional Lifeways, Federal-Indian Relations, and the State's Native People Today* (Portland, OR: Oregon Council for the Humanities, 1991).

Oregon Department of Forestry, *Report on Rock Creek and Highway 38 (M.P. 13) Debris Flows November, 1996,* report from Squier Associates, Inc. (Salem, OR: Oregon Department of Forestry, 1998).

Oregon Progress Board, *Oregon State of the Environment Report* (Salem, OR: Oregon Progress Board, September 2000).

Oregon State Board of Horticulture, *Report of the Secretary, Oregon State Board of Horticulture* (Salem, OR, undated, c: 1900).

Pabst, R.J., and T.A. Spies, "Distribution of Herbs and Shrubs in Relation to Landform and Canopy Cover in Riparian Forests of Coastal Oregon," *Canadian Journal of Forestry* 76 (1998): 298–315.

Pagter, Lawrence B., *Land Classification of Siuslaw National Forest, Oregon* (Corvallis, OR: Siuslaw National Forest, July 31, 1917). Cited in Prior 1998.

Peffer, E. Louise, *The Closing of the Public Domain: Disposal and Reservation Policies 1900–50* (Stanford, CA: Stanford University Press, 1951). Cited in Prior 1998.

Randall, Warren R., Robert F. Keniston, Dale N. Bever, and Edward C. Jensen, *Manual of Oregon Trees and Shrubs* (Corvallis, OR: OSU Book Stores, 1988).

Reeves, G.H., L.E. Benda, K.M. Burnett, P.A. Bisson, and J.R. Sedell, "A Disturbance-based Ecosystem Approach to Maintaining and Restoring Freshwater Habitats of Evolutionarily Significant Units of Anadromous Salmonids in the Pacific Northwest," *American Fisheries Society Symposium* 17 (1995): 334–349.

Rich, E.E., ed., *The Letters of John McLoughlin from Fort Vancouver to the Governor and Committee, First Series, 1825-38* (London: The Champlain Society, 1941). Cited in Bunting 1993.

Ripple, William J., "Historic Spatial Patterns of Old Forests in Western Oregon," *Journal of Forestry* 92, no. 11 (1994): 45-49.

Ripple, William J., K.T. Hershey, and Robert G. Anthony, "Historical Forest Patterns of Oregon's Central Coast Range," *Biological Conservation* 93 (2000): 127-133.

Robbins, William G., *Landscapes of Promise: The Oregon Story, 1800-1940* (Seattle: University of Washington Press, 1997).

Rollins, Philip, ed., "Robert Stuart's Narratives," in *The Discovery of the Oregon Trail* (New York: Charles Scribner's Sons, 1935).

Ross, Alexander, *Adventures of the First Settlers of the Oregon or Columbia River: being a narrative of the expedition fitted out by John Jacob Astor, to establish the "Pacific Fur Company;" with an account of some Indian tribes on the coast of the Pacific* (1849; reprint, New York: The Citadel Press, 1969).

Russell, Emily W.B., *People and the Land through Time: Linking Ecology and History* (New Haven, CT: Yale University Press, 1997).

Scouler, John, "Dr. John Scouler's Journal of a Voyage to N.W. America," *Oregon Historical Quarterly* VI (June 1905): 124.

Slacum, William A., "Slacum's Report on Oregon 1836-7," *Oregon Historical Quarterly* XIII, no. 2 (June 1912).

Spies, T., D. Hibbs, J. Ohmann, G. Reeves, R. Pabst, F. Swanson, C. Whitlock, J. Jones, B.C. Wemple, L. Parendes, and B. Schrader, "The Ecological Basis of Forest Managment in the Oregon Coast Range," in *Forest and Stream Management in the Oregon Coast Range* (in press).

"Spruce Division camps, 1918," *Seaside (Oregon) Signal*, 16 May 1991.

Swanson, F.J., and J.F. Franklin, "New Forestry Principles from Ecosystem Analysis of Pacific Northwest Forests," *Ecological Applications* 2, no. 3 (1992): 262-274.

Swanson, F.J., G.W. Lienkaemper, and J.R. Sedell., *History, Physical Effects and Management Implications of Large Organic Debris in Western Oregon Streams*, USDA Forest Service General Technical

Report PNW-56 (Portland, OR: USDA Forest Service Pacific North-west Forest and Range Experiment Station, 1976).

Swanson, F.J., J.A. Jones, and J.K. Agee, *Analysis of Disturbance History by Fire, Windthrow, and Related Land Management Activities in the Bull Run Watershed, Mt. Hood National Forest, Oregon* (submitted to the City of Portland Water Bureau and Mt. Hood National Forest in partial fulfillment of cooperative agreement PNW 92-0220, 1998).

Swetnam, Thomas W., Craig D. Allen, and Julio L. Betancourt, "Applied Historical Ecology: Using the Past to Manage for the Future," *Ecological Applications* 9, no. 4 (1999): 1189–1206.

Suzuki, N., and W.C. McComb, "Habitat Classification Models for Beaver (*Castor canadensis*) in the Streams of the Central Oregon Coast Range," *Northwest Science* 72, no 2 (1998): 102–110. Cited in Rainbolt, unpublished report.

Tappeiner, John C., II, David Hibbs, and William H. Emmingham, "Silviculture of Coast Range Forests," in *Forest and Stream Management in the Oregon Coast Range* (in press).

Taylor, Terri A., and Patricia C. Erigero, *Cultural Landscape Report: Fort Vancouver National Historic Site,* vol. 1 (Seattle, WA: U.S. Department of Interior, National Park Service, 1992).

Teensma, Peter D.A., John T. Reinstra, and Mark A. Yeiter, *Preliminary Reconstruction and Analysis of Change in Forest Stand Age Classes of the Oregon Coast Range from 1850 to 1940,* Technical note T/N OR-9 (Portland, OR: USDI Bureau of Land Management, 1991).

Towle, Jerry C., "Changing Geography of Willamette Valley Woodlands," *Oregon Historical Quarterly* LXXXIII, no. I (spring 1982): 67–87.

Townsend, John Kirk, *Narrative of a journey across the Rocky Mountains, to the Columbia River, and a visit to the Sandwich Islands, Chili &c., with a scientific appendix* (1839; reprint, Corvallis: Oregon State University Press, 1999).

Tsukada, M., S. Sugita, and D.M. Hibbert, "Paleoecology in the Pacific Northwest. I. Late Quaternary vegetation and climate," *Proceed-*

ings—*International Association of Theoretical and Applied Limnology, 1980*, vol. 21, pt. 2 (1981): 730–737.

USDA Forest Service, *Monitoring and Evaluation Report, Fiscal Year 1998* (Mount Hood National Forest: USDA Forest Service, 1998).

USDA Forest Service, *County Portraits of Oregon and Northern California*, General Technical Report PNW-GTR-377 (Portland, OR: USDA Forest Service, 1996).

USDA Forest Service, *Log Production in Washington and Oregon: An Historical Perspective,* Resource Bulletin PNW-42 (Portland, OR: USDA Forest Service, Pacific Northwest Forest and Range Experiment Station, 1972).

USDA Forest Service, *Forest Statistics for Clatsop County, Oregon* (Portland, OR: USDA Forest Service, Pacific Northwest Forest and Range Experiment Station, 1938).

Victor, Frances Fuller, *All Over Oregon and Washington: Observations on the Country, its Scenery, Soil, Climate, Resources, and Improvements* (San Francisco: John G. Carmany & Co., 1872).

"Views on road ban to pour in," *Salem (Oregon) Statesman-Journal,* 16 July 2000.

Waite, R.M., "Copy of a document found among the private papers of the late Dr. John McLoughlin," in *Transactions of the Eighth Annual Re-Union of the Oregon Pioneer Association for 1880*, p. 46. Cited in Erigero 1992.

Wallin, David O., Frederick J. Swanson, Barbara Marks, John H. Cissel, and Jane Kertis, "Comparison of Managed and Pre-settlement Landscape Dynamics in Forests of the Pacific Northwest, USA," *Forest Ecology and Management* 85 (1996): 291–309.

Waring, R.H., and J.F. Franklin, "Evergreen Coniferous Forests of the Pacific Northwest," *Science* 204 (1979): 1380–1386.

Warre, Henry, and Mervyn Vavasour, "Documents Relative to Warre and Vavasour's Military Reconnoissance in Oregon, 1845–6," in *Oregon Historical Quarterly* X, no. 1 (March 1909): 1–99.

Wells, Gail, *The Tillamook: A Created Forest Comes of Age* (Corvallis: Oregon State University Press, 1999).

Wheeler, Olin D., *The Trail of Lewis and Clark 1804–1904,* vol. II. (New York: G.P. Putnam's Sons, 1904).

Wilkes, Charles, *Narrative of the United States Exploring Expedition: during the years 1838, 1839, 1840, 1841, 1842* (Philadelphia: Lea and Blanchard, 1845, c. 1844). Cited in Boyd 1999.

Williams, Gerald W., *Pacific Northwest Region (R-6) of the USDA Forest Service: a Brief History of the Early Days* (Portland, OR: USDA Forest Service, 1993). Cited in Prior 1998.

Williams, Michael, *Americans and Their Forests: A Historical Geography* (Cambridge: Cambridge University Press, 1989).

Wimberly, Michael C., Thomas A. Spies, Colin J. Long, and Cathy Whitlock, "Simulating Historical Variability in the Amount of Old Forests in the Oregon Coast Range," *Conservation Biology* 14, vol. 1 (2000): 1–15.

Worona, M.A. And C. Whitlock, "Late Quaternary Vegetation and Climate History near Little Lake, Central Coast Range, Oregon," *Geological Society of America Bulletin* 107 (1995): 867–876.

Unpublished Sources

Agee, James K., "Historic forest disturbance on Oregon's North Coast" (paper presented at the symposium Oregon's forests as encountered by Lewis and Clark, Seaside, OR, August 24, 2000, sponsored by Oregon Forest Resources Institute, Portland, OR).

Bowen, William Adrian, "Migration and Settlement on a Far Western Frontier: Oregon to 1850" (Ph.D. dissertation, University of California, Berkeley, 1972).

Bunting, Robert Reed, "Landscaping the Pacific Northwest: A Cultural and Ecological Mapping of the Douglas-fir Region, 1778–1900" (Ph.D. dissertation, University of California, Davis, 1993).

Crown Zellerbach Corp., Clatsop County Tree Farm, unpublished report dated 1946. Information on West Coast tree farms for annual progress report to joint committee. Copy in possession of the authors.

Crown Zellerbach Corp., press release on completion of company reforestation activities, dated 1954. Copy in possession of the authors.

Davidson, T.L., "By the southern route into Oregon" (Salem, Oregon, 1878) (Bancroft Library mss. P-A 23, p. 1, University of California, Berkeley, CA). Cited in Bowen 1972.

Deady, Matthew P. "History and Progress of Oregon after 1845" (Portland, Oregon, 1878) (Bancroft Library mss. P-A 24, p. 59, University of California, Berkeley). Cited in Bowen 1972.

Eld, Henry, "Journal. Statistics etc. in Oregon and California . . . Sept. 6th to Oct 19th inclusive (1841)" (Beinecke Library WA MS 161, in the Western Americana Collection, Yale University, New Haven, CT). Cited in Boyd 1999.

Grant, C. Frank, unpublished family memoirs, 1990: 18. Cited in Prior 1998.

Hedlund, C., "The late Pleistocene and early Holocene paleoecology of Oregon," unpublished report. Copy in possession of the authors.

Graumlich, L., "Long-term Records of Temperature and Precipitation in the Pacific Northwest Derived from Tree Rings" (Ph.D. dissertation, University of Washington, Seattle, 1985). Cited in Ripple 1994.

Heigh, Lisa. Unpublished draft report on Young's Bay history. Copy in possession of the authors.

Horlin, Hazel Crooks [Shelby]. "The life story of Leora Watkins Crooks Anderson (and her family)," unpublished manuscript dated 1975, cited in Prior 1998.

McLoughlin, John, Private Papers 1825-1856, (Bancroft Library mss. P-A 155:2, University of California, Berkeley). Cited in Bowen 1972.

Nierenberg, Tara R. "A Characterization of Unmanaged Riparian Overstories in the Central Oregon Coast Range" (master's thesis, Oregon State University, Corvallis, OR, 1996).

Northam, Ray M., "Rural Settlement and Resources of the Alsea Valley" (master's thesis, Oregon State College, Corvallis, OR, 1955).

Prior, Jan M., "Kinship, Environment, and the Forest Service: Homesteading in Oregon's Coast Range" (master's thesis, Oregon State University, Corvallis, OR, 1998).

Rainbolt, Raymond E., "Historic beaver populations in the Oregon Coast Range," unpublished report dated Dec. 15, 1999. Copy in possession of the authors.

Stamm, E.P., statement for Santa Barbara conference, 1957. Unpublished information on timber holdings, logging, and manufacturing by Crown Zellerbach Corp. in Oregon and Washington. Copy in possession of the authors.

Teensma, P.D.A., *Fire History and Fire Regimes of the Central Western Cascades of Oregon* (Ph.D. dissertation, University of Oregon, Eugene, OR, 1987).

Tobie, H.E., "The Willamette Valley before the Great Immigrations" (master's thesis, University of Oregon, Eugene, OR, 1927).

Tunnell, Chester Leonard, "History of Oregon City to 1870" (master's thesis, University of Oregon, Eugene, OR, 1940).

United States Department of Interior, General Land Office, survey notes, 1875a:451–2. Cited in Prior 1998.

USDA Forest Service, Loyd Drorbaugh LAC case file (Siuslaw National Forest, August 2, 1919). Cited in Prior 1998.

Weisberg, Peter J., and Frederick J. Swanson, "Regional synchronicity in changing fire regime patterns of the western Cascades, U.S.A.," paper in review. Copy in possession of the authors.

Whitlock, Cathy, and Lyn Berkley, "Fire and vegetation history in the Cascade Range, Oregon," unpublished paper. Copy in possession of the authors.

Zybach, Bob, "Historical overview of Columbia Gorge forestlands: Dynamics and fragmentation, 1792-1996," unpublished report. Copy in possession of the authors.

Common and Scientific Names

Birds and Mammals

Beaver	*Castor canadensis*
Deer	*Odocoileus* spp.
Elk	*Cervus* spp.
Marbled murrelet	*Brachyramphus marmoratus*

Fish

Chinook (king) salmon	*Oncorhynchus tshawytscha*
Coho salmon	*Oncorhynchus kisutch*
Cutthroat trout, coastal	*Oncorhynchus clarki clarkii*
Steelhead	*Oncorhynchus mykiss*

Trees and Shrubs

Alder, red	*Alnus rubra*
Bigleaf maple	*Acer macrophyllum*
Blackberry	*Rubus* spp.
Chinkapin, golden	*Castanopsis chrysophylla*
Coastal redwood	*Sequoia sempervirens*
Cottonwood	*Populus* spp.
Crabapple, wild	*Malus diversifolia*
Douglas-fir	*Pseudotsuga menziesii*
Elderberry	*Sambucus racemosa*
Grand fir	*Abies grandis*
Hawthorn	*Crataegus* spp.
Hazel, California	*Corylus cornuta californica*
Huckleberry	*Vaccinium* spp.
Indian-plum	*Oemieria cerasiformis*
Madrone, Pacific	*Arbutus menziesii*
Manzanita	*Arctostaphylos* spp.
Maple, bigleaf	*Acer macrophyllum*

Maple, vine	*Acer circinatum*
Mountain hemlock	*Tsuga mertensiana*
Noble fir	*Abies procera*
Oak, Oregon white	*Quercus garryanna*
Oceanspray	*Holodiscus discolor*
Oregon ash	*Fraxinus latifolia*
Oregongrape	*Mahonia* spp.
Pine, lodgepole	*Pinus contorta*
Pine, ponderosa	*Pinus ponderosa*
Pine, western white	*Pinus monticola*
Poison oak, Pacific	*Toxicodendron diversilobum*
Port-Orford-cedar	*Chamaecyparis lawsoniana*
Rhododendron, Pacific	*Rhododendron macrophyllum*
Sagebrush	*Artemisia* spp.
Salal	*Gaultheria shallon*
Salmonberry	*Rubus spectabilis*
Sedges	*Carex* spp., *Scirpus* spp.
Serviceberry	*Symphoricarpos albus*
Silver fir	*Abies amabilis*
Sitka spruce	*Picea sitchensis*
Subapline fir	*Abies lasiocarpa*
Thimbleberry	*Rubus parviflora*
Western hemlock	*Tsuga heterophylla*
Western redcedar	*Thuja plicata*
Willow	*Salix* spp.
Yew, Pacific	*Taxus brevifolia*

Grasses and Forbs

Brackenfern	*Pteridium aquilinum*
Camas	*Camassia quamash*
Fescue	*Festuca* spp.
Reed canarygrass	*Phalaris arundinacea*
Swordfern, western	*Polystichum munitum*
Vetch, American	*Vicia americana*
Wapato	*Sagittaria latifolia*

Illustration Credits

Cover photo (OrHi 798) courtesy of Oregon Historical Society.

Introduction. Portraits of William Clark and Meriwether Lewis courtesy of the Independence National Historic Park, Philadelphia, PA. Photo of big trees courtesy of USDA Forest Service, PNW Research Station. Photos of Cascades and Willamette Valley forests courtesy of College of Forestry, Oregon State University.

Chapter 1. Pleistocene and Holocene timeline, Ice Age map of North America, figure of Milankovitch cycles, and map of America's Ice Age forests are adapted from Bonnicksen 2000. Map of glaciers covering western Washington is adapted from Heusser 1977. Graph of shifting forest composition over time is adapted from Worona and Whitlock 1995. Photos of spruce-hemlock stand and young Douglas-fir seedlings courtesy of USDA Forest Service, PNW Research Station. Map of Cascadia subduction zone is adapted from Atwater and Yamaguchi 1991. Figure showing receding Lyman Glacier in the Washington Cascades is adapted from Jumpponen et al. 1998.

Chapter 2. Graphs of forest community development in western hemlock and Sitka spruce zones are adapted from Hemstrom and Logan 1986. Graph of fire severity and return intervals is adapted from Agee 1989. Graph of fire frequency from 1500 to present is adapted from Weisberg and Swanson, in review.

Chapter 3. Broughton's map courtesy of London Office of Public Records. Images of Captain Gray (OrHi 26699) and his ship (OrHi 984) courtesy of Oregon Historical Society.

Chapter 4. Clark's map (OrHi 87702), Wilkes' map (OrHi 51819 or 21093), image of longhouse (OrHi 4465), and Clark's drawing of trout (OrHi 8180) courtesy of Oregon Historical Society.

Chapter 5. Astoria in 1841 (OrHi 702), Slacum's chart (OrHi 379), John McLoughlin portrait (OrHi 248), photos of cabin in the woods (OrHi Gi 7199), identification of Fort Clatsop (OrHi 1692-93), St. Paul cemetery (OrHi 927), and Lewis and Clark

Trail Commission at the reconstructed Fort Clatsop (OrHi 403-A) courtesy of Oregon Historical Society. Photos of Youngs Bay log dump and Columbia County tax-forfeited land courtesy of USDA Forest Service, PNW Research Station. Tillamook Head aerial photos courtesy of Willamette Industries. Timber harvest data from Oregon Department of Forestry.

Chapter 6. Covington illustration of Fort Vancouver courtesy of Vancouver National Historic Reserve Trust. Modern-day photo of Oregon City courtesy of William E. Hill and Caxton Press. Willamette Valley vegetation maps are adapted from Towle 1982. Wind River photos and Clark-Wilson Lumber Co. photo courtesy of USDA Forest Service, PNW Research Station. Jason Lee portrait (OrHi 8342), Willamette Falls engraving (OrHi 102007), Warre's painting of Oregon City (OrHi 791), Lorain's photo of Oregon City (OrHi 21079), photo of Portland in 1852 (OrHi 39197), and Summit House on the Barlow Road (OrHi 47135) courtesy of Oregon Historical Society. Logging railroad photo courtesy of Oregon Forest Resources Institute. Timber harvest data for Clackamas County from Oregon Department of Forestry. Timber harvest data for Mount Hood National Forest from USDA Forest Service. Kinney Ridge panoramic photos 1937 courtesy of Iamwho Panoramic Imaging. Kinney Ridge panoramic photos 1987 courtesy of USDA Forest Service and Michael Hanemann.

Chapter 7. Photos of Alsea River and Cascade Head courtesy of OSU College of Forestry. Burning hillside in Tillamook County 1933 (OrHi 49536) courtesy of Oregon Historical Society. Beaver stream photo courtesy of Bob Gilman. Map showing occurrence of forest fires since 1849 adapted from Morris 1934. Data on historical Oregon forest fires from Oregon Department of Forestry. Maps showing Coast Range burned areas and ages of surrounding forests created from Bureau of Land Management data. Maps of fire history, land cover by decade, and managed stands courtesy of Bureau of Land Management, Salem District. Charles Brown homestead c. 1910 photo (neg. no. 88-2C) courtesy of Oregon Coast History Center. Photo of Charles Brown homestead 1993 courtesy of Jan Prior. Photo of aftermath of 1933 Tillamook fire and photo of cut-over pasture site courtesy of USDA Forest Service, PNW Research Station. Aerial photos of Marys Peak and Burnt Woods areas in 1948 and 1997 courtesy of Starker Forests, Inc. Timber harvest data from Oregon Department of Forestry. Saddle Mountain panoramic photos 1937 courtesy of Iamwho Panoramic Imaging. Saddle Mountain panoramic photos 1988 courtesy of USDA Forest Service and Michael Hanemann.

Chapter 8. Photo of Oak Creek courtesy of College of Foresty files. Photo of Salmon Creek restoration project courtesy of Caryn Davis. Graph on range of scales addressed by historical-ecology data is adapted from Swetnam et al. 1999. Historical and current land use maps and graph of historical and estimated sustainable harvest levels by ownership are from Oregon Progress Board 2000. Graph comparing patterns of forest development is adapted from Kimmins 1997.

Index

U

U.S. Army Spruce Division 85
Umpqua River 145-146, 161

V

Vancouver (city) 53, 55
Vancouver, George 44-47
Vancouver Island 26, 43, 67
Vavasour, Mervyn 104, 106, 109
Victor, Frances Fuller 78, 80, 116
Villard, Henry 116
volcanoes 178

W

wapato (Sagittaria latifolia) 53, 99
Warre, Henry 104, 106, 109
West Linn 105
western redcedar (Thuja plicata) 10, 22-26, 32, 35, 38, 54, 58, 73, 98, 157, 213
wetlands, reclamation of 65, 75
Weyerhaeuser, Frederick 120
Wilderness Act of 1964 125
Willamette Falls 8, 103, 106, 115
Willamette River 17, 65, 95-99, 104, 106, 110, 115, 145, 162

Willamette Valley 8, 10-11, 17, 19, 23, 25, 35, 52, 72, 74, 105-113, 117-118, 127, 138-140, 143, 146, 153, 156-157, 162, 186
willow (Salix spp.) 9-10, 18-21, 31, 47, 55, 75, 101, 108, 143
wind, as disturbance agent 35-38, 44, 83, 88, 177-178
windstorms 11, 37-38, 83, 177-178
Winship, Nathan 65, 71
woody debris 34, 142, 179
Wyeth, Nathaniel 69, 100-101

Y

Yaquina Bay 138, 148-151, 162
Yaquina River 138, 141, 149-150
yew, Pacific (Taxus brevifolia) 22, 24, 157
York (Clark's slave) 57
Young, Ewing 112
Youngs Bay 77, 81

About the Oregon Forest Resources Institute

The Oregon Legislature created the Oregon Forest Resources Institute (OFRI) in 1991 to improve understanding of forestry and the state's forest resources. Funded by a portion of the harvest tax on forest products producers, OFRI provides information and education programs on forestry in Oregon and encourages sound forest management.

About the Authors

Gail Wells is a writer and the director of the Communications Group at the College of Forestry at Oregon State University. She is the author of *The Tillamook: A Created Forest Comes of Age* (OSU Press, 1999). Dawn Anzinger is a graduate student in forest ecology at Oregon State University.